MK Lawson.

£5·95

MEDIEVAL MONASTICISM

D0348184

8

MEDIEVAL MONASTICISM

Forms of religious life in Western Europe in the Middle Ages

C. H. Lawrence

LONGMAN
London and New York

LONGMAN GROUP LIMITED
Longman House, Burnt Mill, Harlow
Essex CM20 2JE, England
Associated companies throughout the world

*Published in the United States of America
by Longman Inc., New York*

© Longman Group Limited 1984

All rights reserved; no part of this publication may be
reproduced, stored in a retrieval system, or transmitted
in any form or by any means, electronic, mechanical,
photocopying, recording, or otherwise, without the
prior written permission of the Publishers

First published 1984

BRITISH LIBRARY CATALOGUING IN PUBLICATION DATA
Lawrence, C. H.
 Medieval monasticism.
 1. Monasticism and religious orders – Europe
 – Middle Ages, 600–1500
 I. Title
 271′.0094   BX2470

 ISBN 0-582-49185-1
 ISBN 0-582-49186-X   Pbk

LIBRARY OF CONGRESS CATALOGING IN PUBLICATION DATA
Lawrence, C. H. (Clifford Hugh), 1921–
 Medieval monasticism.

 Bibliography: p.
 Includes index.
 1. Monasticism and religious orders – History – Middle
Ages, 600–1500. I. Title.
BX2470.L39 1984   271′.0094   83-19921
ISBN 0-582-49185-1
ISBN 0-582-49186-X (pbk.)

Set in 10/11 Linotron 202 Times
Printed in Hong Kong by
Wah Cheong Printing Press Ltd

CONTENTS

Contents

PREFACE

History is a language of explanation. This book has grown out of the experience of many years spent endeavouring to explain to students the presence and function of monasteries in the medieval world. Huge though the literature of the subject is, indeed because it is so vast, it seemed to me that there was use for a short study that traced the growth of the Western monastic tradition as a whole in its social context, from its origins in late antiquity down to the later Middle Ages. This unifying purpose is my justification for the title. For although I have included the friars, they were not properly speaking monks, nor were the Brethren of the Common Life and the members of other fringe groups that figure in the later chapters. But the Mendicant Orders and the other religious movements of the later Middle Ages were nevertheless offshoots of the same monastic tradition and would be unintelligible without reference to it.

In the course of writing, I have often been aghast at my presumption in attempting to survey such a vast and rich manifestation of the human spirit in the compass of one short book. Drastic selectivity has been forced upon me both by the scale of the subject and by the limitations of my own scholarship. I am conscious that Spain gets scant treatment, and that although I have written about the Military Orders, the other monks of *Outremer* should also have had a place in the story.

I have done my best to indicate my literary debts in the chapter endnotes (where place of publication is given only for works produced outside the UK). Other intellectual debts are less easy to define. Like all workers in this field, I owe much to the teaching and inspiration of the late David Knowles; also to a kind of infused understanding derived from the conversation of the late Father Daniel Callus. To me he always seemed to personify the essence of the ideal of the scholar-friar. I should like to acknowledge with gratitude the help of my wife, who encouraged me to write the book and cast a judicious eye over each chapter as it was finished.

ABBREVIATIONS USED IN THE NOTES

AA SS	*Acta Sanctorum*, edited by the Bollandists
CCM	*Corpus Consuetudinum Monasticarum*, ed. K. Hallinger (Siegburg 1963 ff.)
CSEL	*Corpus Scriptorum Ecclesiasticorum Latinorum* (Vienna and Prague 1866 ff.)
MGH	*Monumenta Germaniae Historica*
MGH SRM	*Monumenta Germaniae Historica, Scriptores rerum Merovingicarum*
MGH SS	*Monumenta Germaniae Historica, Scriptores*
PG	*Patrologia Graeca*, ed. J. P. Migne (Paris 1857–66)
PL	*Patrologia Latina*, ed. J. P. Migne (Paris 1844–64)
RS	Rolls Series: *Chronicles and Memorials of Great Britain and Ireland*

To the monks of Fleury Saint-Benoit, who thirty-seven years ago helped a wandering student find peace of mind after the turmoils of war, this book is gratefully dedicated.

Chapter 1

THE CALL OF THE DESERT

The history of Christian monasticism begins in the Middle East. It made its earliest appearance in Egypt and Palestine towards the end of the third century. In its primitive form it was a way of life adopted by solitaries, or anchorites, living in the desert. The word 'monk' itself derives from the Greek word *monos*, meaning alone. Monks were people who had withdrawn from society to pursue the spiritual life in solitude. As Jerome, one of the early Western converts to the monastic life, wrote to another convert, Paulinus of Nola, in the year 395, 'If you wish to perform the office of a priest, live in cities and townships, and make the salvation of others the gain of your soul. But if you desire to be what is called a monk, that is a solitary, what are you doing in cities, which are after all the dwelling places not of solitaries but of the many?'[1] Some monks, the greater number in fact, lived in organised communities of their own kind; but the first in time were the hermits. By the fourth century, the desert of Nitria, on the western edge of the Nile Delta, and the wilderness of Judea were peopled by scattered colonies of hermits. For the most part these people were not clergy but lay Christians, who had migrated into the solitude from the urban society of late antiquity.

Writers on the subject, both ancient and modern, have suggested two alternative explanations for the movement. Some, including Jerome (*c.* 331–420), have claimed that the first Christian anchorites were refugees who sought safety in the desert from the persecution launched against the Church by the imperial government under Decius and Diocletian. Others have argued that the movement resulted from the softening of the moral fibre of the Christian community after Constantine had given peace to the Church in 313. From this angle, the asceticism of the desert solitaries represented a reaction by choicer spirits against the laxer standards and the careerism that crept into the Church once imperial approval had given it respectability and brought it endowments; the advent of large numbers of merely nominal Christians, which followed upon public recognition of Christianity, drove those who were more deeply committed to the religious life to separate themselves from their congregations. Both these explanations have some basis in our sources, but neither is completely satisfying in itself.

Ascetical withdrawal from the world, that is the renunciation of marriage, property, and the ordinary pleasures and comforts of life, in order to discipline the senses and free the mind for supernatural contemplation, is a feature of other world religions besides Christianity. Buddhism has its monks. And Judaism, which is not conspicuously ascetical in its ethos, had its Essene tradition, which modern archaeology has done much to elucidate. The study of the Dead Sea Scrolls and excavation of the Qumran site have revealed the existence of a Jewish ascetical settlement at the time of Christ that displayed many of the characteristics of a later Christian monastery. There was also an ascetical tradition in Greco-Roman philosophy, represented by the Stoics and the Neoplatonists, which counselled the man who aspired to perfect wisdom to avoid the distractions of marriage and social intercourse and live the life of a recluse. As we can see from the career of St Augustine, this pagan image of the sage, or philosopher recluse, exercised a powerful influence over the minds of educated Christians who had been schooled in the classical tradition. But the earliest Christian anchorites were not for the most part highly educated men, and we must look elsewhere for the source of their inspiration.

Christian renunciation of the world was rooted in the Gospel. St Mark – writer of the earliest of the Gospel narratives – begins his account with the voice of the Baptist crying in the wilderness. Before beginning his public ministry, Christ was led by the Spirit into the desert; and ecclesiastical tradition saw in this a parable of the conflict within the soul of the Christian: the quest for God involved separation from the world and the conquest of sensuality and human ambition. One of the passages in the Gospels that launched many ascetics on their spiritual career was the invitation of Jesus to the rich young man who asked 'What must I do to be saved?' He was told, 'Keep the commandments, love your neighbour as yourself.' But he was not satisfied: he had done all this, or so he claimed, and he pressed for more. And in reply he received the devastating advice, 'If you would be perfect, go, sell what you possess and give to the poor, and you will have treasure in heaven; and come, follow me.' In fact, the desert monks were responding to a vocation which they found in the Christian tradition – to follow the 'evangelical counsels', to renounce property and ordinary human ties in the quest for spiritual perfection. They accepted the challenge of total surrender to Christ through the abandonment of worldly goods and prospects. But the quest for perfection involved more than this. Renunciation was only the beginning of the journey of the monk. His ultimate goal was union with God through contemplation. But man's predicament since the Fall made the journey of the soul to God a hard one. Original Sin had left man's reason darkened and his senses in disorder. Thus the newness of life, of which the Gospel spoke, could only be realised in this life by the continual mortification of the natural appetites and the progressive purification of the mind. In the solitude, beyond the frontiers of human society and freed from its distractions and temptations, a man might achieve that detachment from created things that prepared him for the supreme encounter with God.

In the first centuries of the Christian era, before Constantine proclaimed the peace of the Church, the ascetical spirit of renunciation was fostered by periodic persecution and the very real possibility of martyrdom. Many Christian congregations contained individual ascetics of both sexes, who renounced marriage and devoted themselves to a life of prayer and service to the deprived. This form of idealism was kept alive, too, by the expectations of the early Church, which stressed the need to live in constant readiness for the hour of divine judgement and the second coming of the Lord, an event that was believed to be imminent: 'the appointed time has grown very short; from now on, let those who have wives live as though they had none, and those who buy as though they had no goods, and those who deal with the world as though they had no dealings with it. For the form of this world is passing away.'[2] But the passage of time gradually dampened the urgency of this appeal. In the fourth century, the change from persecution to imperial recognition of the Church brought a sense of security and creeping worldliness in its train; and in this situation those who hankered for a more intense religious commitment were increasingly attracted by the idea of total withdrawal from the community. The pull of the desert gained added force from the popular esteem that was accorded to the solitary holy man. For as the age of the martyrs passed into historical memory, their role as the heroes of the faith was increasingly occupied in the eyes of devout Christians by the monks. These were the new confessors, who had renounced the security of property and the ordinary comforts of hearth and home in order to conquer the spirit of the world and scale the heights of contemplative prayer. As Sulpicius Severus wrote of St Martin of Tours, protagonist of the monastic movement in fourth-century Gaul, 'to fast, to keep unceasing vigil, to lacerate the flesh, this also is a martyrdom'.[3] He was echoed in the ninth century by Abbot Smaragdus of Verdun: 'Let no one say, brethren, that in our times there are no combats for martyrs. For our peace has its martyrs also.'[4]

The deserts to which the early ascetics were drawn were those of Egypt, Syria, and Palestine. Egypt, in fact, was the cradle of the monastic movement, which gradually spread into all the lands penetrated by the Church. It was on the fringe of the Western Desert, in the hinterland of the city of Alexandria, and in the fertile lands higher up the Nile valley, that there appeared in the course of the fourth century two variant modes of ascetical life, each of which became the source of a distinct and enduring monastic tradition. The first was the way of life adopted by the desert hermits – the eremitical life of the solitaries, which took its name from *eremos*, the Greek word for a desert. Its acknowledged leader and inspiration was St Antony (*c*. 251–356), a Coptic-speaking Christian of the Alexandrian region. The other and commoner way was the coenobitical life, that is the ascetical life practised within an organised community or monastery, which Greek-speaking Christians called a 'coenobium'. According to tradition, the originator of the Christian coenobium – the first fully communal monastery – was St Pachomius (*c*. 292–346), who established a monastic community beside the upper Nile somewhere about the year 320. These two, Antony the hermit and Pachomius the abbot, represent the twin fountain-head of two traditions – the eremitic and the coenobitic – which constantly inspired and reinvigorated distinct types of monastic organisation in the Middle Ages, both in Western Christendom and in the Byzantine East.

The fact that Egypt was the arena for the pioneers of Christian monasticism is explicable. It reflects the dominance of the East Roman provinces in the polity of the early Church, and particularly the leading role played by the Church of Alexandria in the theological world of the patristic age. Christianity, after all, had arisen and made its first conquests in the teeming cities of the Eastern Empire. Alexandria, with its famous schools of Platonic philosophy and Jewish Rabbinic learning, was a major centre of Christian speculation, the forcing-ground of major heresies, as well as of Clement of Alexandria, Origen, and Athanasius, the three greatest of the Greek Fathers. Its large Christian population offered a fertile seed-bed for fresh interpretations of the Christian life. And the intellectual element in the early monastic movement should not be overlooked. For not all the ascetics who fled to the desert were simple and unlearned people. The writings of Origen (184–254) were circulated and read in the desert monasteries; and Origen, who had made himself a eunuch for the sake of the kingdom of heaven, provided an ascetical theology of total renunciation. The two worlds of ascetical retreat and doctrinal controversy constantly interpenetrated one another. Athanasius (*c*. 296–373), patriarch of Alexandria and hero of the struggle against the Arian heresy, when driven from his see, found a refuge among the monks of Pachomius. Later, Alexandria was invaded by mobs of excited monks demonstrating in the cause of orthodoxy.

THE DESERT HERMITS

We do not really know when the flight to the desert began. Antony first embarked on the life of a hermit shortly before the year 270; but it seems that he had predecessors. The *Life of St Antony*, said to be the work of Athanasius, makes it clear that he was not the first of the anchorites. Athanasius tells us that when he experienced the call to the spiritual life, Antony renounced his inherited property and sought out an aged holy man living as an anchorite on the fringe of the village, and placed himself under his guidance, and that during this phase of his ascetical training he was helped by other solitaries in the district. But if he was not the originator of Egyptian monasticism, it was his life-story, as it was told by Athanasius, that provided the eremitical life with its first and most widely read manifesto and attracted a significant number of imitators. After his spiritual apprenticeship, he retired to live in a tomb within reach of his village; then, as he attracted growing numbers of sightseers, he withdrew to a ruined fortress on the edge of the desert, and lived there in solitude for twenty years. At the end of this period he emerged as a charismatic teacher and leader of monks: 'from that time', says Athanasius, 'there were monasteries in the mountains and the desert was peopled with monks'.[5] In the final stage of his career he retreated from the increasing pressure of his admirers to a remote oasis near the Red Sea, where he died at a great age in 356.

The saga of Antony represents the earliest traceable age of Egyptian monasticism. By the time of his death, the mountain of Nitria to the west of the Nile Delta and the inner desert of Scetis, forty miles to the south, had been settled by colonies of hermits. And similar settlements had appeared in Palestine and Syria inspired, according to Jerome, by St Hilarion, who had been instructed in the ascetical life by Antony.[6] These colonies contained several hundred solitaries living in caves or huts out of sight, and generally out of earshot, of one another. A group of this kind was called a *laura*, a Greek word meaning a pathway or passage, and apparently derived from the common pathway that connected the caves in the mountain monasteries of Judea. At the centre of the settlement stood a complex of buildings, including bakeries and a church, where the entire group of hermits gathered on Saturdays and Sundays for common prayer and the weekly celebration of mass. There was also accommodation for guests – something had to be done to provide for the constant flow of pious sightseers. Even anchorites required a modicum of food and clothing to stay alive, and the leaders of the movement enjoined their disciples to work for their livelihood. Out of the raw materials available in the region of the Nile they produced baskets, mats, ropes, and linen, which were exchanged for basic necessities. The marketing of their products was left to agents in the local villages, so that the monks themselves could preserve their solitude.

The life of the anchorite was not structured for him by any monastic rule. The only form of community support was the weekly gathering for common prayer. The abbot, the father-figure who directed the group, was available for counsel; it was he who trained the neophytes, for it was a cardinal principle of ascetical teaching that the beginner should place himself under the guidance of an experienced instructor. But apart from this the spirit of the *laura* was intensely individualistic. 'Except a man shall say in his heart', said Abbot Allois, 'I alone and God are in this world, he shall not find peace.'[7] The aspirant was taught how to brave the unbroken solitude of his cell, to meditate, and to engage in lonely combat with his own passions and illusions and with the demons of the waste places, who haunt the literature of the desert.

Fasting, deprivation of sleep, and other forms of bodily mortification, were the standard weapons of the ascetic's armoury in his struggle for self-conquest. The novice was stiffened in his resolution by stories of the feats accomplished by the heroes of this spiritual warfare. In about the year 420 Palladius wrote down what he had discovered about the lives of the desert anchorites in his *Lausiac History*. He had been a monk himself, but he could not stay the course; he still hankered after the flesh-pots; but he garnered some good anecdotes from the brethren. One of these was about the Alexandrian Macarius (d. 393), a giant of the first generation among the hermits of Nitria. Macarius had heard of the superhuman austerities practised by the monks of St Pachomius in the desert of the Thebaid in upper Egypt; and he resolved to outmatch them. So he went to the monastery of Tabennesis, disguised as a man of the world, and sought admission as a novice. The abbot was doubtful of his staying powers, but was prepared to let him try. As Lent came on, Macarius observed that some of the brethren fasted for two days together, and one of them for a whole week, while others spent half the night standing in prayer. So he made his dispositions to outdo them all. He took up his stand in a corner, and remained there praying and plaiting mats, without food, drink, or sleep, until Easter. This performance caused an outcry among the brethren, who complained to the abbot that this curious old man was making fools of them. But Pachomius fell to prayer, and it was revealed to him who his novice was. All the same, after thanking Macarius for knocking the conceit out of his youngsters, he gently asked him to leave: 'Now therefore return to the place from which you came; we have all been sufficiently edified by you.'[8]

The kind of competitive asceticism that drew a cool response from Pachomius seems to have been a characteristic of the eremitical movement in its early age. Later, wiser counsels prevailed. The classical masters of monastic lore discountenanced the more extravagant forms of Eastern mortification. But spectacular feats by individual anchorites continued to excite feelings of veneration and awe among the people. Some of the wildest and most bizarre manifestations of the ascetical spirit appeared in the fifth century among the anchorites of Syria, who inhabited the desert in the region of Antioch and Chalcis. It was here that the most dramatic form of withdrawal from the world was personified by the weird figure of St Simeon the Stylite, who took up his residence on top of a pillar, where he remained, exposed to sun and weather, for forty-seven years. Simeon commanded much admiration in the ecclesiastical world of his time, and he even had a few emulators, but his strange feat has no relevance for the history of the monastic tradition.

ST PACHOMIUS AND THE COMMUNITY LIFE

The example of the desert hermits continued to inspire individuals and groups in the Middle Ages, but the vocation of the hermit was an exceedingly rare one. Man is a social animal. The life of the solitary was full of difficulties and hazards. Only the strong dare be lonely. Lesser mortals can all too easily sink into mental breakdown or despair. It was easier and safer to follow the ascetical life with the support of a community engaged in the same task and within the framework of a rule. This, the fully shared life of monks living in an organised community, appeared in upper Egypt almost as soon as the anchoritic movement. Its originator, according to tradition, was Pachomius (*c.* 292–346), another Coptic-speaking Egyptian, who had been a conscript in the Roman army before his conversion to Christianity. At first it was the life-style of the anchorites that attracted him; but after a time the need to organise and direct a growing colony of disciples persuaded him to create a collective establishment at Tabennesis, the site of a deserted village beside the upper Nile, in the region of the Egyptian Thebes. As recruits multiplied, fresh colonies were established in the district, and by his death in 346 there was a congregation of women's as well as men's monasteries planted in the Thebaid. Each community had its own head, but Pachomius presided patriarchally over the whole group.

The Pachomian monastery was a large community, numbering upwards of 1,000 monks or nuns. Within the walls, which enclosed a wide precinct, a central focus was provided by a church, common refectory, and hospital. There was also a guest-house, where the Rule required that visitors should be housed with comfort. The residences of the monks consisted of a series of simple houses, laid out with a functional precision reminiscent of the legionary camps Pachomius had known in his youth. Each house contained some twenty monks under the direction of a prior. The distinctive things about the life of the monastery were its fellowship – the daily round of collective worship and the common meal – and the insistence upon total obedience to the commands of the superior. This surrender of personal will to that of a superior was a cardinal principle of the Pachomian ascesis. Another axiom was the virtue of work. There could be little provision for intellectual activities in the Pachomian settlement; in any case, many of the monks were unlettered men of peasant origin. Manual tasks were prescribed, however, because the product could be sold to support the monastery and because work was a sovereign remedy for the mental state of 'accidie' – that insidious demon of the burning noonday which tempted solitary and coenobite alike to abandon his vocation through boredom and disgust. The Pachomian monks were grouped in their houses according to their skills. Many of them occupied themselves with manufacturing linen and making mats and baskets from the rushes of the Nile, which they ferried down the river to market.

ST BASIL

An important part in taming the ascetical idealism of the desert monks and integrating it into the organisation of the Church was played by St Basil of Caesarea. Basil represents a new kind of monastic convert. Unlike most of the Egyptian ascetics, he was a highly educated man from a professional family, educated in the schools of rhetoric at Caesarea and the academies of Constantinople and Athens. Drawn to the ascetical life, in the years 357–58 he set out on a tour of Palestine and Egypt in search of a spiritual director. He visited the eremitic colonies of Nitria and Scetis; but the deepest impression seems to have been made on him by the Pachomian communities in the Thebaid. On his return home, he retired to a remote place near Annesi in the north of Asia Minor, where he was joined by a group of ascetics. But after experiencing the solitary life for a few years, he concluded that the organised life of the coenobium offered a better way, and he founded a community at Caesarea, which became a model for many other monasteries in Asia Minor. As a writer, and in later years as bishop of Caesarea, Basil not only helped to bring the monastic movement under the control of the ecclesiastical hierarchy; he left a lasting mark upon the monastic tradition.

Basil left no 'rule' in the sense of a blueprint for the interior organisation of a monastery, like the Rule of St Benedict. His so-called Longer and Shorter Rules are really a series of disconnected precepts, or conferences, set out in the form of question and answer, the random harvest of the years he spent counselling the monks of Cappadocia and Asia Minor. But these, and his letters, reveal what he considered the essential principles on which a monastery should be based. In the first place, it should be fully coenobitical – an inter-grated community. Basil's monks constitute a spiritual family living under one roof, a kind of house-monastery, as opposed to the erem-itic *laura* or the huge subdivided Pachomian colony. The significant thing is that, after touring the eremitical settlements of Palestine and Egypt and himself trying his vocation as a solitary recluse, he concluded that the ascetical life followed in community was better than the life of the anchorite. The reason for this was that the community was based upon the social nature of man, and alone provided the opportunity of fulfilling the Christian commandment to love one's neighbour: 'charity seeks not her own; but the solitary life removed from all others has only one aim, that of serving the ends of the individual concerned. But this is manifestly opposed to the law of charity. . . . We have been called in one hope of our calling, are one body and members one of another.' The defect of the solitary life was that it provided no opportunity to practise the virtues of humility and patience or to perform practical works of mercy – 'If you live alone, whose feet will you wash?'[9] Basil did not totally reject the vocation of the hermit; he recognised that the man who sought freedom in the desert to be alone with the Alone was fulfilling the first and greatest of the commandments; but he regarded the erem-itical life as a less perfect fulfilment of the Gospel than the life of the monk in community.

Basil left his mark upon monastic thinking in other ways. His conception of obedience to the head of the community was more subtle and far-reaching than that of Pachomius, and it represented an important refinement of the ascetical tradition. The novice renounces his own will and obeys the superior in everything, in spirit as well as in act, on the model of Christ, who was obedient unto death. There was no room in Basil's monastery for the individualism and the spectacular ascetical feats of the Egyptian anchorites; the only kinds of mortification allowed were those that the superior had authorised. It was only thus that the fanatic who was bent on taking the kingdom of heaven by storm could be saved from falling into the pit of pride. There is a rationality and moderation in Basil's ascetical teaching which is the hallmark of a cultivated Greek intelligence.

Another theme of Basil's teaching that was to be influential was his insistence upon the virtue of work in the monastery. Work was a means of perfecting the soul as well as supporting the community and providing for the poor. He would have the novice taught a trade, if he did not possess one when he joined the community, preferably one of the sort that produced marketable essentials, such as agriculture, weaving, or shoemaking. Perhaps it was from the monks of the Thebaid that Basil derived his high regard for manual work. At all events, it was a doctrine that made a deep imprint upon the minds of subsequent monastic legislators.

Although he left no systematic Rule, Basil's collected counsels for the ordering of a coenobitical community gave him a unique status in the Eastern Church, where he came to be regarded as the father of Orthodox monasticism. Nevertheless, despite his preference for the community life, in the monastic world of the Byzantine Empire the eremitical tradition continued to hold a prominent place alongside that of the organised coenobium. A long series of Orthodox ascetical theologians, from St Maximos the Confessor in the seventh century to St Gregory Palamas in the fourteenth, bear witness to the persistence of the desert ideal. And the major centres of Orthodox monasticism, such as the peninsula of Mount Athos, in northern Greece, and the rocky canyons of the Meteora in Thessaly, were peopled by anchorites living in caves as well as by thousands of monks living in communities.[10]

THE DESERT TRADITION TRANSMITTED TO THE WEST

Knowledge of the monastic movement, which had spread across the Eastern provinces of the Empire during the fourth century, was transmitted to Western Europe through various channels. Interest was awakened by the dissemination of literature about the desert monks, by migration to the West of refugee bishops like Athanasius and of individual ascetics like Cassian, and by the accounts brought back by pilgrims and pious sightseers.

It was the literature of Egyptian monasticism that brought the first flood of converts. More than any others, the work that made the deepest and most long-lasting impression upon Western readers was the *Life of St Antony* by Athanasius. Athanasius explains that he has written it to give encouragement to the brethren across the seas. And the strange ferment it caused must have fully satisfied his expectations. It was quickly translated into Latin, and by the year 374 Evagrius of Antioch, the friend and patron of Jerome, had improved on the earlier version with a more elegant translation, for, as he explained, 'a literal translation from one language into another occludes the sense and strangles it, as does couchgrass a field of corn'.[11] It was read with passionate interest in Christian circles at Rome and Milan and at Trier, where the imperial court was located. It was in his house at Milan, in the summer of 386, that Augustine heard an account of it from a visitor who had come from Trier, and it was the story of the desert anchorites that brought on the crisis of his conversion. He was only one of the first of a long line of Western Christians who were to fall under the spell of the Antonian desert.

In the course of the following decades, other literary accounts of the lives of the Desert Fathers became available to Latin readers. Stirred by the success of Evagrius, Jerome wrote a colourful *Life of Paul the Hermit*, and translated the Rule of Pachomius. His friend Rufinus of Aquileia, who had settled in a monastery at Jerusalem, translated the *History of the Monks in Egypt* from Greek into Latin. Like the *Lausiac History* of Palladius, this was an account written by a monk – a member of Rufinus's own community – who had made a pilgrimage to Egypt and had gathered the recollections of the aged anchorites on the spot. There were other travellers, too, who extracted literary capital from their tours of Nitria and the Thebaid, like Postumianus, who supplied Sulpicius Severus with anecdotes about the desert monks for the first book of his *Dialogues*, which he wrote in 430. As time went on, a mass of oral tradition accumulated and gradually assumed written form in the various versions of *Apophthegmata*, or Sayings of the Fathers, collections of maxims and anecdotes which circulated in Greek and Coptic and were eventually translated into Latin. But, more faithfully than anywhere else, the ethos of the desert and the teaching of the famous abbots were encapsulated in the *Conferences* of the Scythian monk John Cassian.

About the year 385 Cassian left his monastery at Bethlehem in the company of Germanus to tour the monastic settlements of Egypt. He stayed at Nitria and Scetis, and sat at the feet of the veterans in their cells. He was a good listener, and years later, when the violent controversy over the theology of Origen had driven him from the East, he settled in the south of Gaul and sat down to distil the wisdom of the anchorite-abbots for the benefit of Western readers. In these conferences the reader is given the freedom of the cells of Scetis and is allowed to listen to the aged masters of the contemplative life talking about their experience. Of course, memory is an incorrigible improver. We cannot be sure how much Cassian's recollections improved upon the discourses of the Egyptian abbots, for twenty-five turbulent years intervened before he committed them to writing. But the work became a classic of Latin spirituality – part of the essential reading of every monk. Cassian was the maestro whose writings taught St Benedict and his successors the ascetical lore of the East. His *Conferences* provided an inexhaustible treasury of axioms and reflections on the techniques and trials of the interior life of prayer; and the *Institutes*, a treatise he wrote for a community of monks he helped found at Apt in Provence, contained the first body of instruction on the coenobitic life to be produced in Western Europe. Together these two works did much to form the spirit and shape the pattern of early Western monasticism; and they continued to provide daily food for meditation in the cloisters of the Middle Ages.

THE FIRST WESTERN MONKS

According to Jerome, it was the visit of Athanasius to Trier and Rome during his years of exile (335–7 and 339–46) that gave Western monasticism the kiss of life. Certainly he was an enthusiastic propagandist for the ideals of the Egyptian monks, but the process of cross-fertilisation between the two traditions was too complex to be the work of a single individual.[12] Probably Hilary of Poitiers (*c.* 315–67) played just as big a part in transplanting Eastern monastic practices to the lands of the Western Empire. Hilary had been driven into exile in Asia Minor by the ascendancy of the Arian heresy at the imperial court, and during his enforced travels he must have encountered the monastic movement. On his return, he sponsored a group of ascetics in his episcopal city of Poitiers and became the patron and mentor of St Martin of Tours, who settled in Gaul about the year 360.

Martin (d. 397) is the first major figure in Gallic monasticism. He had had a career in the Roman army before his conversion. Having decided to adopt the life of an anchorite, he installed himself in a cell near Milan, where he remained until the hostility of the Arian bishop persuaded him to migrate to Gaul. The reputation of Hilary drew him to Poitiers, and it was at Ligugé, in the vicinity of the town, that he settled in a hermitage, which became a focal point for like-minded souls. His devotion to the monastic vocation was in no way diminished by his appointment to the see of Tours. Even as a bishop he persisted in maintaining the life-style of an anchorite; and after 372 he organised his disciples as a colony of hermits at Marmoutier, outside Tours. The settlement of Marmoutier looks very like an Eastern *laura*, but we cannot tell whether Martin had ever been to Egypt or how much he owed to the example of the Desert Fathers. Certainly the *Life of St Martin* by Sulpicius Severus, like the *Dialogues*, betrays the influence of Nitria and Scetis on every page; but Sulpicius was writing after 400, with the enthusiasm of a disciple, and his purpose was to show that the sanctity of St Martin placed him in the same league as the greatest of the Egyptian ascetics: 'You have conquered, O Gaul', shouted Postumianus, 'all the eremites and anchorites.'[13] The biography by Sulpicius proved to be a classic of medieval hagiography. It stamped the portrait of St Martin upon the imagination of medieval Christendom and it provided a powerful stimulus to the monastic movement in Gaul.

As the fame of the Eastern ascetics spread, a tiny but growing stream of aspirants from the West began to flow into Syria and Egypt. One of the first generation of converts was the wealthy Roman widow, Melania, who visited the Egyptian anchorites in 372. During her stay in Nitria she met Rufinus, the friend of Jerome, who was on a similar pilgrimage. Both of them eventually settled at Jerusalem, where they established and directed two coenobitical monasteries, one for men and one for women, on the Mount of Olives. These twin outposts of Latin Christianity were to form the nucleus of an expatriate colony of Western ascetics living in the Holy Land.

Jerome himself did much to promote the ideals of Oriental monasticism at Rome. Like Rufinus, he had felt the pull of the desert, and towards the end of 374 he took the plunge and went off to try his vocation as a hermit in Syria. But he could not bear to be parted from his library. His cave in the desert was hardly more than a secluded study, where his pen maintained an unbroken lifeline to the turbulent world of ecclesiastical politics. His experiment in the anchoritic life lasted upwards of two years and was then abandoned. Back in Rome in 382, after an interval, he assumed direction of a pious group of wealthy women, who had already adopted an ascetical lifestyle. Chief among them were two widowed noblewomen, Marcella and Paula. Marcella had already learned about the desert fathers through reading the *Life of St Antony* and through conversations with Peter, the exiled patriarch of Alexandria. Now, under the direction of Jerome, she turned her spacious house on the Aventine into a kind of conventual establishment for a circle of like-minded friends and servants. But Jerome's heart still lay in the East, and in the summer of 385 he set off for Palestine, were he was joined by Paula. Together they toured the Holy Places and the eremitical colonies of lower Egypt before finally settling at Bethlehem. There Paula financed the construction of a monastery for men and a convent for nuns, where she and Jerome spent the rest of their lives.[14]

The migration of ascetics was a two-way traffic. While the monasteries at Jerusalem and Bethlehem were constantly reinforced by new arrivals from the West, the monastic movement in Western Europe derived a powerful stimulus from the migration of Eastern ascetics, like John Cassian, who were driven to seek refuge in the West from the violent theological controversies that had their storm centre at Alexandria. After staying a while at Rome, Cassian moved to Gaul; and about the year 410 he established twin monasteries, one for men and one for women, at Marseilles. Although he was convinced that the anchorite represented the highest form of Christian life, he regarded the coenobitical life as a necessary preparation – one that differed in degree rather than in kind from the contemplative life of the hermit. So both his communities at Marseilles were organised as coenobitic monasteries; and so too was the monastery he founded later at the request of Bishop Castor of Apt.

Another wanderer, more obscure than Cassian but who left a memorial that was nearly as famous, was Honoratus (d. 429). Hilary of Arles says he sold his patrimony in Gaul and went on a pilgrimage to the East. But soon after 410, about the time when Cassian was organising his communities at Marseilles, Honoratus returned and founded a monastery on one of the islands of Lérins, off the coast of the Riviera. Here the whole range of the desert experience seemed to be institutionalised: there was a central coenobium under an abbot, and also a cluster of satellite hermitages where the elders, who had been trained in the community, could venture out to the solitary struggle of the desert.

With the foundation of Marseilles and Lérins monasticism was firmly rooted in Gaul, and it continued to spread throughout the fifth century. Lérins came to be a magnet and a school for aspiring monks and monastic founders from the northern parts of Europe; and its role was not confined to training ascetics: Lérins was a flourishing centre of learning in a world from which classical education was fast disappearing. Its scholars provided some heavy artillery in the Pelagian controversy over grace and free will. It was also a nursery of monk-bishops.

The appearance of monks in the ranks of the episcopate signified the assimilation of monasticism into the ecclesiastical organism. At the beginning of the fifth century the monastic movement was still widely regarded as a fringe phenomenon. It had not yet won acceptance by the secular world or even the general approval of the ecclesiastical hierarchy. Those sections of the old senatorial aristocracy that had remained pagan viewed the ascetics of the new religion with incomprehension and disgust. Rutilius Namatianus, prefect of Rome in 414 and champion of the old imperial cultus, referred disdainfully to the monks whose island he passed on his voyage[15]:

> A filthy island filled by men who flee the light.
> 'Monks' they call themselves, using a Greek name,
> Because they will to live alone, unseen by man.
> Fortune's gifts they fear, dreading its harm:
> Mad folly of a demented brain,
> That cannot suffer good, for fear of ill.

Rutilius spoke for the cultivated pagans. But even Christian society at Rome remained cool towards the practice of ascetical withdrawal that was advocated by Jerome.[16] Despite the promotion by Athanasius and the example of St Martin, many bishops regarded the monastic movement with distrust. This was heightened by the conspicuous and often violent part played by monks in the theological controversies that rent the Eastern Church. The increasingly public role that the monks were assuming seemed to pose a threat to the hierarchical order of the Christian community.

The mistrust was not all on one side. In the East, the ascetical movement had sprung up alongside, but quite independently of, the secular Church. The communities of Nitria had their own priests, but the movement did not derive its inspiration from clerical leadership, and in its early stages it often manifested mistrust of the ecclesiastical hierarchy. 'The monk ought to flee women and bishops' wrote Cassian.[17] And he warned the brethren against the diabolical temptation of seeking clerical office out of a desire to bring spiritual help to others. The author of the *Life of St Romanus*, the fifth-century founder of the monastery of Condat in the Jura, reserves some of his best invective for monks who get ordained: 'gaining clerical office out of rabid ambition, they are straight away inflated with pride and exalt themselves, not only over their worthier contemporaries, but even over their elders; mere youths, who for their juvenile vanity ought to be put in their place and whipped'.[18] Ecclesiastical office was part of that world of secular distractions the monk had renounced.

All the same, unless it was to suffer the fate of all fringe movements, monasticism had to be domesticated and brought under the roof of the institutional Church. It needed episcopal approval and encouragement. Athanasius had already pointed the way. At the height of the Arian dispute he had found a refuge among the monks of the Thebaid and had become a devoted friend and admirer. St Augustine, after his election to the African see of Hippo, lent his immense authority to the idea that the proper life-style for a bishop was monastic. And the *Life of St Martin* pointed the same moral. Thus a dangerous dichotomy between the ascetical movement and the ecclesiastical hierarchy was averted. The monasteries of Gaul and Italy enjoyed the patronage and protection of bishops. In fact, despite Cassian's warning, they came to be a favoured recruiting ground for zealous pastors. Honoratus left Lérins to become bishop of Arles, and in 429 he was followed in the see by Hilary, who had been one of his monastic disciples. In the following centuries the monk-bishop, from the Irish Aidan to the English Boniface, played a major role in evangelising the Germanic peoples. Monasticism was thus intergrated into the structure of the Church. But monks in general remained part of the lay section of the Christian community. It was some time before it became the normal practice for those who entered a monastery to be ordained.

By the fifth century, then, the ascetical tradition of the Eastern desert had been transmitted to the West. Monasticism had struck roots in Italy and southern Gaul. The writings of Cassian had provided the Western ascetical movement with a theology. But it was not until the sixth century that the first treatises appeared which offered a coherent plan for a monastic community. The earliest of these were the Rules composed by St Benedict and the unknown Master who provided him with a literary model. Both were compiled in Italy, and both drew deeply upon the oriental tradition.

NOTES

1. *Epistulae*, *PL* 58, 583.
2. I Cor. vii. 31.
3. *Sulpicii Severi Epistulae*, *CSEL* 1 ii, 144.
4. *Diadema Monachorum*, *PL* 102, 688.
5. *Vita S. Antonii*, *PG* 26, 866. On Antonian monasticism see Derwas J. Chitty, *The Desert a City* (1966), Ch. 1, and the works there referred to.
6. For the question of primitive Christian monasticism in Palestine see Chitty, *op. cit.* pp. 14–16.
7. *Apophthegmata Patrum*, *PG* 65, 134. For extracts of the Sayings of the Fathers in translation see Helen Waddell, *The Desert Fathers* (1936).
8. *Historia Lausiaca*, *PL* 73, 1116.
9. *Regulae Fusius Tractatae*, *Interrogatio VII*, *PG* 31, 934; translated in W. K. Lowther Clarke, *The Ascetical Works of St Basil* (1925). See also the same author's *St Basil the Great* (1913).
10. On the Byzantine monastic tradition see D. M. Nicol, *Meteora: The Rock Monasteries of Thessaly* (1963).
11. *Evagrii ad Innocentium prologus*, *PL* 73, 125–6.
12. For the process by which the monastic lore of Egypt and Syria was transmitted to the West see R. Lorenz, 'Die Anfänge des abendländischen Mönchtums im 4 Jahrhundert', *Zeitschrift für Kirchengeschichte* 77 (1966), 1–61; Owen Chadwick, *John Cassian* (1950).
13. *Sulpicii Severi Dialogi* i, *CSEL* 1 ii, 186.
14. J. N. D. Kelly, *Jerome* (1975), pp. 129–40.
15. *Claudii Rutilii Namatiani De Reditu Suo*, ed. L. Mueller (Leipzig 1870), ll. 440–8. For a translation see H. Isbell, *The Last Poets of Imperial Rome* (1971), p. 233.
16. Kelly, *op. cit.*, pp. 104–15.
17. *Instituta* xi, 18, *CSEL* 17, 203. On Cassian's view of clerical office as a form of temptation see the *Collationes* i 20, *CSEL* 13, 31.
18. *Vita S. Romani* in *Vie des pères du Jura*, ed. F. Martine (Sources chrétiennes No. 142, 1968), p. 262. The whole question of the relationship of the early monastic movement to the ecclesiastical hierarchy has recently been investigated by P. Rousseau, *Ascetics, Authority and the Church, in the Age of Jerome and Cassian* (1978).

Chapter 2

THE RULE OF ST BENEDICT

ST BENEDICT AND HIS BIOGRAPHER

For many centuries in the medieval West the Rule for Monks composed by St Benedict provided the standard pattern of monastic observance. Richly endowed, and sometimes exploited, by lay rulers, the great Benedictine abbeys came to hold a prominent position in the social landscape of Europe as landowning corporations, ecclesiastical patrons, and centres of learning. But we have to be on our guard against projecting the assumptions of a later period backwards upon the earlier age when the Rule was slowly establishing its reputation. In his own day, St Benedict (*c.* 480–550) – the patriarch of Western monks – was a quite obscure Italian abbot, and we know surprisingly little about the origins of his Rule. In many ways the first half of the sixth century, when he lived, is a bad period for literary sources. The Roman Empire in the West had been succeeded by a cluster of unstable Germanic barbarian Kingdoms. Italy had been subjected to a century of Ostrogothic settlement, at the end of which the peninsula was plunged into a prolonged and destructive war by Justinian's efforts to recover it for the East Roman Empire. Siege and counter-siege had gone far to reducing the city of Rome itself to ruins, inhabited by a much shrunken population. During this troubled period the West produced little in the way of historical writing that could be compared with the literary histories of antiquity. 'Among all our people', lamented Gregory of Tours when he took up his pen to fill the gap, 'there is not one man to be found who can write a book about what is happening today.' By contrast, Gregory's contemporaries nurtured a rich crop of biographies in the literary genre that had been pioneered by Athanasius and Sulpicius – the hagiographical Lives of saints, designed to promote their cultus and stimulate popular devotion. It is to a work of this kind that we owe what little we know about the author of the Benedictine Rule.

17

We depend in fact upon a single source: the *Life of St Benedict* written by Pope Gregory the Great about 593–94,[1] some forty-five years after Benedict's death. Attempts have sometimes been made to reconstruct a kind of identikit character study by examining his Rule; but modern textual criticism has shown most such efforts to be worthless: the very passages that were once thought to express the personal ideas of the author have been shown to be derivative. For St Benedict's life-story we have no alternative but to rely upon the biography which constitutes the second book of Gregory's *Dialogues*. These are a collection of Lives of Italian abbots and bishops cast, according to a well-established literary convention, in the form of dialogues between a questioner and his informant. It was the *Dialogues* that launched the cultus of St Benedict, for the book enjoyed immense popularity in the Middle Ages; and it is the earliest reference to him that we have. It evidently contains all that was known about him in Rome at the end of the sixth century; possibly rather more than was known. For Gregory's work is a piece of hagiography. It represents Benedict as both a holy man and a powerful miracle-worker or thaumaturge. His prayers conjure a spring from a barren cliff-top, enable his disciple Maurus to run on the surface of a lake, and restore to life children who have died by mishap. By contrast with the miraculous matter, there is a shortage of verifiable detail and a frustrating absence of chronological landmarks, except perhaps for an alleged visit to Cassino by the Goth Totila shortly before his entry to Rome.[2] These failings, and the lack of any contemporary source to corroborate Gregory's account, have caused some scholars to dismiss it as a work of allegory or pure fiction, and even to question the historical existence of St Benedict.

Such comprehensive scepticism is unjustified. We must not allow Gregory's concern with miracles to distort our evaluation of his work. His purpose in writing the *Dialogues* was, of course, didactic; and the miraculous anecdotes were an integral part of his message. His object was to record and celebrate the conquests made by Christian asceticism in Italy in the early decades of the sixth century, when the country was under Gothic rule, to show that Italy too had its saints and heroes of the ascetical life, like Egypt. In fact, he was doing for Italy precisely what Sulpicius had done for Gaul in the previous century; and the work of Sulpicius provided him with a literary model. There too were to be found anecdotes about holy abbots and, as the centre-piece, an extended *Life of St Martin*. The heroic saga of the Desert Fathers was being repeated in Gaul. Gregory's *Dialogues* carried the same message for Italy. The Roman population, impoverished and humiliated under a barbarian regime, and further demoralised by plague and by Justinian's short-lived *reconquista*, was to understand that it had not been abandoned by God.

The sanctity of its monks and bishops, and the marvels God had worked for them, were grounds for hope in the future. The theme gained added poignancy from Gregory's own regret for his lost monastic vocation and his lament for the collapse of the old social order.

Thus miraculous signs were essential to Gregory's purpose. The more sophisticated part of Gregory's readership, consisting of the clergy and monks, would have understood their symbolic significance. For less cultivated readers, they simply accorded with a popular conviction, widespread in late antiquity, that the holy man wielded mysterious powers over the forces of nature. For the historian, the important part of the miracle stories is their context, and there is no reason to think this was fictitious. Gregory, after all, was writing oral history for a live Italian readership. If his readers were to accept his message, he could neither invent the topographical setting of the anecdotes, nor could he invent personalities who had existed within living memory. Author and reader alike were surrounded by the visual evidence of the past. Cassino and Subiaco were lying ruinous and deserted, as St Benedict had prophesied; and there were still living those who could remember the life at Cassino before the Lombards burnt it, and who had known the founder. Some of them are named by Gregory as the source of his information.

Gregory tells us that Benedict was born in central Italy in the province of Nursia – the conventional date of 480 is pure surmise – and was sent to Rome for his education in liberal letters. But distressed by the debauched life of his fellow-students, he abandoned the schools, 'knowingly ignorant and wisely untaught', and fled with his nurse to the village of Afide, some twenty miles away. From there he withdrew to the solitude near Subiaco, a deserted spot in the Sabine Hills, where he lived in a cave for three years. During this time he was supplied with bread by a monk named Romanus from a nearby monastery, who also instructed him in the practice of the ascetical life. Gradually disciples settled round him, and he organised them into groups of twelve, appointing an abbot over each group. Finally he migrated to the hilltop of Monte Cassino that towers above the Via Latina midway between Rome and Naples. And there he built a monastery for a fully coenobitical community, which he directed for the rest of his life. He died, Gregory seems to tell us, sometime between the years 546 and 550, and was buried at Cassino. In the *Dialogues* Gregory makes only a single reference to St Benedict's Rule: 'He wrote a Rule for monks remarkable for its discretion and the lucidity of its language. If anyone wishes to know more about his life and conversation, he can find all the facts of the master's teaching in this same institution of the Rule, for the holy man could not teach otherwise than he lived.'[3] This is the earliest known reference to the Rule and it is all that Gregory has to say about it. There is nothing in the *Dialogues* to indicate that he had read it.[4]

THE RULE AND ITS SOURCES

Among the innumerable manuscripts of the Rule, the earliest extant is probably one that was made in Anglo-Saxon England about the year 750, which is now at Oxford in the Bodleian Library. But a more precious copy is one that survives in a manuscript of St Gall. This is the copy made at Aachen early in the ninth century from a codex which Theodemar, the abbot of Monte Cassino, had sent to Charlemagne. Charles had written to request an authentic text for use in his own dominions, and the codex that Theodemar sent him was copied at Cassino from the manuscript that was believed to be St Benedict's own autograph. It seems then that we have in the St Gall manuscript a text derived at only one remove from the author's original – a rare thing for a widely disseminated text of such antiquity.

Although we cannot be sure when Benedict compiled it, there are internal signs that the work in its existing form was not composed all at once, but was amended and expanded over a period of some time in the light of his experience. This is indicated by a number of dislocations in the logical sequence of the subject-matter and by the fact that the last seven chapters appear to have been added to the original conclusion as an afterthought. The Rule in fact consists of a prologue and seventy-three chapters, and, apart from the occasional discontinuities in the argument, it sets out a coherent and detailed plan for the organisation of a monastic community. The monastery it describes is a fully coenobitical society, living in a single building or complex of buildings, under the direction of an abbot who is elected by the brethren. Those who seek admission to it are required to pass a year in the noviciate to test their suitability and perseverance, following which they totally renounce all personal property, and take vows binding them to observe the rules of the monastic life and to remain in the community until death.

The prologue and first seven chapters of the Rule comprise an exhortatory treatise on the ascetical life, explaining its aims and the characteristic virtues the monk should strive to cultivate, foremost among which are obedience and humility. The following thirteen chapters contain detailed instructions for the order of divine service – the regular round of prayer, readings, and psalmody, which constituted the framework of the monk's day. After this there are a series of chapters dealing with such constitutional matters as the election of the abbot and the role of other monastic officers, regulations for the hours of sleep, manual work, and reading, and for meals, and intercalated among these various instructions, a penitential code, which lays down penalties for breaches of the monastic discipline. Much attention is given to the reception and training of recruits. It is impossible to do justice in a few words to the wealth of detail and the subtlety of insight contained in St Benedict's treatise. Some of his cardinal ideas will be examined below. As a whole, the Rule offered an eminently practical guide both to the government of a coenobitical community and to the spiritual life of the monk.

Although internal evidence suggests that it was composed in the years after 535, we know very little about the circumstances in which St Benedict worked. The sources of his teaching pose a special problem. One thing at least has been made clear by modern critical scholarship: it is no longer possible to regard the Rule as the isolated work of an original genius; it formed one of a group of closely inter-related monastic Rules composed in Italy and southern Gaul in the first half of the sixth century. Close to it in time were the two Rules – the one for women and the other for men – written by Caesarius of Arles (*c.* 470–542).

Like most Gallic bishops of his time, Caesarius was an offspring of the Gallo-Roman aristocracy. He had taken monastic vows at Lérins as a lad of twenty, but his health could not stand the life. He was sent to Arles, where he went to the schools and the bishop made him a clerk. But his heart remained at Lérins. They had to drag him out of hiding to make him a bishop; but years later, he compensated a little for his lost vocation by founding and directing a community of nuns at Arles. It was for them he wrote the first and longer of his Rules after persistent nagging by their abbess.[5] The document he produced consisted of a rather disorganised collection of precepts and an order of psalmody for use in the divine office. Many of the instructions on such matters as the novitiate, the renunciation of personal ownership, and lifelong stability, were cardinal principles adopted by St Benedict, and there are verbal echoes in his Rule which suggest that he knew the work of Caesarius. But the borrowing was not all in one direction. Caesarius himself had clearly read the Italian *Rule of the Master*, a text which, as we shall see in a moment, provided Benedict with his major literary source. These complex literary relationships show that in the sixth century Italy and Provence formed part of a single monastic world united by a common body of ascetical doctrine.

Some of the literary products of this milieu have recently been identified, like the Rule for monks composed by Eugippius.[6] Eugippius was abbot of a monastery at Lucullanum near Sorrento. His other work, a *Life of St Severin*, was written some twenty years before St Benedict founded his establishment at Cassino. It was probably in

21

one of the monasteries south of Rome that, soon after the year 500, an unknown abbot wrote the *Rule of the Master*.[7] It is now generally accepted by scholars that this text was St Benedict's chief literary source.

Benedict's debt to the anonymous Master was a heavy one. He derived from him not only most of his basic principles and organisational details; some of the most famous passages in the Rule, such as the chapters on obedience and the grades of humility, were taken over verbatim; and many other passages were transplanted with little change. In fact, all the essentials of St Benedict's Rule are to be found in the work of his unknown predecessor who, to judge by his liturgical instructions, was writing some forty years earlier. Appropriation of other people's work without acknowledgement was commonplace with medieval writers. To us it is plagiarism; to them it was a mark of humility and deference to greater wisdom. When Benedict decided to compile a book of instruction for his monks at Cassino, it would have seemed perfectly natural to him to model his Rule on a treatise composed by some other acknowledged veteran of the ascetical life.

St Benedict emerges then not as a solitary genius with a unique gift for monastic legislation, but rather as the representative of a school of ascetical teaching current in sixth-century Italy, which derived its primary inspiration from Egypt. He does not stand alone. Behind him we can dimly discern a shadowy company of abbots and hermits inhabiting the hill-places east and south of Rome, who were linked to one another by personal contact and the exchange of books. Nevertheless, it was his Rule, and not that of the anonymous Master, that gradually won universal recognition in Western Europe. What were the reasons for this? Gregory's biography was certainly a major factor. It made him famous and aroused interest in his Rule. But its success cannot be explained solely by Gregory's propaganda. The intrinsic merits of Benedict's treatise were equally important in promoting its circulation. For he was no slavish copyist. Both structurally and stylistically his Rule is better than the model he used. He and the Master both wrote in the *lingua vulgaris* – the ordinary Latin spoken by educated people in the sixth century, as opposed to the literary Latin of the classical age. But Benedict's language, where he is not copying from his source, is terser and his phraseology is more finely chiselled than the Master's. Again and again he arrests and pleases the reader with a lapidary phrase or epigram: 'Idleness is the enemy of the soul'; 'wine is certainly not suitable for monks'; 'let nothing have precedence over divine service.' By contrast, the Master's treatise is verbose, rambling, and poorly co-ordinated.

It was not only stylistically that Benedict improved on his source. His thought is more refined and his argument is less cluttered with irrelevant detail. Also, at several points where he is discussing the government of the monastery, he reveals a more genial spirit than the Master's and a greater tolerance of human weakness. 'We hope', he writes, 'we shall ordain nothing that is harsh or burdensome.'[8] In both treatises the sheet-anchor of the community is the personality of the abbot, and both authors were clearly influenced here by Roman notions of paternal authority. But the authority of Benedict's abbot is less autocratic. In decision-making he is instructed to take the opinion of the whole community, including its most junior members, whereas the Master insists that no one is to proffer advice unless it is asked for. And Benedict's abbot is elected by the brethren, whereas the Master's abbot is given the power to designate his successor. Unquestioning obedience to the will of the superior is demanded by both Rules, but Benedict tempers this doctrine with a repeated emphasis upon the bond of mutual love. All in all, his Rule is gentler and more humane than its prototype.

THE MONK'S PROFESSION ACCORDING TO THE RULE

St Benedict's idea of the monastic life is completely coenobitic. His community of monks is a family, living under one roof or, at any rate, round one patio, under an abbot who is father to the community – in fact, a villa monastery. Indeed the classical layout of the Benedictine abbeys and priories of the Middle Ages was descended from the plan of the Roman country villa of late antiquity. Following the Master, Benedict allows for the vocation of the hermit; but he obviously considers it a rare and dangerous one; those who are called to it must first undergo their training by sharing the life of the monastic community – 'who not in the first fervour of the ascetical life, but in the daily testing of the monastery have been taught to fight the devil, and go out well armed from the battle-line of their brethren to the solitary combat of the desert',[9] The military imagery is a pervasive feature of early monastic literature. The spiritual life of the monk was a ceaseless warfare against demons, who roved the world seeking to exploit the weaknesses of man's fallen nature. The anchorite needed to be well equipped for his lonely confrontation with the rulers of the world's darkness.

Benedict's cautious approval of hermits was not lost on his disciples in later times. It was not unusual for a Benedictine abbey of the Middle Ages to have one or two members of its community who were living as hermits at some remove from the parent monastery. As late as the fourteenth century, the cathedral priory of Durham dispatched a succession of monk-solitaries to occupy a cell on the island of Inner

Farne off the Northumbrian coast. But it was not for people like this that Benedict composed his Rule. He was writing for the coenobites – 'the brave race who conduct their warfare subject to a Rule and under an abbot'.[10]

There are several hints in the Rule that he had a wider monastic public in mind than his own community at Cassino. But although he included advice for other communities who were living in different conditions, he did not envisage anything that could be called a monastic order. The kind of monastery described by the Rule was an autonomous unit, economically self-supporting, and having no constitutional links with any other religious house. A man who sought to become a monk must knock on the gate of a particular community, and if after a period of trial he was admitted to membership, he promised to remain in that establishment until his death.

The ritual set out in the Rule for receiving new brethren throws much light on Benedict's thoughts. The postulant was not to be allowed easy entry; he must persist in his request for four or five days before the door is opened to him, and he must then complete a year's probation in the cell of the novices. If he stayed the course, he made his profession in the oratory in the presence of the community. He took a vow of stability, promising to persevere in the same house for the rest of his life, a vow to embrace the religious life, and a vow of obedience; he then prostrated himself before each member of the community in turn. If he had any property, he was required either to distribute it to the poor or confer it on the monastery by a solemn deed of gift.

Benedict's insistence on the need for stability was not novel. 'A monk out of his cloister', said St Antony, 'is a fish out of water.' And Caesarius agreed with him. What was new was the incorporation of the principle into the monk's vows. Its importance for Benedict is apparent from the fierceness with which he condemns the *gyrovagi* – the wandering monks, who were for ever on the move, trading upon the hospitality of other houses, 'concerning whose miserable way of life it is better to be silent than to speak'. The Master had been less reticent: his Rule includes a Rabelaisian picture of the gluttonous wanderers descending upon their impoverished host and picking him bare. The professional guest – whether he was a wandering monk or a vagabond clerk – was a constant nuisance to the medieval Church. For centuries bishops and councils fulminated against him in vain. Benedict's uncharacteristic sharpness on the subject is understandable: the wanderer not only disrupted the cohesion of the brethren by his restlessness; by abusing hospitality he exploited one of the most solemn obligations imposed by the Rule, for Benedict insisted that a monastery should receive a guest as though he were Christ himself. Of course, a monk might be sent elsewhere under higher orders without damaging the general principle of stability. So Abbot Hadrian was dispatched by the pope to England with Archbishop Theodore of Tarsus to make sure he introduced none of his dubious Greek customs into the English Church; and the Irish monks, who were notorious wanderers, evangelised Northumbria and planted monasteries across the face of Europe from St Gall to Bobbio.

Another feature of Benedict's thought that is highlighted by the instructions for novices is his thoroughly Roman insistence upon the absolute sovereignty of a written Rule. The law of Rome was a written law – at the time that the Rule was taking shape in his mind the jurists of the Emperor Justinian were busy codifying the great mass of classical legislation and jurisprudence. So it was that the would-be monk should have the Rule read to him repeatedly during the year of his noviciate, and after two months he was to be told, 'Here is the law under which you wish to fight; if you can observe it, enter; if you cannot, depart freely.'[11] In other monasteries the customs of the house were determined by the superior. But in Benedict's plan the Rule is sovereign, and even the abbot is allowed no discretion to depart from it. He is warned of his duty to maintain it in every detail. Because the Rule reflected the social customs and liturgical practices of the sixth century, later modifications there were bound to be. But the essence of Benedict's idea impressed itself upon the Western ascetical tradition. Men came to think of monks as people whose religious life was governed by a written code: the monastic life came to be described as the 'regular life' – life according to a rule.

When the monk made his profession he was required to renounce personal ownership completely: 'from that day he will not even have proprietorship of his own body'.[12] All property was held by the community in common. The individual must regard nothing as his own. Even the possession of a stylus and writing-tablets required the abbot's permission. Property is an extension of personality. Its renunciation was an act of self-negation that the Gospel had commended to those who sought spiritual perfection. But it did not involve destitution where it was made within the context of corporate ownership. Benedict makes it clear that he expected a monastery to possess buildings and land. He assumes that in most cases the labour on the estate will be performed by tenants, though where poverty forced the monks to help gather the harvest they were to do so without grumbling, 'for then are they truly monks when they live by the labour of their hands as the apostles and fathers did before them.'[13] But it is unlikely that he visualised monasteries possessing great wealth. Monks were *ex professo* 'the poor of Christ', and as such they attracted support from pious benefactors. Yet the poverty of the individual, living in a spacious and wealthy institution, tended to be psychological rather than material. Centuries of endowment turned many abbeys into rich and powerful corporations displaying all the characteristics of group acquisitiveness. Was wealth on this scale compatible with the Rule? In the twelfth century, the question was put to Cluny by St Bernard. 'In saying "any property"', writes Peter the Venerable defensively, 'the Rule makes no exception. Monks hold these things in a quite different way . . . they exist as having nothing, yet possessing all things.'[14] It was a stock answer. But the question could not be so easily silenced in a society where those vowed to poverty enjoyed the security and comfort of palatial surroundings, while most of those in the outside world were living at subsistence level.

Following the teachings of the Eastern masters, Benedict makes obedience the cardinal principle of the monastic life. Along with stability and conversion of ways, it was the subject of the monk's threefold vow. Its significance for Benedict is shown by its place in the opening words of the Rule: 'Hear, O son, the precepts of the master; so that by the labour of obedience you may return to Him from whom, through the sloth of disobedience, you fell away.' So the monk's task was to undo the primeval act of man's disobedience to the divine will by modelling himself on Christ, who 'was obedient unto death'. The monastic life began with the intention to renounce self-will and to place oneself under the will of a superior, who represented the person of Christ. What was demanded was not mere outward conformity, but the inner assent of the will to the commands of the abbot. Obedience must be prompt, willing, and without murmuring. The sixty-eighth chapter of the Rule raises the question of what a brother should do if he is ordered to undertake something too burdensome or impossible. He is told he should receive the command gently and obediently; and if the task required seems utterly beyond his powers, he is to explain patiently to his superior the reason for his inability to carry out the instruction, but without resisting or contradicting. If, after his explanation, the superior persists, the monk is to obey, trusting in the help of God. The conundrum was a classical one in the training of ascetics. Total docility to the will of the master was the essential safeguard against spiritual pride.

It followed from such an uncompromising doctrine of obedience that the personality of the abbot was the linchpin of the monastic community. St Benedict's abbot cannot lawfully command anything that is contrary to the law of God or to the Rule, but otherwise his discretion is absolute. He can appoint and dismiss subordinates, allocate punishments, and direct the relations of the monastery with the outside world as he thinks best. He is urged by the Rule to take the advice of the brethren before taking policy decisions, but he is not bound by it. Constitutionally then, St Benedict's monastery is a paternal autocracy tempered by the obligation to listen to advice. But the abbot is much more than an absolute ruler. He has a pastoral role towards his community. He is the teacher, confessor, and spiritual guide of his monks. This side of his role is illuminated by Benedict's instructions for Lenten observance. Each monk is to decide what form of mortification he is going to undertake; he must then propose it to the abbot and only undertake it with his permission. Thus by performing his ascetical acts under obedience the monk is protected against spiritual pride or complacency. As the pastor of his community, the abbot is reminded that at the Judgement he will have to render account for their souls. The Rule constantly warns him against ruling tyrannically or harshly; he is to regard himself as the servant of the brethren rather than their master; he should study to make himself loved rather than feared.

The authoritarian character of the regime is softened not only by St Benedict's insistence upon governing with counsel but also by his provisions for appointing the head of the monastery. The abbot is to be chosen by the brethren themselves and usually, it is implied, from their own number. Even the most junior member of the community is to be considered eligible if his prudence and learning make him suitable. Once elected, the abbot is presented to the bishop for consecration, and he holds office for life. Benedict allows for active intervention by the bishop or by neighbouring abbots only in an emergency situation, where a lax or disorderly community has elected a candidate who is obviously unworthy. In this case, they may have an abbot imposed upon them; but otherwise the choice remains with the monks.

In a community of any size the abbot would need assistants to help him rule the monastery. The Rule refers to a provost or prior, deans, a cellarer, who is in charge of provisioning the establishment, a gatekeeper, and brethren deputed to take charge of the novices, the guest-house, and the infirmary. Benedict's main concern here seems to be to preserve the monarchic regime of the abbot from any dilution. All the monastic officers are to be appointed by him and to be directly subordinated to him. In the great Benedictine abbeys of the Middle Ages, where the abbot was a prelate constantly taken from his community by public duties, the effective head of the brethren was the claustral prior. But in the Rule St Benedict contemplates the prior with misgiving as a possible source of discord: 'some there be, puffed up with the malignant spirit of pride, who reckon themselves second abbots'.[15] He prefers a system of deans, each of whom is placed by the abbot in charge of a group of ten monks. The deans were, so to speak, non-commissioned officers – name and rank were in fact derived from the imperial army, and the system was adopted in the Pachomian monasteries of Egypt. Abbot Smaragdus, commenting on the Rule in the ninth century, observed that the deans were not merely rulers of their sections; they were their spiritual mentors and should know the inmost thoughts of their charges. Smaragdus wrote from experience, for the system was still practised in the Carolingian monasteries, but it hardly outlived him. In the reformed abbeys of the eleventh century, the devolution of authority followed different lines, determined by economic and administrative convenience.

THE MONK'S LIFE ACCORDING TO THE RULE

'We must', wrote Benedict in his preface, 'create a *scola* for the Lord's service.' In the language of the sixth century the word *scola* had a military as well as an academic sense; it meant a special regiment or *corps d'élite*. In the early Middle Ages the Roman Borgo – the region of the city that lay outside the Aurelian walls between St Peter's and the Tiber – was defended by *scolae* or units of militia, supplied by the various nationalities settled in the district. Benedict was using the word in this sense. His monastery was not a place of quiet retreat or leisure, nor a school in the academic sense; it was a kind of combat unit, in which the recruit was trained and equipped for his spiritual warfare under an experienced commander – the abbot. The objective was the conquest of sensuality and self-will that made a man totally receptive to God. For this purpose the Rule prescribed a carefully ordered routine of prayer, work, and study, which filled the day, varying only according to the liturgical year and the natural seasons. It was a regime of strict discipline but, wrote Benedict, casting an eye over his shoulder at the fiercer austerities of the Eastern ascetics, there was to be 'nothing harsh or burdensome'. His was 'a little Rule for beginners'. And in fact the timetable made no intolerable demands. It allowed eight hours of sleep in the winter and six hours, with an afternoon siesta, in the summer. The allowance of food, if not lavish, was adequate. The eating of meat was forbidden except to the sick, but a meal could include two or three dishes of cooked vegetables with bread and a measure of wine; but if the brethren lived in a region where wine was not to be had, they were to accept the fact without grumbling. 'We read', observed Benedict, 'that wine is certainly not for monks'[16] yet here, as elsewhere in the Rule, he was willing to make concessions to human weakness.

The first task of the monastic life was prayer in common – the singing of divine service in the oratory, what Benedict calls the Work of God or *Opus Dei*. This provided the basic framework of the day and everything else was fitted round it. Following the Rule of the Master, but with significant variants, Benedict gives elaborate instructions for the celebration of these daily services, which are of great interest to the historian of Christian worship, as they are the earliest detailed description of the divine office that we have. It had long been the common practice in the greater churches to conduct public prayers daily at dawn and in the evening; these were the offices of Lauds and Vespers. By St Benedict's time, the monastic communities had added to these services and evolved a daily round of eight offices that were recited in common at certain hours of the day.

The monk's routine of worship began during the hours of darkness, at 2 a.m. or shortly after in winter, and at 3 a.m. or shortly after in summer, with the singing of the office of Vigils or Nocturns (later called Matins). Lauds was sung at first light, and there followed at intervals the relatively short offices of the day, sung at the first, third, sixth, and ninth hours, and the evening office of Vespers. The day ended with the brief service of Compline, which was sung at sundown. The night office was the longest and most elaborate of the services. It was divided into parts called Nocturns, each of which consisted of six psalms and four lessons together with responsories, or meditative verses, relating to the subject of the lessons. On Sundays and feast-days the night office contained three Nocturns, and it must have taken nearly two hours to complete. Benedict's Rule laid down detailed instructions for the order of psalmody so as to ensure that the entire Psalter was recited in the course of each week. The lessons were to be drawn from the Bible and the Scriptural commentaries of the Fathers. In the course of the following centuries the office was greatly elaborated, musically as well as textually, but the basic pattern as it is outlined in the Rule persisted and came to be the standard framework of daily worship in the Western Church; and its traces are clearly visible in all the service-books, Protestant as well as Catholic, that are derived from the medieval tradition.

Rather surprisingly to the modern reader, the Rule, which provides in such detail for the daily prayer of the community, has only a few and incidental references to eucharistic prayer. This was because the order of the eucharistic liturgy was determined by the bishop; it was not something on which an abbot could legislate. And St Benedict was observing the custom of the early Church, which was still maintained in his time, by which the celebration of mass was reserved to Sundays and the feasts of the Lord. As the whole community would attend the weekly eucharist, the monastery would not need more than one or two men in priest's orders, and those to be ordained would be selected by the abbot. Benedict assumed that the majority of the monks would not be ordained. Those chosen to be priests or deacons are sternly warned against arrogance: they are to do nothing except on the abbot's orders and they must remain in the rank already assigned to them in the community, unless they should be promoted to one of the monastic offices.

The community did not go back to bed after Nocturns; there was a short interval, after which the office of Lauds was sung at first light, and then the office of Prime at sunrise. Then the monks processed out of choir and went about their work. The timetable varied like the tides in response to the rhythm of the seasons. The computation of time that was followed was that of classical antiquity, which was still in use in the sixth century. By this reckoning the periods of daylight and darkness were each divided into twelve hours of equal length. Thus in winter the night hours would be longer than sixty minutes, and day hours would be correspondingly short; and conversely, in summer the day hours would be long and the night hours short. The job of getting everybody out of bed at the correct time for the night office and ringing the bells for the canonical hours must have posed problems before the advent of the mechanical clock in the fourteenth century. Before this, water clocks were widely used. Some monastic custumals recommend astronomical observation as a check during the night hours. Clearly somebody had to stay awake during the night to rouse the community at the proper time. In the Master's Rule the duty falls upon each tithing of the brethren in turn. They watch the clock in pairs, lest one of them fall asleep, and when the hour comes, they go the abbot's bed and say 'Lord, open thou my lips', tapping his feet gently until he wakes.[17]

Outside the hours of common prayer the Rule divided the monk's day into periods of manual work and periods of reading. The summer timetable, which began at Easter, allocated upwards of seven hours to work and three hours to reading; in winter the period of work was shortened and the time for reading increased. In the longer summer days the Rule provided for two meals, the first shortly after midday and the second in the early evening; whereas the winter timetable allowed only a single meal, which was eaten at about 2.30 in the afternoon, or later still in Lent. No talking was permitted during meals; the brethren ate in silence while a member of the community read to them. The thing that is most conspicuously absent from the Rule is any provision for leisure. 'Idleness', Benedict observes severely, 'is the enemy of the soul.' His insistence upon the value of manual work is in the Eastern monastic tradition; it had an ascetical as well as an economic function; it kept men humble, and it provided for the material wants of the community. Any of the monks who were craftsmen were to ply their skill at the abbot's discretion and their artefacts might be sold. The rest of the community would go to work in the fields or be occupied with house duties. Benedict's careful balance between periods of manual work and study was destroyed by later medieval developments. The addition of a daily chapter mass and the increasing elaboration of the liturgical offices, which reached its climax at Cluny, encroached upon the rest of the day. And the acquisition of great estates meant that growing numbers of monks in the Benedictine abbeys were preoccupied with managerial tasks. But Benedict's simple plan offered a model that later monastic reformers constantly sought to revive.

What did St Benedict intend his monks to read during the many hours of each week that were allocated to study? Did the phrase he used – *lectio divina*, sacred or divine reading – include literary or intellectual pursuits? Here was one of the enigmas of the Rule over which later commentators spilt much ink. The ninth century was an age of learned abbots, when the Benedictine monasteries of the Meuse and the Rhineland played a major role in transmitting the literary culture of antiquity to the medieval world. In fact, until the scholastic movement of the twelfth century, most of the leaders in the world of learning were monks. But did this tradition represent an authentic interpretation of St Benedict's plan? In the seventeenth century, Rancé, the founder of the Trappist reform, had no doubt that it did not, and charged the learned Benedictines of St Maur with subversion of the Rule: 'St Benedict and the whole of antiquity is on my side . . . and what is called study has only been established at a period of relaxation.'[18] Rancé displays all the blind rigidity of the self-appointed dogmatist, and the chief merit of his shrill polemic was that it provoked the great monk-scholar Jean Mabillon to write his magnificent apologia for monastic learning; but from the viewpoint of the sixth century, he had a point.

Churchmen of the sixth century displayed an ambivalent attitude towards classical letters. Christianity had conquered the Empire, but the pagan deities which haunted the poets and orators of antiquity were still too close to be trifled with. Venus and the Muses were dangerous beguilements for the man who had heard the Gospel call to renunciation. It was this that gave the *coup de grâce* to the ancient schools of rhetoric. They had lingered on in Italy and Gaul after the collapse of the imperial civil service, only to be finally smothered under a cloud of ecclesiastical disapproval. But the poets and orators were not so easily exorcised. The Latin Fathers who rail against them most had been reared on them, and their prose betrays their debt on every page. There were some who sought a reconciliation, like the old Roman aristocrat Cassiodorus, who was a contemporary of St Benedict. After serving the Ostrogothic King Theodoric, he retired to a monastery which he created on his own estate at Vivarium, in southern Italy. And he composed a programme of studies for his monks which included the classical orators and Aristotle's logic; the programme was to be divided into two parts, or Institutes – one of divine and one of secular letters – and, as he explains, the purpose of studying the pagan classics was to equip the student for a better understanding of the sacred Scriptures.[19] It was the strategy that

31

Augustine had approved: Christian education might exploit the classics for its own purposes, just as the Israelites had plundered the Egyptians.

The *Institutes* of Cassiodorus were much read, but his educational scheme did not win general approval with early monastic legislators. The learned leisure of Vivarium owed more to the classical tradition of the scholar-recluse than it did to the ascetical spirit that was blowing from the East. That spirit was more faithfully encapsulated in Jerome's account of a dream he had after he had decided to embrace the ascetical life. He was on his way to the Syrian desert, but he could not bring himself to leave his Cicero out of his luggage. One night, during a bout of illness, he dreamed he was brought before the divine judgement seat and asked his profession. His answer that he was a Christian produced the stern response: 'Thou liest. Thou art no Christian, but a Ciceronian; where thy heart is, there is thy treasure also.' And he was sentenced to a cruel flogging.[20] In his fright he vowed never to read the pagan classics again, and for some years at least he seems to have kept his promise. The anecdote, which was intended to warn one of his spiritual protégés off reading Horace and Virgil, is a paradigm of the attitude of the early monastic world towards the classics. Apart from the Old and New Testaments, the only works that St Benedict expressly commends to his monks are the books of the Catholic Fathers, the Lives of the Fathers, Cassian, and the Rules of St Basil. It is the ascetic's quintessential library. His phrase 'divine reading' by implication excludes the pagan classics; and his instructions for the issue of books to the community imply that the purpose of reading is to acquire food for pious meditation: every year, at the beginning of Lent, each monk received a codex from the library, which he was required to read in entirety, without skipping pages. The ritual was maintained at Canterbury in the eleventh century, in Lanfranc's day: the books for Lenten reading were laid out on a carpet in the centre of the chapter-house; the books of the previous year were returned, and anyone who had failed to finish his volume, prostrated himself, and confessed his fault.[21]

Yet even in St Benedict's cloister there had to be some study of the classics. The Rule provides for child-oblates, donated to the monastery by their parents. The practice already existed in the time of the anonymous Master. In the Rule the parents make the vows on the child's behalf, wrap his hand in the cloth used for the mass offerings, and as it were place him in the offertory plate, together with a suitable gift. So the boys, aged seven and upwards, formed a normal group in the Benedictine communities of the early Middle Ages. In the eighth-century commentary of Paul the Deacon, they are shepherded about the house in crocodile formation by a posse of masters and they are required to take their place in choir for all the offices. And they had of course to be taught their letters through the standard grammars of Priscian and Donatus, which provided a fair anthology of the Latin poets. The classics might be dangerous fare, but they could not be wholly dispensed with in educating the young. Thus of necessity the monastery contained a school, but it was a school for child-monks, which did not normally admit pupils from outside.

St Benedict's Rule did not deny entry to men from any class of society. But in practice the requirements of the monastic life restricted adult recruitment to those social groups that were educated. In fact in the following centuries the foundation and endowment of monasteries was largely the work of the princes and nobility in the Germanic kingdoms, and the recruitment of monks was mainly from the same class. The practice of child oblation, distressing though it may be to the mind of a modern parent, became increasingly popular. Among landed families it offered a welcome means of providing for surplus children who could not be endowed without a dangerous partition of the family estate. It was equally valued as a way of providing for girls for whom no suitable marriage alliance could be found. Thus the child oblates were a major source of recruitment to the medieval monasteries. Sentiment turned against it in the twelfth century. The Cistercians refused to accept children – though more out of a desire to avoid the worldly entanglements involved than from any appreciation of child psychology – and in 1215 the practice was forbidden by the Fourth Lateran Council. But in the heyday of Benedictine monasticism the practice produced some remarkable people. The Northumbrian Bede, 'Candle of the Church' and proto-historian of England, and Eadmer, the precentor of Christ Church and biographer of St Anselm, were both reared in the cloister from childhood. So too was Matilda, the abbess of Quedlinburg, a daughter of the Emperor Otto I, who had been veiled at the age of eleven, and who proved herself equal to ruling a kingdom in the absence of her nephew. After the Lateran Council it was still permissible to accept children for education so long as they were not committed to the monastic profession. But from this time the numbers of children in monastic houses dwindled rapidly, and there seems no doubt that the ending of child oblation was one of the reasons for the reduced size of Benedictine communities in the later Middle Ages.

St Benedict's Rule provided a model for a close-knit, well-organised ascetic community, following a carefully planned routine of prayer, work, and study. Though the writer's debts to the ascetical teaching of the East are obvious, what gave his scheme its distinctive character was his concern for the essentially Roman virtues of stability, order, and moderation. It was a wise and reassuring prescription for religious groups recruiting their members from the intelligentsia of late antiquity. Amid the debris of classical civilisation, in a world grown barbarous, violent and unpredictable, Benedict's monastery offered an enclave of peace and order. But it was vulnerable; and the survival of his institution was by no means assured. Some twenty years after his death, the Lombards broke into Italy and carried devastation through the peninsula. The military presence left by Byzantium was too weak to offer any effective resistance. In 577 Monte Cassino was sacked and its monastic buildings were burned down. Benedict's other foundations at Subiaco and Terracina suffered the same fate. The monks at Cassino scattered, some to Rome, where the pope offered them a refuge in one of the satellite monasteries of the Lateran basilica. The site at Cassino remained ruinous and deserted for the following 140 years. Elsewhere, the Lombardic settlement seems to have arrested the development of Italian monasticism. It is obvious from Gregory the Great's reference that the Benedictine Rule was known at Rome at the end of the sixth century, but there is no evidence of any monastery at Rome following the Rule nor, significantly, is there evidence of any cultus of St Benedict at Rome, either in iconography or church dedication, before the tenth century. The future of the Rule lay in fact, not in Italy, but north of the Alps in the Germanic kingdoms; and above all in Gaul.

NOTES

1. *PL* 66, 126–204; modern edition by U. Moricca, *Gregorii Magni Dialogi* (Fonti per la Storia d' Italia 57, 1924).
2. The story of Totila's visit and St Benedict's alleged prophecy of his entry to Rome has literary antecedents in the Lives of the Fathers and the *Life of St Martin*, which raises the question of its historical authenticity, see P. A. Cusack, 'Some literary antecedents of the Totila encounter in the second Dialogue of Pope Gregory I', *Studia Patristica* **12** (1975), 87–90. On the allegorical sense of the stories in the Dialogues see W. F. Bolton, 'The supra-historical sense in the Dialogues of Gregory I', *Aevum* **33** (1959), 206–13, and J. H. Wansborough, 'St Gregory's intention in the stories of St Scholastica and St Benedict', *Revue Bénédictine* **75** (1965), 145–51. In his introduction to the Dialogues in *Grégoire le Grand: Dialogus I* (Sources chrétiennes 251, Paris 1978) A. de Vogüé rejects a comprehensively sceptical approach to the historical matter in the Dialogues, and distinguishes between narration and Gregory's tropological exposition. I agree with him.
3. *PL* 66, 162.
4. The point was convincingly made by K. Hallinger, 'Papst Gregor der Grosse and der heilige Benedikt', *Studia Anselmiana* **42** (Rome 1957), 231–319, that those of Gregory's letters that contain advice on

monastic matters display no acquaintance with the Rule and in some respects contradict it.

5. *Sancti Caesarii Arelatensis Opera*, ed. G. Morin (Maredsous 1942), II, pp 129–30.
6. A. de Vogüé, 'La Règle d'Eugippe retrouvée', *Revue d'ascétique* **47** (1971), 233–65.
7. Text edited by A. de Vogüé, *La Règle du Maître* 3 vols (Sources chrétiennes 105, Paris 1964–65). For the discussion surrounding this document see M. D. Knowles, *Great Historical Enterprises and Problems in Monastic History* (1963), pp 137–95; and de Vogüé, 'Saint Benoît en son temps: règles italiennes et règles provençales au vi^e siècle', *Règulae Benedicti Studia* I (Rome 1972), 170–93.
8. *The Rule,* prologue.
9. *Ibid.,* c. 1.
10. *Ibid.,* c. 1.
11. *Ibid.,* c. 58.
12. *Ibid.,* c. 58.
13. *Ibid.,* c. 48.
14. *The Letters of Peter the Venerable*, ed. G. Constable (Cambridge, Mass. 1967), i, p. 84.
15. *The Rule,* c. 65.
16. *Ibid.* c. 40.
17. *La Règle du Maître*, ii, pp. 172–3.
18. *Lettres de Armand Jean le Bouthillier de Rancé*, ed. B. Gonot (Paris 1846), p. 226.
19. *Cassiodori Senatoris Institutiones*, ed. R. A. B. Mynors (1937), pp. 68–9.
20. *Epistulae* 22, 30; J. N. D. Kelly, *Jerome* (1975), p. 42.
21. *The Monastic Constitutions of Lanfranc.* ed. M. D. Knowles (1951), p. 19.

Chapter 3

WANDERING SAINTS AND PRINCELY PATRONS

COLUMBANUS IN GAUL

By the time Lombards sacked Cassino, monasticism had struck deep roots in Gaul. It took a variety of forms. In the northern kingdom of Neustria centred on the Paris basin, and in the West, St Martin's colony of Ligugé had provided the dominant model. The writings of Sulpicius had propagated his cultus among the Germanic peoples of the North. According to Gregory of Tours, when Clovis the Frank set out to conquer the Arian Visigoths, he first sent messengers to the shrine of St Martin to ask for a sign of divine approval.[1] Whatever the truth of the story, the Merovingians adopted the pioneer of Gallic monasticism as their *Reichsheiliger* – the national saint of the Franks – and this must have done much to boost his fame and promote his ideal of the ascetical life. Eremitical groups inspired by his example sprang into existence in the region of the Loiret and Aquitaine. Martin, however, left no known Rule, and we know little about the internal organisation of these communities. Many of them were only short-lived. A more stable type of monasticism flourished in the south-east, in Provence, and the Rhône valley. Here there existed a number of well-organised fully coenobitical communities, which stemmed from the early plantations at Lérins and Marseilles, the most famous of which was the convent for women founded by Caesarius in the suburbs of Arles. These establishments were located in or adjacent to episcopal cities and were under the supervision of bishops. As a rule they recruited their superiors, and probably most of their membership, from the old Gallo-Roman aristocracy of the area.

Although cultural contact between the two areas seems to have been limited, at least one significant link was forged by St Radegund's foundation at Poitiers, where the Rule of Caesarius was adopted. The founding of the convent of the Holy Cross at Poitiers inaugurated a new social era for the monastic movement. It now began to enjoy the patronage of the Merovingian kings and started to recruit its leadership from the nobility of the Germanic kingdoms. Radegund's own life-story has something of the quality of a fairy-tale by the brothers Grimm. She was a Thuringian princess, who was captured while still a child by the Frankish king Chlotar I during a campaign in her father's kingdom. Chlotar carried her off as a spoil of war, had her brought up on a royal manor and educated in letters, and eventually married her. But she had already made up her mind to adopt the ascetical life, and the marriage was an uneasy one for both partners. They joked at court that the king had married a nun.[2] In the end, after her husband had had her brother murdered, she quitted the royal household and settled at Poitiers, where she constructed and endowed a convent with Chlotar's help and took the veil. Her life was written by Venantius Fortunatus, the expatriate Italian poet, who settled close to the monastery and became her life-long friend and admirer. It was to celebrate her acquisition of a relic of the Cross – a gift from the Eastern emperor – that he composed the triumphal procession hymn of the *Vexilla Regis*. Fortunatus acted as counsellor and business manager to the community, and the elegantly contrived verses he wrote for Radegund and Abbess Agnes allow us one of a very few glimpses into the life-style of a royal nunnery of the sixth century. Radegund refused to direct the community herself. She preferred to serve as a nun under a superior whom she had appointed. Fortunatus was aghast at the thought of her washing dishes and doing her share of the menial jobs about the house.[3] Nevertheless the planning of the institution was hers, and it was her decision to adopt the Rule that Caesarius had composed for the nuns of Arles. And it was an integral part of her plan that the foundation should be subject to the supervision of the bishop of Poitiers. The oversight of a community of royal women proved, in fact, to be a thorny task. After Radegund's death in 587, two daughters of King Charibert led a rebellion of forty of the nuns against the abbess – 'for we are humiliated here as if we were the offspring of low-born serving-women, instead of being the daughters of kings'.[4] Not all princesses who were placed behind the walls of a convent or took refuge there felt a vocation to the ascetical life.

At the period of Radegund's death the ascetical tradition of southern Gaul, represented by the Rule of Caesarius, was beginning to penetrate the North, but permanent monastic foundations in the Frankish kingdoms of Neustria and Austrasia were still sparse. In Provence, the ancient centres of Lérins and Marseilles had sunk into obscurity. But in the last decade of the sixth century Gallic monasticism received a sudden infusion of new life from Ireland. The prime mover in this transformation was St Columbanus, the most famous wanderer of the early Middle Ages, from a nation notorious for its mobility. Columbanus was a monk and schoolmaster of the great monastery of Bangor in County Down. The Irish passion for leaving home, and the ascetical ideal of exile for the sake of Christ, had driven him to quit his monastery to evangelise areas that were still semi-pagan. In or about the year 591 he landed in Gaul with twelve companions, and made his way to the court of Childebert in Burgundy to seek the king's collaboration. He was first allocated a wild spot at Annegray in the Vosges. Recruits flowed in, and the foundation of Luxeuil – the most illustrious Celtic monastic establishment on the Continent – soon followed, and that of Fontaine shortly afterwards. But the role of moralist at Merovingian courts was a dangerous one. Columbanus's outspokenness about the sex-life of the young King Theuderic gained him the enmity of the formidable Queen Brunhild, the king's grandmother, and she had him expelled from Burgundy. He narrowly escaped being transported back to Ireland, resumed his wanderings, visited the Neustrian court at Soissons, and moved on over the Vosges into Swabia. By Lake Constance he parted from his faithful companion Gallus, whose cult centre grew into the great abbey of St Gall, and made his way to Italy. He was graciously received at the court of the Lombard King Agilulf and granted a site in the Apennines, at Bobbio, where he created his last monastic colony. He died and was buried at Bobbio in 615.

Like Luxeuil and St Gall, Bobbio became a focus for expatriate Irish monks and scholars. Columbanus was, in fact, the spearhead of the first invasion of the Continent by the culture of Celtic Christianity. The impact of his advent upon the religious life of Gaul was like that of a spring tide bursting into a stagnant pool. His foundations excited a wave of religious enthusiasm among the Frankish aristocracy and inaugurated a new era of growth for Gallic monasticism. To understand the sources that energised this growth it is necessary to turn to the development of monastic life in the Celtic lands.

EARLY IRISH MONASTICISM

We do not know how or when organised monasticism reached Ireland. It may have been imported from Britain or from Gaul or even directly from the East Mediterranean. The weight of evidence has forced modern scholars to abandon the old notion that the Anglo-Saxon invasion and settlement severed the Celtic Christians of western Britain and Ireland from contact with Continental Christianity. Missionaries from both Britain and Gaul had played a part in evangelising Ireland; there is also evidence that monastic life existed in Wales and Strathclyde in the fifth century, and that individual ascetics moved freely between the Celtic lands and the Continent. The mission of St Patrick, who died in 461, created an episcopal organisation in Ireland. It seems that alongside the secular hierarchy the ascetical movement was already gaining ground: Patrick refers in his *Confession* to great numbers of virgins who had consecrated their lives to Christ. Before the end of the century St Brigit had formed her monastery at Kildare. But the great age of monastic foundation in Ireland was the sixth century. Hagiographical tradition ascribed the cardinal role to St Finnian, 'master of saints', who was led by an angel to the site of Clonard, where he built his cell which became the nucleus of his famous monastery.[5] Clonmacnoise, Clonfert, and Terryglass, and many other monasteries claimed foundation by saints who had been disciples of Finnian at Clonard. In the same period, St Columba (Colmcille) founded Derry and Durrow and planted a colony on Iona off the coast of Pictland; St Comgall founded Bangor; and towards the end of the century, St Kevin founded Glendalough.

The inspiration for these ascetical colonies came ultimately from Egypt, but we do not know how it travelled from there. In some ways their mode of life resembled what we know of St Martin's semi-eremitical establishments in the west of Gaul, and perhaps it was from there rather than from the west of Britain that the pattern was derived. The Irish monastery was like a walled city. The whole settlement was enclosed by a rampart of earth and stones, within which monks lived singly or in small groups in detached huts, made either of wattle or of stones morticed in the characteristic beehive fashion. The crudity of the building technique imposed limitations of scale, and larger monasteries like Bangor and Clonmacnoise, that were unable to house the whole community in a single building for liturgical purposes, contained several relatively small churches; kitchen, guest-house, and other offices were also housed in separate structures. Each settlement was an autonomous unit, presided over patriarchally by a presbyter-abbot – a monk in priest's orders.

These were coenobitical communities, but they also made room for anchorites on their fringe. Cassian's teaching that the contemplative life of the hermit was superior to the coenobitical life had been absorbed, and the Celtic monastic movement contained a strong anchoritic tradition. A text called the *Catalogus Sanctorum Hiberniae*,[6] now recognised to be a compilation of the ninth century, divides the early saints of Ireland into three orders and assigns the highest place in the spiritual hierarchy to the third order – the anchorites. Not only monks, but Celtic abbots and bishops, moved freely and often from community life to solitude. Jonas of Bobbio, who wrote the *Life of Columbanus*, describes him periodically quitting his monks at Luxeuil and living in a cave. During one of these eremitic spells, it was revealed to him that several of the brothers had fallen ill, and he hurried back to the monastery to care for them.[7] When St Cuthbert at the end of his life withdrew from his community on Lindisfarne to settle in a hermitage on the island of Inner Farne, he was following a well-recognised practice. The pull of the desert – 'the wave cry, the wind cry, the vast waters of the petrel and the porpoise' – that sounds so strongly in Celtic hagiography, peopled many desolate islands and rocks round the coasts of Ireland and northern Britain with hermits. In some places their derelict stone huts and oratories are still visible.

No Irish monastic rule is known earlier than the Rule of St Columbanus. This, together with his Penitential and sermons, give us a glimpse of the spirit that governed Celtic practice. These documents, in fact, describe an ascetical regime so harsh and uncompromising that they chill the blood. For Columbanus, the life of the monk was a heroic and unremitting warfare to conquer his own self-will and sensuality[8]:

> The chief part of the monk's rule is mortification.. . . Let the monk live
> in a community under the discipline of one father and in the company
> of many. . . . Let him not do as he wishes, let him eat what he is bidden,
> keep as much as he has received, complete the tale of his work, be
> subject to him whom he does not like. Let him come weary and as if
> sleep-walking to his bed, and let him be forced to rise while his sleep is
> not yet finished. Let him keep silence when he has suffered wrong. Let
> him fear the superior of his community as a lord, love him as a father,
> believe that whatever he commands is salutary for himself.

This austere programme is underpinned by a Penitential of merciless severity. A brother who drops food or spills drink while serving is to do penance in church, lying prostrate and motionless during the singing of twelve psalms; breaking the rule of silence at meals is to be punished with six lashes; forgetting prayer before or after work, with twelve lashes; smiling during the divine office, with six lashes; using the words 'mine' or 'thine', with six lashes; contradicting the word of another, with fifty lashes.[9]

The object of this ferocious discipline was to hurry the monk along the road to the unitive experience of God, which was the crown of the contemplative's efforts. Columbanus explained it in the letter he wrote from exile to the brethren he had been forced to leave at Luxeuil. He writes tearfully and in haste, for a messenger has come to say that the ship that will carry him back to his own country is loaded and ready to sail. 'Keep to the highway of perfection . . . we must pass by the royal road to the city of God, through affliction of the flesh and contrition of the heart, through the toil of the body and the humiliation of the spirit . . . if you remove the battle, you remove the crown as well.'[10] The tone of this advice is echoed in Celtic hagio-graphical literature. The saints perform heroic acts of mortification; they recite the Psalter standing in icy waters, or stand for long periods in prayer with arms outstretched like a cross – the crossfigill; Kevin of Glendalough maintained the posture for seven years, unsleeping and motionless, so that the birds nested in his upturned hands[11]; they fast continually, and use bare rocks for bolsters. On the other hand, there are hints in the Lives that the actual regime in the Irish monasteries was more compassionate on human weakness than the Penitentials suggest. In the midst of the ascetical heroics, glimpses of a gentler and more humane spirit break through, of the abbot's solicitude for his monks to see they are not overworked and are prop-erly fed, of the love of animals and an appreciation of the natural world.

The Irish monks seem to have been free from the dread of the classics that afflicted Jerome and Gregory the Great. Latin was taught in the Irish monasteries of the seventh century, and it was not only the Latin of the Scriptures and the Fathers. The Latinity of Columbanus, who had taught the monks of Bangor before he embarked on his Continental odyssey, shows reminiscences of Virgil, Ovid, and Juvenal, as well as the Christian poets.[12] By the seventh century, their enthusiasm for learning and their zeal in teaching had made the monastic schoools of Ireland the most famous in Europe. Bede referred to them with awe. They were also important centres of book production. Children brought up in the monastery were taught to copy texts in the distinctive half-uncial script that was trans-mitted by the Irish missionaries to Anglo-Saxon England and by migratory monks to the scriptoria of St Gall and Bobbio and many other Irish monastic colonies on the Continent. St Columba was an accomplished scribe. Adamnan, who wrote his Life nearly a century later, tells us that at Durrow, when there was drought, they carried the books written in Columba's own hand into the fields and opened them, so as to induce rain.[13] The tenth-century author of the Life of St Comgall has a pleasing story of one of the boys in the monastery who was learning to write, but his writing was so appalling that nobody could tell whether it was a human script or meaningless marks made by the claws of a bird. His teachers despaired, but Comgall blessed his eyes and hands, and after that he made fine progress until he surpassed all the other scribes.[14] It was the fusion of this tradition of Irish calligraphy and love of zoomorphic animal forms with the artistic tradition of northern Britain, following the Celtic mission to Northumbria, that was to produce the great series of illuminated Gospel books, like the Book of Durrow, the Book of Kells and the Lindisfarne Gospels, which are the supreme monu-ments of Hiberno-Saxon art.

Historians have long puzzled over the peculiarities of the monastic structure that developed in the Celtic Church. The Church of the early centuries had modelled its organisation upon the administrative structure of the Roman Empire. In Gaul, as in other lands of the old Empire, diocesan organisation rested upon monarchic bishops, who were city-based. Everywhere the bishop's see was located in the old Roman *civitas* – an arrangement that was expressly authorised by the council of Chalcedon (451). Monasticism had developed in the West alongside, and in close connection with, this urban episcopal structure. Monasteries of men and women were founded in or adjacent to cities, and were under the supervision of bishops. But Ireland had never been within the Empire and lacked any urban life that could provide a basis for a Roman diocesan structure. It was a pastoral society, bonded together by the ties of tribe and kindred. There is evidence that the mission of St Patrick created an episcopal organisation of the traditional Roman type; but lacking the kind of social base that existed elsewhere, it seems to have withered; and before the end of the sixth century it had been largely superseded by a different type of ecclesiastical organisation centred upon the monasteries. The pastoral unit or 'paruchia' was the area dependent upon a monastery, and its spiritual ruler was the abbot, who in some cases might be a bishop, but was usually only in priest's orders. The ecclesiastical hierarchy included bishops, of course; they were essential for those sacramental functions that only a bishop could perform, such as ordinations and the consecration of churches; but they operated within the monastic paruchia and under the authority of an abbot. In the language of the later canonists, the power of jurisdiction (*potestas jurisdictionis*) was vested in abbots, and bishops exercised the power of order (*potestas ordinis*), that is their sacramental powers. The paruchia of some of the greater monasteries extended beyond their immediate territory to embrace an empire of daughter-houses founded across the seas, each with its own superior, but all subject to the overriding authority of the abbot of the founder-house.

This monastic church structure was peculiar to the Celtic lands. It is found in sixth-century Wales as well as Ireland, and the Irish missionaries from Iona imported it into northern Britain. But it made no headway on the Continent against the long-established Roman episcopal organisation. In Britain, its further development was arrested by the Synod of Whitby (664), where Colman of Lindisfarne representing the Irish mission, and Wilfrid of Ripon the Roman, argued out the case for their respective traditions, and King Oswiu declared for the Roman party. Ostensibly the object of the conference was to settle the Easter Controversy – the two traditions differed over the dating of Easter because the Celts still adhered to an older system of computation which Rome had abandoned. But behind this frontal issue lay deeper differences of culture and ecclesiastical organisation.

The monastic organisation of the Celtic Church, so different from that of Rome, was rooted in the socio-political structure of Irish society. The ascetical movement of the sixth century found its recruits chiefly among the aristocracy, and the wave of monastic foundations was largely the work of devout princes. It provided an outlet for their religious zeal without diminishing the property or power base of local dynasties. The monastery was the spiritual focus of the tribe or kindred group. The ruling dynasty which endowed it with a portion of the family lands retained a continuing interest in its property. The abbot was normally a member of the dynasty, and his successors were also co-arbs, co-heirs that is, of the founder's family. The paruchia of the monastery was not only an area of spiritual jurisdiction where the abbot held sway; it also reflected the political dominance of the founding dynasty. The place of Iona in the polity of the Celtic Church is a conspicuous case. Its founder, St Columba, was a prince of the Ui Neill, the most powerful dynasty in Ireland. Iona was to be the royal cult centre for the Scottish kingdom of Dalriada, an Irish colony established in Argyll, on the edge of the Pictish kingdoms. As the evangelisation of the Picts and the northern Angles proceeded at the hands of monks from Iona, the paruchia of the monastery expanded eastwards, and it came to hold a position in the Celtic churches of Britain analogous to that of a metropolitan see in Southern Europe. But it continued to be, as it had begun, a spiritual base for Scottish colonisation of the territory of the Picts. A century after Columba's death, Adamnan the abbot, was still a member of the ruling Irish dynasty of the Ui Neill.

COLUMBANUS AND THE MEROVINGIAN NOBILITY

This special relationship between the monastery and its founding dynasty helps to explain the success of St Columbanus and his disciples in promoting Irish monasticism in Gaul. From the outset Columbanus directed his mission to the Merovingian court and he made his most influential conquests among the court aristocracy. This was the area of society from which Luxeuil, despite the severity of its regime, chiefly recruited its monks.[15] It became a focus from which the ideals and usages of Celtic monasticism were widely diffused on the Continent; and in the seventh century it stimulated a wave of monastic foundations which went forward under the enthusiastic patronage of kings and queens and members of the Frankish nobility. Part of the attraction the Columbanian type of monastic organisation must have had for this class lay in its independence of episcopal control and the continuing control that the founding family might exercise over the monastery's landed property and leadership. Within a few years of the death of Columbanus, Luxeuil had mitigated the deterrent effects of his fearsome penitential by tempering it with the gentler and more humane Rule of St Benedict; and it was this 'mixed rule' of Luxeuil that was introduced into the many abbeys that adopted the new model.

Like Lérins in an earlier age, Luxeuil was a nursery of monk-bishops. At least eleven of its monks were appointed to Gallic sees in the course of the seventh century.[16] Besides these, the chief agents in promoting the ideals of Columbanian monasticism were secular bishops, like Audoenus – the St Ouen of hagiographical tradition – of Rouen and St Eligius of Noyon, who had previously held high office at the Neustrian court of Paris. Audoenus was the son of an Austrasian nobleman who had given hospitality to Columbanus during his exile from Burgundy, and his childhood encounter with the holy *émigré* inspired a lifelong devotion to the ascetical life. Audoenus became *Referendarius* (Secretary) to King Dagobert, and with the king's assistance he founded a monastery at Rebais in Brie in 635 which was modelled on Luxeuil. After 640, when he was appointed to the see of Rouen, a new field was opened to him. 'If anyone would know', wrote his hagiographer excitedly, 'how many monasteries for either sex have been founded by him and under his episcopate, let him but perambulate his diocese and marvel at the throngs of monks; he might think he was in Egypt.'[17] St Wandrille, Jumièges, Pavilly, and Fécamp, all owed their existence to his patronage and to the favour of the king, which he was in a position to tap. Enthusiasm for the monks of Columbanus seems to have gripped the whole family of Audoenus: two of his brothers collaborated with him in the foundation of Rebais, and one of them, Ado, established the famous double monastery of Jouarre on his portion of the family estates in the valley of the Marne.

The family of Audoenus were typical members of the Frankish court aristocracy who responded with enthusiasm to the inspiration of Columbanus and his disciples. In their activities as monastic founders they had the active help of the Merovingian kings, who seconded their efforts with charters of confirmation and grants of immunity. But royal assistance was not confined to ratifying the acts of others. Several women of the reigning dynasty also played a conspicuous role in promoting Columbanian monasticism of the type practised at Luxeuil. This kind of direct royal sponsorship reached a climax in the activity of Queen Balthild, the wife of Clovis II who ruled the joint kingdom of Neustria and Burgundy. Balthild is a startling instance of the tendency of the Merovingians to follow their fancy in choosing their brides from the lower strata of society. She came of an obscure Saxon family settled in Britain. She had been sold into slavery as a girl and had been acquired by Erchinoald, the mayor of the Neustrian palace. According to her hagiographer, Erchinoald was much taken with her and offered her marriage, but Clovis, the son and heir of King Dagobert, snapped her up instead – 'a reward for her humility', adds the writer unctuously.[18] She did much for the family of her adoption: she bore her husband three subsequent rulers, and her posthumous career as a royal saint conferred on the dynasty a valuable aura of supernatural approval. It was possibly a mixture of piety and policy that made her the devoted friend of zealous churchmen like Audoenus and St Eloi and the patroness of monks, for ecclesiastical support could be invaluable in reinforcing the position of a legitimate wife.[19]

Both during her husband's lifetime and after his death in 657, when she presided matriarchally over the conjoint kingdom as regent for her son Chlotar III, Balthild worked steadily to promote the monastic customs of Luxeuil. It was through her efforts that the 'mixed rule' of Luxeuil was imposed upon the royal abbey of Saint-Denis. She also used her influence with many of the bishops to introduce the same regime to the loosely structured communities that served the basilicas housing the tombs of the saints, so that Saint-Martin of Tours, Saint-Germain of Auxerre, Saint-Medard of Soissons, Saint-Pierre-le-Vif of Sens, and Saint-Aignan of Orleans all became regular monasteries following the 'mixed rule' of St Columbanus and St Benedict. Shortly after 657 she founded and endowed the abbey of Corbie and peopled it with monks brought from Luxeuil. But her darling was the abbey of nuns at Chelles. The original convent there had been established on a royal villa by Clotilde, queen of the first Clovis; but Balthild refounded and rebuilt it on a grander scale. The first abbess, Bertille, and a community of nuns were imported from Jouarre. In the end a political upheaval that was probably connected with her policy of monastic endowment forced her to relinquish power[20]; and the Wagnerian drama of her life ended in the peace of Chelles, where she took the veil and lived out her remaining years humbly under the abbess she had appointed.

THE DOUBLE MONASTERIES OF GAUL

Both Chelles and Jouarre were double monasteries, housing communities of men and women within the same enclosure.[21] They formed part of a group of aristocratic foundations for women that sprang up in the north-east region of Gaul in the three decades following the death of St Columbanus. The double monastery was not of course a mixed society. It consisted of separate communities of men and women living in proximity, in some cases using a common church for the liturgical offices, and directed by a single head. There was a precedent for the arrangement in the early monasticism of the East. Both Pachomius and St Basil had organised communities of nuns in the vicinity of their houses of monks for the purpose of mutual support. The point of the arrangement was that communities of women required the liturgical ministrations of priests; the male community also provided help with manual tasks and managerial skills that were thought to be beyond the capacity women. The Columbanian double monasteries of seventh-century Gaul were essentially communities of nuns, to which communities of monks were attached in order to provide priests and heavier manual services. The head of the joint congregation was invariably an abbess. Although the inspiration for these foundations had come from the mission of Columbanus, he himself did nothing to provide religious institutions for women, nor was there any clear precedent for double monasteries in the Celtic lands.[22] The initiative came from the same court circles that founded the abbeys for men. The regime of Luxeuil provided the model for observance, and encouragement seems to have come from Eustace and Walbert, the two abbots who succeeded Columbanus at Luxeuil.

The proprietary attitude of the founding families towards these establishments is vividly displayed in the matriarchal abbesses who ruled autocratically over both their male and female subjects. The contemporary *Rule of a Father for Virgins*, which may have been the work of Walbert of Luxeuil, gives the abbess much the same role as a male abbot – including the power to hear the confessions of her nuns and absolve them. 'An abbess', writes the author significantly, 'ought to be noble in wisdom and holiness, as well as noble by birth.'[23] The noble abbesses of Merovingian hagiography are learned and masterful women who govern their monasteries with the authority and self-assurance that society regarded as their birthright. Through them and the successors they appointed from their own kindred, the families which had endowed monasteries out of their own land continued to retain an interest in the property. The apotheosis of the abbess after death at the hands of the hagiographers provided the family with a domestic saint – a *Hausheiliger* – who enhanced its standing with a special kind of sacral prestige.[24] This was the role that St Gertrude, the abbess of Nivelles, discharged for the Carolingian family of Austrasia, which provided mayors of the palace before they aspired to the throne.

Nivelles in Brabant was the earliest of the family's monastic foundations. It was constructed and endowed by Itta, the wife of Pippin the Elder, after her husband's death in 640. Itta appointed her daughter Gertrude as its first abbess, while continuing to direct the abbey's external affairs herself. Gertrude organised it as a double monastery following the 'mixed rule' of Luxeuil. The fact that she intended it to be a Columbanian establishment following Celtic liturgical customs is evident from the fact that she sent to Ireland for monks to come and instruct the sisters in the chant. She was also determined to infect her nuns with the Irish zest for letters: she sent agents to Rome to get books to educate them, being herself, writes her hagiographer, almost an entire library of sacred lore.[25] Like other aristocratic abbesses, she appointed her successor, choosing her niece, whom she had educated in the abbey. Gertrude's powerful figure so dominated the imagination of her community that ten years after her death she reappeared to rescue the house from a crisis. A fire had broken out. The community had abandoned all hope of saving the buildings and the nuns had taken refuge outside the enclosure, when the monastic steward of the estates caught sight of the familiar figure, clothed in her habit, standing on the summit of the refectory roof and battering back the insolent flames with her veil.[26]

The 'mixed rule' of St Benedict and St Columbanus that was followed by both men and women in the newly founded Gallic monasteries of the seventh century derived its authority from the example of Luxeuil. The first reference to this hybrid regime, in the foundation diploma of Solignac, indicates that it was adopted at Luxeuil under Walbert, who became abbot in 629.[27] We do not know enough about the observance at Luxeuil in this period to say with confidence which features of the Benedictine Rule were adopted; but it is a reasonable assumption that the successors of Columbanus preferred St Benedict's gentler penitential discipline as well as various practical directions for the management of the community that the Rule of St Columbanus ignored. How knowledge of the Italian rule reached the northern kingdoms of the Franks remains a historical puzzle. But it is clear that through the spiritual colonies of Luxeuil knowledge and appreciation of it were gradually disseminated among the bishops and ascetical communities of northern and central Gaul. The spread of the Benedictine conception of the monastic life was closely associated with the cultus of St Benedict; and somewhere about the end of the seventh century this gained added impetus from a sensational relic theft which brought the bones of the patriarch himself to a Frankish monastery. The perpetrators and immediate beneficiaries of this furtive translation were the monks of Fleury abbey, the modern St Benoît-sur-Loire.

Fleury was founded in 651 by Leodebodus, the abbot of Saint-Aignan of Orleans, and it was richly endowed with land by Chlotar III and Theuderic III. But the days of its fame began with its acquisition of St Benedict. The great Romanesque basilica erected over the shrine in the eleventh century still stands beside the rapid waters of the middle Loire as an eloquent memorial to its importance as a major cult centre of Northern Europe. The eighth-century tradition, represented in its most reliable form by Paul the Deacon, contained only a few facts about the translation. These were that a party of monks from the Orleanais came to Monte Cassino which had lain deserted and ruinous for the past century, disinterred the bones of St Benedict and his sister St Scholastica, and carried them back to their homeland. This sparse stock of information was copiously improved by Adrevald of Fleury in the ninth century. He wrote a *History of the Translation of St Benedict*, which proved a welcome model to other monasteries anxious to authenticate the acquisition of their patron saints.[28] Adrevald attributed the plan of retrieving the relics to Abbot Mommoleus who sent a party over the Alps to find St Benedict's tomb. They were joined in the enterprise by a party dispatched by the bishop of Le Mans, who wanted the body of St Scholastica. There was the classical *mise-en-scène*: the unsuccessful search for the graves, miraculous guidance to the spot, a night break-in and a dramatic flight home from the pursuit of pope and Lombards. The monks of Monte Cassino, of course, later contested the authenticity of the translation, and medieval pilgrims had a choice between two St Benedicts. But Adrevald was widely read, and the fact that the author of the Benedictine Rule had chosen Gaul as his final resting place was of much significance for the development of Gallic monasticism. The Franks had taken possession of St Benedict. And it was in the Frankish realms that the Rule eventually acquired its authoritative status as the standard norm of monastic observance.

NOTES

1. *Historia Francorum* ii, 37.
2. *Sanctae Radegundae Vita*, *MGH SS RM* II, 366–7.
3. *MGH Auctorum Antiquissimorum* IV, 289; Fortunatus returns to this theme in the *Vita*, *MGH SS RM* II, 372.
4. *Historia Francorum* ix, 39.
5. On Irish monastic foundation in general see J. Ryan, *Irish Monasticism, its Origins and Early Development* (1931); for an evaluation of the sources see J. F. Kenney, *The Sources for the Early History of Ireland* (New York 1929); Kathleen Hughes, *Early Christian Ireland: Introduction to the Sources* (1972). The most valuable modern studies are those of Kathleen Hughes, *The Church in Early Irish Society* (1966), and Nora Chadwick, 'Celtic Christianity and its literature' in *The Celtic Realms*, ed. M. Dillon and Nora Chadwick (1967), pp. 202–94.
6. Text in A. W. Haddan and W. Stubbs, *Councils and Ecclesiastical Documents* (1869–78) II, 292; see discussion of its date and significance by Kathleen Hughes, *The Church in Early Irish Society*, pp. 69–70.

7. *Vitae Columbanae abbatis discipulorumque eius auctore Iona*, *MGH SS RM* IV, 75, 76–8.

8. *Sancti Columbani Opera*, ed. G. S. M. Walker, *Scriptores Latini Hiberniae* II (1957), pp. 140–2.

9. *Ibid.*, pp. 142–68.

10. *Ibid.*, pp. 26–36.

11. L. Gougaud, *Christianity in Celtic Lands*, translated by M. Joynt (1932), p. 95.

12. On the literary culture of St Columbanus see M. Manitius, *Geschichte der Lateinischen Literatur des Mittelalters* (1911–31), I, p. 181; and Walker, *op. cit.*, introduction.

13. *Adomnan's Life of Columba*, ed. and translated by A. O. and M. O. Anderson (1961), pp. 450–2.

14. *Vitae Sanctorum Hiberniae*, ed. C. Plummer (1910), ii, p. 13.

15. The best account of the spread of Columbanian monasticism in Gaul is by F. Prinz, *Frühes Mönchtum im Frankenreich* (Munich – Vienna 1965), pp. 121–41. I am especially indebted to this work.

16. Prinz, *op. cit.*, p. 123.

17. *Vitae Audoini*, *MGH SS RM* V, 557. On the foundations of Audoenus and his family see Prinz, *op. cit.*, pp. 124–27.

18. *Vitae Sanctae Balthildis*, *MGH SS RM* II, 482–3; cf. *Vita Eligii*, *MGH SS RM* II, 32, 37–8, 41, 48.

19. A point made by Dr Janet Nelson in her stimulating study of the careers of Brunhild and Balthild in *Medieval Women*: ed. D. Baker (Studies in Church History, Subsidia 1, 1978), pp. 31–77. On Balthild's monastic patronage see E. Ewig, 'Das Privileg des Bischofs Berthefrid von Amiens für Corbie u. die Klosterpolitik der Königin Balthild', *Francia i* (1973), 62–114.

20. Ewig, *op. cit.*, p. 109. He makes the point that the conversion of the basilican churches to the monastic life involved loss of control and valuable property for the bishops.

21. On Jouarre and the other women's foundations see G. A. Rohan Chabot, Marquise de Maille, *Les Cryptes de Jouarre* (Paris 1971); Prinz, *op. cit.*, pp. 142–5. On double monasteries, Mary Bateson, 'The origin and early history of double monasteries', *Trans. Royal Hist. Soc.* NS xiii (1899), 137–98; C. J. Godfrey, *The Church in Anglo-Saxon England* (1962), pp. 157–62.

22. The argument of Mary Bateson and J. Ryan that St Brigid's Kildare was a double monastery has not found favour with modern Celtic scholars.

23. *Regula cuiusdam Patris ad Virgines*, PL 88, 1069.

24. On this aspect see Prinz, *op. cit.*, pp. 489–503.

25. *Vita Sanctae Gertrudae*, *MGH SS RM* II, 458.

26. *Ibid.* 466.

27. Prinz, *op. cit.*, pp. 268.

28. *MGH SS* XV, 474–7. For Adrevald and his work see W. Goffart, 'Le Mans, St Scholastica, and the literary tradition of the translation of St Benedict', *Revue bénédictine* 77(1967), 107–41; P. J. Geary, *Furta Sacra: Thefts of Relics in the Central Middle Ages* (Princeton 1978), pp. 146–9.

Chapter 4

ENGLAND AND THE CONTINENT

ROMAN AND CELTIC FOUNDATIONS

It must have been the aristocratic tone of the women's abbeys of northern Gaul, as well as their reputation for asceticism and learning, that commended them to the notice of the nobility in the Anglo-Saxon kingdoms of Britain. Bede had heard that for lack of suitable nunneries nearer home, Earcongota, the daughter of the king of Kent, had become a nun at Faremoutiers-en-Brie; and he reports that many girls of the English nobility were sent to Chelles and Andelys and other Gallic monasteries to be educated and in some cases to enter the religious life.[1] Abbess Hilda, who was related to the royal family of Northumbria and who had been baptised by Paulinus together with the rest of the Northumbrian court, had a sister at Chelles. She had intended to go to Chelles herself until Aidan undertook her direction, and by so doing saved her for English monasticism and the English Church.

In seventh-century Britain the three traditions, Roman, Gallic, and Irish, met together and fused. Monastic life grew step by step with the conversion of the heathen English to Christianity and, as the life of Hilda shows, it recruited among first-generation converts. Britain was the field of two missionary efforts – that of Augustine sent from Rome by Gregory the Great, and the Celtic mission dispatched from Iona at the request of King Oswald – and two distinct monastic traditions were planted in their wake. Augustine and his companions had been monks before setting out on the mission to Kent, and besides erecting a cathedral at Canterbury he founded a monastery dedicated to Saints Peter and Paul outside the city – the later St Augustine's abbey – which became the mausoleum of the first archbishops and the early kings of Kent. We know nothing of the observance there at this early period, but it is a fair assumption that it followed the customs of the Roman monastery of St Andrew on the Coelian Hill, from which Augustine himself came. It has often been suggested that Augustine imported the Rule of St Benedict into England and that the abbey outside Canterbury was the first Benedictine foundation outside Italy.[2] But there in no evidence for this. It rests upon the mistaken notion that St Andrew's and other monasteries in Rome had adopted the Benedictine Rule. In fact, the usages of the Roman monasteries of the seventh century were various and eclectic. Some were Greek establishments following the tradition of St Basil; others, which had sprung up as satellites round the patriarchal basilicas of the city, used the liturgical order of the basilica they served, and their internal regime, as it is revealed by the early Roman *ordines*, was determined by the varying experience of their founders. The Rule of St Benedict was known at Rome, but there is no evidence that any Roman monastery adopted it as an exclusive model before the tenth century.[3]

The first great burst of English monastic foundation followed Aidan's mission to Northumbria. True to the tradition of the Celtic Church, he set up his missionary see in a monastery on the island of Lindisfarne, which had been granted him by King Oswald in 635. Although he was an active bishop with a diocese that covered the whole of Northumbria, he continued to live the life of a monk, retreating periodically to Lindisfarne, where the community was governed by an abbot, and even on occasion withdrawing to a hermitage on the Inner Farne. The rule of life followed at Lindisfarne was that established by Columba at Iona. And the same Celtic observance presumably governed the other northern monasteries that sprang from the headwater of Aidan's mission: Melrose, Gateshead, and Hartlepool, all founded by Aidan, Ripon which originated as a colony of Melrose, and Lastingham which was founded by Cedd, the apostle of the East Angles, who had been a monk at Lindisfarne. The strategy of the missionaries from Iona was the same as that of Columbanus in Gaul: they addressed themselves initially to the court aristocracy, and monastic foundation went forward with the active collaboration of the Northumbrian kings, who provided the landed endowment. The main effort of Iona was concentrated on the North; but a number of Celtic monasteries were planted in the southern kingdoms by Irish missionaries from elsewhere. Fursey, an Irish princeling who, like Columbanus had taken a vow to spend his life as a pilgrim for love of Christ, was welcomed by the East Anglian King Sigebert, and given the old Roman shore-fort at Burgh Castle in Suffolk, within which he erected a monastery. Malmesbury in Wessex was also an Irish foundation.

One of the most striking results of the links between English courts and the women's abbeys of northern Gaul was the introduction of double monasteries of the Gallic type into England. Like their Gallic counterparts, the English double monasteries of the seventh century were primarily nunneries to which communities of men were attached and they were governed by abbesses. In England also they were largely aristocratic foundations, housing the daughters and dowagers of kings and ruled by abbesses of royal or noble blood. Wimborne in Dorset was founded and directed by two sisters of King Ine of Wessex. St Mildred, the founder and abbess of Minster-in-Thanet, came from the royal family of the Hwicce. St Etheldreda, the founder of Ely, herself the daughter of a king, had been queen of King Ecgfrith of Northumbria. At court she came under the influence of the domineering personality of Wilfrid, adopted an ascetical style of life, and resolved to become a nun. According to Bede, Ecgfrith tried without success for twelve years to persuade her to consummate the marriage.[4] He never forgave Wilfrid, but in the end he allowed her to take the veil at Coldingham. The double monastery she constructed at Ely was built on her own land, which was a dower from a previous marriage. Coldingham, where she was trained in the religious life, was governed by Abbess Aebbe, who was her aunt and a sister of King Oswiu.

No rule in use by an English monastery of the seventh century is known to survive. But the prototype of the English double monasteries was the Columbanian double monastery of Gaul; and the custumal they followed was probably the 'mixed rule' of Saints Columbanus and Benedict that was observed at Chelles and Faremoutiers. The Irish element is certain. Hilda, successively abbess of Hartlepool and Whitby, had been trained in monastic observance by Aidan. And Coldingham, which was a nursery of royal saints and abbesses, had Irish monks. It was an Irish member of the community who complained to Aebbe that her nuns were eating and gossiping in their cells when they should have been at prayer, and wasting their time weaving fine clothes. He predicted the abbey would be punished by fire, like Nineveh.[5] And it was. The story is Bede's, and we need not take the accusation of laxity too seriously. The double monasteries may not have conformed to the fiercely ascetical standards of Columbanus, but they had inherited the Hiberno-Frankish tradition of religious fervour and learning, and they stood high in contemporary esteem.

The royal abbesses of Anglo-Saxon England, like their sisters in Gaul, ruled with the imperious self-assurance conferred on them by their birth, and many of them exerted an influence on ecclesiastical affairs far beyond the confines of their monasteries. St Hilda's regime at Whitby from its foundation in 657 until her death in 680 made it one of the most vital and creative centres of English Christianity in the generation before Bede. She had renounced the world but not been forgotten by it. Bede wrote that kings and princes came to her for advice.[6] It was indicative of the prestige of her abbey in Northumbrian society that King Oswiu chose it as the venue for the momentous synod of 664 that settled the Easter Controversy in favour of the Roman party and determined the future course of the English Church. Whether for political reasons or out of loyalty to those who had trained her in the Celtic tradition, she sided with the spokesmen for the Irish practice and remained a stubborn opponent of Wilfrid. But her involvement in ecclesiastical politics was less important than the direction she gave to her monastic community. She vigorously promoted education and learning in the abbey. Her enlightened regime thus performed a vital service by educating clergy for what was still a missionary church operating in an oral society. Five monks of her community in fact became bishops. Probably it was her perception of the catechetical possibilities of religious epic that made her quick to befriend and encourage the peasant poet Caedmon. When late in life he discovered his gift for song, she persuaded him to join the monastery and had him compose poems on the great Biblical themes of creation and redemption. Both as an intellectual centre and as a focus for pastoral activity Hilda's Whitby stood faithfully in the Irish monastic tradition.

Wilfrid claimed he had been the first to organise an English monastery entirely on the basis of the Rule of St Benedict. The monastery was Ripon, and Wilfrid had been given it to rule after Abbot Eata and a group of the Irish monks had left it rather than conform to Roman customs. Wilfrid regarded enforcement of the Benedictine Rule as part of his campaign 'to root out the poisonous weeds planted by the Scots'.[7] His residences in Rome and Gaul had given him a taste for grandeur and a contempt for the insular traditions of the Celts. He had effectively pleaded the case for conformity with Rome at the Synod of Whitby. After 669 as bishop of Northumbria his state was kingly; and something of his magnificence rubbed off on Ripon and the sister abbey he founded at Hexham in c. 670. The straggling monastic colonies of the Irish, with their humble structures of drystone or timber, must have looked barbarous to the eye that had feasted on the spacious Christian basilicas of Rome. At both Ripon and Hexham Wilfrid embarked on elaborate building operations, which included the erection of stone churches, the crypts of which still survive, with their narrow passages encased by great blocks of ashlar. There seems no reason to doubt the claim of his biographer, Eddius Stephanus, that Ripon and Hexham were the first Benedictine monasteries in England in the sense that their custumal was based exclusively upon the Rule. But it was not a model imitated by other monastic founders of the seventh century. Knowledge of the Rule was gaining ground, and it might be referred to for guidance on practical matters such as the procedure for electing an abbot; but in general, monastic custumals were still eclectic.

WEARMOUTH AND JARROW

This conjunction of *Romanitas* with the monastic traditions of Gaul and Ireland is nowhere more apparent than in the two famous foundations of Benedict Biscop at Wearmouth and Jarrow. Like Wilfrid, Biscop belonged to the Anglian court nobility and was an inveterate traveller. At twenty-five he abandoned everything and set out on pilgrimage for Rome.[8] He learned the discipline of the regular life at Lérins, where he took monastic vows; but Rome repeatedly drew him like a magnet. In 669 he returned to England with Archbishop Theodore and was placed in charge of the abbey of Saints Peter and Paul at Canterbury. But within a couple of years he was off to Rome again in search of books and relics. The great Northumbrian monastery he began building on the north bank of the Wear in 674 was erected on land given him by King Ecgfrith. To help him in the enterprise and to govern the new community he obtained the assistance of another young nobleman, Ceolfrith, who was a monk at Ripon. Some years later, Biscop erected a sister monastery at Jarrow on the Tyne, and colonised it with monks brought from Wearmouth under the headship of Ceolfrith. The original inscription, incised in Roman capitals and miraculously preserved above the chancel arch of the existing church at Jarrow, records that it was dedicated to St Paul on 23 April 685, the fifteenth year of King Ecgfrith and the fourth year of Abbot Ceolfrith.

The dedication of Biscop's twin foundations to Saints Peter and Paul, the patron saints of the Roman Church, was an outward sign of their spiritual and cultural affinity with Rome. In the course of his constant travels, he brought back numerous trophies of pilgrimage – books from Rome to stock his monastic libraries and scriptoria, and paintings and relics for his churches. He also persuaded John the arch-cantor of St Peter's to come to Wearmouth to teach his monks the Roman chant and liturgical use. For the buildings he imported masons and glaziers from Gaul, who knew how to build 'according to the Roman fashion that he loved'. Modern excavation of the sites has revealed constructional techniques and architectural features, like lathe-turned baluster shafts and flooring material in *opus signinum*, derived from sub-Roman Gaul. Investigation of the layout of the monastic buildings is inconclusive, but indicates a single axial plan that differed from both the clustered enceinte of the Celtic monasteries and the classical Benedictine arrangement round a square cloister-walk.[9]

Were Biscop's foundations Benedictine abbeys in the proper sense of the term, as has often been claimed? We cannot be sure. He demonstrated his own devotion to St Benedict by adopting his name when he entered the religious life. He knew the Rule and expressly commended it to his two communities as an authoritative guide to be followed when they had to elect a new abbot. And Ceolfrith, Biscop's friend and travelling companion of many journeys, who from 688 was sole abbot of both houses, had come from Wilfrid's Ripon, where the Benedictine Rule was observed to the exclusion of all others. Yet in Bede's *Life of Biscop* there seem to be counter-indications that the observance of Wearmouth and Jarrow was not confined whithin the framework of the Rule; the regime was devised by Benedict Biscop and, like other monastic founders of the seventh century, his method of compiling a custumal was eclectic: 'You are not to think', he told the brethren when he was dying, 'that I produced these ordinances from my own untutored heart. In fact, what I transmitted to you to be observed for the health of your souls, were all the best things I learned from seventeen monasteries in the course of my long wandering and frequent pilgrimage.'[10] This valedictory speech seems to conflict with St Benedict's severe insistence on the undiluted sovereignty of his written code. But for all its merits, the Rule of St Benedict was not comprehensive; even later monasteries which were governed by it required a custumal to regulate many of the details of daily observance. Understood in this sense, Biscop's words are compatible with a monastic regime that accorded the Benedictine Rule the status of constitutional law.

Biscop's concern that his monks should follow the Rule in their procedure for choosing a new abbot marks a significant desire to eliminate one of the prevailing features of Celtic and Frankish monasticism. St Benedict's abbot was not a co-arb or member of the founder's kindred; he was elected by the brethren solely on grounds of suitability. This was what Biscop wanted, instead of a choice dictated by considerations of kindred. It was evidently to safeguard this freedom of choice from any outside pressure that he obtained a privilege of Pope Agatho for Wearmouth, which was later confirmed by Pope Sergius and extended to Jarrow. But it was a long time before this precocious ideal made any headway in Northern Europe. It collided with the determination of aristocratic dynasties to retain their control over foundations which had been endowed out of their family estates. Less than fifty years after Biscop's death, the debilitating effect of this domination by founder's kindred was already making itself felt in the monastic movement of Northumbria. In a letter written towards the end of his life to his friend, Archbishop Egbert of York, Bede laments the decline of religious fervour; he attributes much of the trouble to the growth of kindred monasteries, in which the founders assumed the role of abbot while living in the establishment with their wives and families.[11] In England, as in Gaul, the Germanic aristocracy had a way of adapting the ascetical movement to fit their own requirements.

Of course the supreme monument to Benedict Biscop's twin foundations was Bede (*c.* 672–735). His parents, who lived in the vicinity, had given him to Wearmouth as a child-oblate at the age of seven. Shortly after its foundation he was transferred to Jarrow, and there he spent the rest of his life, never stirring outside the monastic enclosure except for a belated visit to his old pupil Egbert at York and possibly a visit to Lindisfarne – for his description of the island has the smell of sense-perception about it: 'I have spent all my life in this monastery, applying myself with all my might to the study of the Scriptures; and, in the midst of observing the discipline of the Rule and the daily care of singing in the church, it has always been my delight to learn or to teach or to write.'[12] This testament of a lifetime of peace and reflection comes at the end of his *Ecclesiastical History of the English People*, which he finished in 731, four years before his death. It is followed by a list of thirty-five works he had written, including commentaries on the books of the Old and New Testaments, homilies and letters, two books on chronology, a martyrology, and a history of the abbots of his own monastery. His treatises on chronology were widely read and copied, and his homilies found their way into the night office of the Western Church; but it is the *Ecclesiastical History* that historians have always gratefully singled out as his masterpiece. Its wealth of detail, its concern for accuracy and documentary evidence, and the classical clarity of its Latin style, make it an astonishing achievement considering the limitations of time and place within which the author had to work. Without it our knowledge of early Anglo-Saxon England would be immeasurably poorer.

The purpose of the *Ecclesiastical History* was avowedly didactic. Its object was to show that God had chosen the English race to receive the light of the Gospel, and a subsidiary theme, but an important one, was the reception by the English of orthodox Roman Christianity. Writing in a Northumbrian monastery a generation after the Synod of Whitby, Bede was preoccupied with the conflict between the Celtic and Roman traditions which had come to a head over the dating of Easter. His account of the synod, which he placed at the centre of the *History*, is the most vivid piece of reportage that the eighth century has to offer. Although he disliked the British and disapproved of the Celtic deviations from Roman practice, he fully appreciated the vital role the Irish monks had played in the conversion of the heathen English. He wrote with enthusiasm about Columba and Aidan, and showed much interest in the monastic life at Lindisfarne. But the real warmth of his admiration was reserved for St Cuthbert – the monk trained by the Irish at Melrose, who came to accept the Roman Easter and who as bishop of Lindisfarne reconciled the two traditions.

THE ANGLO-SAXON MONKS ON THE CONTINENT

The resolution of the conflict not only closed a sore that was draining the strength of the Northumbrian Church; it opened a new phase in the monastic history of Europe. The marriage of the two traditions give direction and impetus to a new missionary effort by English monks on the Continent. English churchmen felt a hankering for the conversion of their heathen kindred in Frisia and Germany, and the monks who undertook the task took with them the notions of *Romanitas* they had acquired in England – of the normative value of Roman custom and the centrality of the see of St Peter in the ecclesiastical cosmos.[13] They also carried a devotion to the Rule of St Benedict. The first objective of their efforts was the evangelisation of Frisia. Wilfrid had initiated the enterprise when he stayed some months in Frisia in 678 on his journey to Rome. But the hero of the Frisian mission was Willibrord, a monk who had been trained in Benedictine observance and devotion to Rome at Wilfrid's Ripon. From Ripon he had migrated to Ireland after Wilfrid's downfall, and there he came under the influence of Egbert, another English *émigré* who had been attracted across the water by the fervour of the Irish monks and the reputation of the Irish schools for learning. Egbert was an adherent of the Roman tradition. It was he who at last persuaded Iona, last bastion of Celtic insularity, to accept it. But he had absorbed the ideals of Irish asceticism and missionary zeal and he hankered for the penitential life of the pilgrim. In 690 he fulfilled his ambition vicariously by sending Willibrord with eleven companions to evangelise Frisia.

The Frisian enterprise went forward under the patronage and protection of Pippin, the Carolingian mayor of the palace, who effectively ruled in place of the king. The strategy of the missionaries was shaped by their Northumbrian training. Educated in the schools of Wilfrid and Egbert, Willibrord sought and obtained papal sanction for his work, and with the collaboration of Pippin he got the pope to create a new ecclesiastical province based on his mission station at Utrecht and was himself consecrated its first bishop by Pope Sergius. And the pope conferred on him the pallium – the yoke of white wool that had first been placed on the tomb of St Peter and symbolised the authority delegated by St Peter's vicar to the bishop of a metropolitan see. The same strategy was adopted by St Boniface, who followed in Willibrord's footsteps and evangelised Thuringia. Boniface was not from Northumbria; he was a Wessex man, given to the monastic life in childhood and reared first at Exeter and then at Nursling near Southampton. But his missionary career manifested the same loyalties that the Northumbrian monks had shown to the

Benedictine Rule and the traditions of Rome. He too went to Rome to seek an apostolic mandate for his work from the pope. Before leaving Rome, his Saxon name, Wynfrith, was changed by the pope to that of Boniface, a Roman martyr whose church was on the Aventine Hill. Later, when he returned to Rome to be consecrated bishop by Gregory II, he took an oath to St Peter and his vicar to 'uphold the faith and purity of holy Catholic teaching' and to 'agree to nothing which is opposed to the unity of the universal Church, but in all things I will show, as I have said, complete loyalty to you and to the welfare of your church'.[14] Like Willibrord before him, he received the pallium, which was sent him in 732, signifying the creation of a new ecclesiastical province for Germany.

This re-exportation to Northern Europe of the Anglo-Saxon idea of Roman ecclesiastical order had momentous consequences for medieval Christendom. After completing the episcopal organisation of the German Church, Boniface was invited by the rulers of Austrasia and Neustria, Carloman and Pippin III, to help reorganise the Church in their dominions. Thus the Frankish Church was brought into direct constitutional relationship with the Roman see and the path was laid for the future expansion of papal jurisdiction. Boniface was also a primary instrument in forging the alliance between the young Carolingian dynasty and the papacy that paved the way to the creation of the Medieval Empire.

The long-term results of the Anglo-Saxon mission were as important for Western monasticism as they were for the secular Church. It had been a monastic enterprise from the start, and this monastic character was maintained by a steady stream of recruits, both men and women, who came from English monasteries to join the mission, and by the exchange of letters which kept the workers in Germany in touch with the brethren at home. 'I thank you for the presents and vestments you have sent', writes Boniface to an English abbess; 'as for copying out the passages of Scripture you asked me for, please excuse my remissness – I have been so much occupied with preaching and travelling about that I could not find time to complete it.'[15] From Bishop Daniel of Winchester he begs the copy of the Prophets that his old Abbot Winbert had, because the text is written in large clear letters: 'such as cannot be procured in this country, and with my failing sight it is impossible for me to read small abbreviated script'.[16] For an instant a bridge is thrown across twelve and a half centuries, and one sees the flickering oil wick and the monastic settlement in the menacing forest, where the monk, Sturmi, constructed a fence every night round his mule to protect it from being eaten by the wild beasts. The missionaries not only drew comforts and reinforcements from the English abbeys; as their work advanced they made recruits to the monastic life among the newly converted peoples, and several famous foundations sprang from the mission. All these were given the Benedictine Rule for their model.

These spiritual colonies of Anglo-Saxon England on the Continent owed their creation to collaboration between the monk-missionaries and the Carolingian dynasty. Echternach, in the region of Trier, was erected by Willibrord in place of a small existing convent and on land given by Pippin and his wife Plectrudis. It provided him with a welcome refuge at times when it was going hard with the Frisian mission. The presence of English monks at the abbey in the eighth century, alongside their German brethren, is visually attested by the manuscripts copied in its scriptorium. The best known of these, the Echternach Gospel Book, now in the Bibliothèque Nationale at Paris, is a superb monument of the Northumbrian school, illuminated and written in the characteristic half-uncial script of the Hiberno-English monasteries. Fulda in Hesse, the most illustrious of Boniface's foundations, was constructed in 744 with the co-operation of Carloman of Austrasia. The story of the foundation is vividly told in the Life of the Bavarian monk Sturmi, who became its first abbot. After Sturmi had spent some weeks in the forest prospecting for a site, he reported back to Boniface, who made straight for the court of Carloman to ask for a royal grant. The hagiographer hints that other landowners besides the king had an interest in the area, and so 'a charter of this gift was ordered to be drawn up, signed by the king's own hand, and all the nobles in the vicinity of Grapfelt were summoned by messengers and asked to follow the king's example, if by any chance they possessed any property in that quarter . . . the donation was accordingly confirmed by all and passed from the possession of men into the possession of God'.[17] But a further act was necessary if God was to enjoy undivided possession: there were still the claims of the bishop. To meet these, Boniface got a privilege from Pope Zachary I, which exempted the abbey from all episcopal authority and placed it under the direct jurisdiction of the apostolic see.

Fulda exemplified in a special way the two poles of Anglo-Saxon monastic loyalty. Its observance was to be strictly modelled on the Benedictine Rule: Sturmi was sent to the fountain-head at Cassino, now repopulated with monks, to imbibe the spirit of the Rule, so that he could return and instruct the brethren. The other English feature was exemplified by the papal privilege of exemption, which accorded with the ideas of Roman authority implanted in their disciples by Wilfrid and Benedict Biscop. Boniface had chosen Fulda to be his place of burial. After his martyrdom in Frisia at the hands of some enraged pagans, local enthusiasts tried to retain his body. But it was well known that the will of the saints was as impossible to frustrate after death as it was in life: the bier became immovable until they placed it on a barge to carry it up the Rhine on the first stage of its journey to Fulda. It was an appropriate mausoleum for a monk who had instructed the Carolingian dynasty in the merits of St Benedict's Rule and the all-powerful authority of St Peter. Later events showed they had learned their lesson well. They invoked the authority of St Peter's vicar to dismiss the last of the Merovingian kings and rule in their stead; and at their direction the Benedictine Rule was imposed upon monasteries throughout their dominions.

NOTES

1. *Historia Ecclesiastica* iii, 8.
2. Thus Philibert Schmitz, *Histoire de l'ordre de Saint-Benoit* (Maredsous 1942), i, p. 38; and J. Godfrey, *The Church in Anglo-Saxon England* (1962), p. 153.
3. On the observance of Roman monasteries of this period see G. Ferrari, *Early Roman Monasteries* (Studi di Antichità Cristiana 23, Vatican 1957).
4. *Historia Ecclesiastica* iv, 19.
5. *Ibid*.iv, 25.
6. *Ibid*. iv,23.
7. *The Life of Bishop Wilfrid by Eddius Stephanus*, ed. B. Colgrave (1927), p. 99.
8. For Benedict Biscop and the foundation of Wearmouth and Jarrow, see A. H. Thompson, 'Northumbrian monasticism' in *Bede, Life, Times and Writings* (1935), pp. 60–101; and P. Hunter Blair, *The World of Bede* (1970), pp. 155–99.
9. Rosemary Cramp, 'Monkwearmouth and Jarrow, the archaeological evidence' in *Famulus Christi. Essays in Commemoration of the Thirteenth Centenary of the Birth of the Venerable Bede*, ed. G. Bonner (1976), pp. 5–18.
10. *Historia Abbatum* in *Venerabilis Baedae Opera Historica*, ed. C. Plummer (1896), pp. 374–5.
11. *Epistola ad Ecgbertum Episcopum in Venerabilis Baedae Opera*, pp. 415–16.
12. *Historia Ecclesiastica* v, 24.
13. On the Frisian mission see W. Levison, *England and the Continent in the Eighth Century* (1946), pp. 45–69.
14. M. Tangl, *Die Briefe des heiligen Bonifatius* (1916), no. 16, translated by C. H. Talbot, *The Anglo-Saxon Missionaries in Germany* (1954), p. 70.
15. Talbot, op.cit., p. 84.
16. *Ibid*. p. 118.
17. *Ibid*. p. 189.

Chapter 5

THE EMPEROR AND THE RULE

THE RELIGIOUS MOTIVES FOR ENDOWMENT

When King Carloman granted fiscal immunities to the monks of Granfelden, he explained the reason for his grant was 'that thereby we may merit pardon from the eternal giver of rewards, and that it may please them to pray perpetually for the stability of our kingdom and in every way to give faithful assistance to our governance'.[1] The same formula was used by his brother Charlemagne in a privilege he gave to Lorsch abbey in 772.[2] The stereotyped language of these royal diplomas indicates the complex attitudes – the mixture of piety and policy – that moved the Carolingians, like other secular rulers, to promote monasticism in their realms. As with all monastic benefaction, the primary motive was that of safeguarding the soul of the benefactor and the souls of his relatives. Medieval rulers shared with their people current doctrinal assumptions about the economy of salvation. And these assumptions included the ideas of vicarious merit and the need to make satisfaction or reparation for sin. The merit that accrued to an individual through prayer and good works could be applied to other people, not only to living people, but also to the dead. This concept played a crucial role in medieval religious practice. To found and endow a community of monks was to ensure for the donor an unceasing fund of intercession and sacrifice which would avail him and his relatives both in life and after death.

The concern with vicarious merit was associated with the belief that people could, and should, make satisfaction for their sins. Repentance attracted divine forgiveness, but without satisfaction it was not enough: compensation must be paid to the wronged party, and in the case of sin, the wronged party was God. The idea of satisfaction was fostered by the early medieval Penitentials. These extraordinary documents belong to the same mental world as the barbarian law codes, with their elaborate tariff of monetary compen-

61

sations for offences against persons and property. They were essentially manuals compiled for the guidance of priests who had to hear confessions and allocate appropriate penances. Private auricular confession and the use of a Penitential were both features of monastic life. It seems that these practices were first extended to Christians living in the secular world by the Celtic Church, and that the Irish monk-missionaries transported them to the Germanic peoples of England and the Continent. Columbanus composed a Penitential for the secular clergy and laity as well as for monks. And under the influence of the Irish treatises, Penitentials were also compiled in England and circulated by the Anglo-Saxon missionaries abroad. From the eighth century lay people were exhorted to confess their sins at least once a year, and a penitential treatise became part of the necessary stock-in-trade of a priest.

The Penitentials laid down a nicely graduated scale of satisfactory penances appropriate to every sin. Thus in the seventh-century Penitential attributed to Archbishop Theodore of Canterbury a priest or deacon who vomits on account of drunkenness is assigned forty days of penance; a layman who commits the same offence is allocated fifteen days; fornication with a virgin involves a year's penance; homicide seven years, and so forth. During his period of penance the sinner was required to fast on bread, salt, and water, and to abstain from the sacraments; if a married man, he must abstain from conjugal intercourse. A year of penance involved performing these ascetical exercises for three Lents – three periods of forty days each. Medieval piety was haunted by the menace of these terrifying documents. The careless could easily accumulate more than a lifetime of canonical penance. What if the sinner should die without having completed his penance? Moralists of the twelfth century declared that the balance of satisfaction still outstanding had to be made up in purgatory. But in earlier centuries, before the doctrine of purgatory had been fully articulated, it seemed doubtful whether the penitent who died without having discharged his debt could be saved. The best hope lay in the possibility of commutation or substitution: periods of canonical penance might be commuted to alms-giving, pilgrimage, or other recognised good works – this was the basic conception underlying the medieval indulgence, which remitted a stipulated period of canonical penance; alternatively, others might be induced to perform the satisfaction on the penitent's behalf.

These features of the medieval penitential system in part explain the eagerness of princes and others to found and endow monasteries. A gift to a monastery was of itself a meritorious act which might remit a long period of penance. More important, the monks, through their penitential life of continual prayer and fasting, acted as surrogates for their benefactor: they performed the satisfaction on his behalf. And, as a deathless society established in perpetuity, they would continue to render him this service until the end of time. These considerations are expressed with uncommon directness in the preamble of the charter with which Duke William III of Aquitaine signified the foundation of Cluny in the year 909[4]:

> desiring to provide for my own salvation while I am still able, I have considered it advisable, indeed most necessary, that from the temporal goods which have been conferred upon me I should give some little portion for the gain of my soul . . ... Which end, indeed, seems attainable by no more suitable means than that, following the precept of Christ: 'I will make his poor my friends' (Luke xvi. 9), and making the act not a temporary but a lasting one, I should support at my own expense a congregation of monks. And this is my trust, this my hope, indeed, that although I myself am unable to despise all things, nevertheless by receiving those who do despise the world, whom I believe to be righteous, I may receive the reward of the righteous.

We have here the primary motivation behind the attention that the Carolingian rulers of the eighth and ninth centuries gave to the endowment and protection of monasteries: in the words of Carloman's charter, they hoped to merit pardon. This also explains the concern of secular minded princes and magnates for the cause of monastic reform, which is a recurrent theme of Charlemagne's capitularies. The prayers and mortifications of holy men would be efficacious with God. But clearly to a benefactor who hoped to participate in the merit acquired by a monastic community, to reap the spiritual dividends as it were, a community of lax and negligent monks was a poor investment.

SOCIAL CONVENIENCE

Besides these spiritual advantages, the patron of a monastery looked to obtain temporal benefits from his foundation. We have already seen how the royal and noble dynasties of seventh-century Gaul used monasteries to make provision for members of their families who could not otherwise be accommodated. Surplus male children, who could not be adequately set up in land without a dangerous diminution of the dynastic estate, and women of the family for whom no suitable marriage alliance could be found, could be placed in monasteries, where they might live with the dignity and esteem that was proper to their rank. In many cases they were given to the monastery as children, together with an endowment in land. The abbeys of the Carolingian age were used in this way by the Frankish nobility, and not least by the ruling dynasty itself. The heads of the richer and more illustrious establishments were often blood relations

63

of the royal family. Fulrad, the abbot of Lobbes, was a grandson of Charles Martel; most of the abbots of Saint-Riquier in the ninth century were members of the family, including Charlemagne's son-in-law and three of his grandsons; and Charles's daughter, Rohaut, was abbess of Faremoutiers. 'Every high dignitary', boasted the chronicler of Saint-Riquier, 'wheresoever he was in the kingdom of the Franks, rejoiced that he had a relative in the monastery.'[5] The abbeys which housed these aristocratic communities tended to exclude postulants who were not of noble birth. The Swabian abbey of Reichenau claimed as much when it petitioned the pope in 1029: 'in the monastery there have always been, and are, only monks of illustrious and noble birth . . . from its foundation there have been none but the sons of counts and barons'.[6] Nor was this social exclusiveness confined to the greater monasteries. Noble founders and benefactors, when they placed their children in a monastery, assumed that they would continue to enjoy the society of their own kind. When the bishop of Eichstätt confirmed the gift of a church to the small Bavarian nunnery of Monheim, he agreed that the benefactress should have the office of abbess among the sisters and gave an undertaking that 'our successors shall see that the abbess has no permission to admit girls of base or ignoble birth to the monastery'.[7]

PUBLIC POLICY

Personal piety and social convenience were the primary motives that prompted rulers to encourage monasticism in their dominions, but they were not the only ones. There were also wider considerations of public policy. These too were referred to in the charters of the Carolingian dynasty: monks were assigned lands and privileges 'that they should pray perpetually for the stability of our kingdom and the safety of our country'. The safety of the realm depended upon the intercession of holy men. The monks were the spiritual counterpart of the secular armies which defended the realm against its enemies, especially against incursions by the heathen. Their prayers and sacrifices averted the wrath of God from the sins of the people and ensured God's blessing upon the king when he went into battle. But it was not only through the invisible services of prayer and fasting that the monks promoted the stability of the realm; the great abbeys on the frontiers of the Carolingian Empire performed an important role in colonising newly conquered territories. Both as landed corporations entrusted with clearance and settlement, and as mission stations for the evangelisation of lesser breeds without the law, they were vital agents of the Carolingian *Ostpolitik*. Charlemagne made it a primary task of his regime to subjugate the warlike and heathen people of Saxony and to incorporate the area into the Frankish realm. This involved the destruction of German paganism and the forcible conversion of the Saxons to Christianity; for religious unity was the counterpart of political dominion: Roman Christianity was the common bond that united the different peoples of Western Europe in obedience to the Frankish ruler. It was here that the monks, alongside the bishops and secular clergy, had an essential role to play. When Charlemagne embarked upon the conquest of Saxony, he summoned an assembly at Paderborn to apportion the task of conversion, and the lion's share was assigned to the frontier abbeys of Hersfeld and Fulda. Abbot Sturmi, grown old and tired, spent his last days preaching to the 'depraved and perverse race',[8] destroying pagan temples, and building churches. The same kind of missionary role was performed in the South by Reichenau from its island fastness on Lake Constance. Its founder, St Pirminus, was a contemporary of St Boniface. He was a Visigoth who had come to the Frankish court as a refugee from southern Gaul, which was being harassed by the Arabs; and Charles Martel sent him to plant monastic communities among the Alamans. The importance of the abbeys as mission stations and centres of Frankish loyalty was reflected in the pattern of royal munificence. A few favoured monasteries in the central heartlands of the Frankish realm received generous gifts; but the most lavish land grants were reserved for the abbeys like Fulda, Hersfeld, and Lorsch, which lay east of the Rhine, and the abbeys of Aquitaine and Septimania, which were close to the Pyrenean frontier.[9]

Concern for the public as well as the private function of the monasteries explains the constant preoccupation of Carolingian legislation with the details of monastic discipline. The decrees of Frankish councils and the royal capitularies harp upon the duties of abbots towards their monks, the rights of postulants to be received without payment, the obligation of monks to maintain strict enclosure and to be zealous in observing the Rule – 'for tepidity is displeasing to God'[10] – to avoid secular business, and to be obedient to their bishop. And from the German Council of 742 until the end of the century, the standard of practice for monks that the decrees appeal to is the Rule of St Benedict. Charlemagne was convinced that the Rule offered the best plan for a well-ordered monastery; so much so that in 787 he sent to Cassino to ask Abbot Theodemar for an authentic copy of the text. This steady promotion through royal propaganda gave the Rule a unique status as the approved code of practice for the monasteries of the Frankish Empire.

Yet despite the cachet of royal approval and the growing adoption of the Rule in the lands east of the Rhine and in southern Gaul, it had still not superseded the 'mixed rule' and other forms of observance by the end of Charlemagne's reign. Customs consecrated by long usage, and traditions embalmed by the veneration of saintly founders, died hard in many of the Gallic abbeys. Not all were willing to swim with the tide. Under the old dispensation the difference between a community of monks and a body of secular canons, which was often called a 'monastery', was not always clear. One of the results of the Carolingian drive for order and uniformity in the affairs of the Church was to clarify the distinction: those who took vows and followed the Rule of St Benedict were monks; other congregations of men and women who lived a communal life of a quasi-monastic kind were canons and canonesses. Thus the clergy who served the basilica of St Martin at Tours, and who clung to the traditions of the past, came in the ninth century to be identified as secular canons. Some of the more famous women's abbeys, including Nivelles, Faremoutier, Chelles, and Jouarre, went the same way and became houses of canonesses. The Benedictine Rule, which had made such spectacular progress in the outer territories of the Carolingian Empire, seems to have encountered more resistance in the central lands of Austrasia and Neustria. At Saint-Denis, in the time of Hilduin, a majority of the community were for adopting the canonical life, and the minority who wanted to follow the Rule of St Benedict had to be hived off to a villa on the Oise. In the year 813 a synod of bishops meeting at Tours lamented that monasteries which had once observed the Benedictine Rule were now lax in keeping it or had abandoned it entirely.[11]

It was not only pious conservatism that hindered the spread of regular Benedictine observance. Many of the older and richer abbeys suffered loss and demoralisation at the hands of their lay proprietors; and the greatest and most exploitive lay proprietor was the king. In this respect, royal practice fell short of the public and repeated avowals of approval for the Rule. The Carolingians extended royal proprietorship over the monasteries of the Frankish empire; bishops and lay benefactors were encouraged to donate their foundations to the king, who could offer them effective protection. But proprietorship meant the right to dispose of the abbey and its property as the proprietor thought fit. Its endowments had been given to God, but God's bailiff was the temporal proprietor. The very lavishness with which lands had been showered upon the monasteries made it inevitable that they would be made to support many secular purposes. Charlemagne was not prepared, any more than his father had been, to divert huge estates solely to the maintenance of relatively small groups of men and women vowed to a life of prayer and seclusion. He used the abbeys freely as a form of property with which he could reward royal servants and relatives or maintain ministers. This royal exploitation took two forms: in some cases a portion of the abbey's estates would be allocated as a fief to a royal vassal; the early Carolingians, hungry for land with which they could reward loyal service, constantly appropriated monastic property in this way; it is to this practice that we owe the *polyptiques* – the early inventories of monastic estates and movable property, made at royal command, which have been of such value to economic historians; in other cases, the king would grant the abbey totally to a lay vassal or a relative. Just as the grant of a secular estate included both the land and the peasant tenants who worked on it, so the grant of an abbey as a 'benefice' or fief to a royal servant included both the lands of the monastery and the monastic establishment itself together with the monks, who were part of the human stock, as it were, of the estate. In this case the recipient of the grant became the lay abbot and could lay claim to most of the rights over the community that were assigned to an abbot by the Rule or by monastic custom.[12]

Where an abbey was given to a layman or a clerk, the allocation of the property and income between the lay abbot and the monks was a matter for negotiation between the parties; so too was the division of responsibility for the direction of the community. The arrangement did not always work to the disadvantage of the monks. Alcuin, scholar, poetaster, and schoolmaster to Charlemagne's palace school, was given six abbeys by his royal master, including Saint-Martin of Tours; and although he was scathing about the 'rusticity of Touraine', he was an appreciative governor. 'I love your holiness', he wrote to the community of Saint-Martin, 'I desire to be one of you.'[13] And in the end he had his desire: after years of struggling to educate the court, from the emperor downwards, he was allowed to retire to his favourite haven beside the Loire, where he ended his days. It must have been his care for the scriptorium of the abbey that made it one of the most famous centres of manuscript production in Europe at the end of the eighth century. Although Alcuin was a clerk, not a monk, he loved the monastic life. But not all those to whom the king gave abbeys were equally sympathetic to the monastic ideal. A layman might exploit the lands of the monastery ruthlessly and disrupt the life of the community by moving his household, with women, servants, and dogs, into the monastic buildings. Those royal abbeys that remained under the direct control of the king tended to fare better. Charlemagne (768–814) treated them as an integral part of the political structure, and himself appointed the abbots, whom he regarded as imperial functionaries. It was of course contrary to the express directions of the Benedictine Rule, which vested the election of the abbot in the monastic community; but nepotism and political prudence did not invariably result in unsuitable appointments. Angilbert, Charles's son-in-law, whom he designated abbot of Saint-Riquier, seems to have felt a genuine if belated vocation to the monastic life, and he rebuilt the abbey and furnished the church on a magnificent scale, as well as restocking the library.[14]

At the end of Charles's reign then, the monastic landscape presented a chequered picture. The abbeys east of the Rhine, which had drawn their inspiration from the Anglo-Saxon missionary effort, contained flourishing Benedictine communities. In Aquitaine and the province of Lyons the Rule was gaining ground. But elsewhere there was a variety of practice; and there are indications that in the Frankish heartlands of northern Gaul and Lorraine the ideal of the coenobitical life was in recession. Charles's desire to see a single and uniform monastic observance serving the spiritual needs of the Frankish Empire was never realised. It was left to his son and successor, Louis and Pious (814–40), to take up the plan and carry it through to a successful conclusion. The emperor's agent in this was St Benedict of Aniane (*c*. 750–821), a monk from the South, who had become a zealot for the strict observance of the Benedictine Rule. Through the collaboration of these two men the Rule was imposed upon monasteries throughout the Carolingian dominions. So, by a development that St Benedict of Nursia could never have envisaged, his Rule was enforced by an act of state, and in this way it came to be the sole standard of monastic observance in the ninth century.

THE RULE IMPOSED: MONASTICISM UNDER IMPERIAL SUPERVISION

Louis's protégé – this second Benedict – was a member of the Gothic aristocracy of southern Gaul. His father, the count of Maguelonne in the March of Gothia, sent him to the court of the Frankish queen to be educated and apprenticed to arms. It was in Italy, on campaign with Charlemagne, that a narrow escape from drowning brought his interior searchings to a crisis and persuaded him to enter the cloister. In 774 he became a monk at Saint-Seine, near Dijon. At first the fierceness of his macerations moved the abbot to remonstrate, but he answered that 'the Rule of St Benedict was composed for beginners or the sick; he himself was endeavouring to rise higher to follow the Rules of the Blessed Basil and the Blessed Pachomius'.[15] The anecdote, which is told by Ardo, who was a disciple and uncritical admirer, conveys more than youthful conceit; there is a foretaste of the puritanical self-righteousness Benedict showed later, when his single-minded enthusiasm caused him to ride roughshod over the traditions of a previous age. Even so, there must have been a warmth in his personality that hardly emerges from Ardo's austere portrait, for Alcuin, who met him at court, could write to him in terms of intimate friendship. Perhaps he mellowed with the years. Being dissatisfied with Saint-Seine, he left it to pursue the ascetical life on his own patrimony, in a cell beside the river Aniane. Faced with the task of organising disciples, he came to the conclusion that the Benedictine Rule was after all the best model for a coenobitical community; and it must have been at this time that he adopted the name of Benedict in place of his Gothic name of Witiza. In 782 he laid the foundations of a new monastery on the banks of the Aniane, which was to be the prototype of many others. In conformity with a growing practice, he gave the abbey and its estate to Charlemagne, who took it under his protection and removed it from the jurisdiction of count and bishop. Its exclusive code of observance was to be the Rule of St Benedict.

The rest of Benedict's life was spent in actively propagating knowledge and practice of the Rule. The hagiographer has probably inflated the list of southern monasteries reformed by him in the early years;[16] but it is clear that he came to be regarded as the leading exponent of the Rule in Provence and Gothia. These activities brought him to the notice of Charles's son, Louis, who was then king of Aquitaine, and he was given a commission to visit the abbeys of Aquitaine and instruct their communities in Benedictine practice. When Louis succeeded his father to the Empire in 814, a much wider field of action was opened to Benedict. Louis saw in this single-minded zealot the vicar-general he needed to implement Charlemagne's plan for a uniform and universal pattern of monastic observance. He summoned him to court at Aachen, and in order to keep him within reach, he had constructed for him a new abbey in the valley of the Inde, a few miles away from the imperial palace. Inde was to be more than a convenient residence for the emperor's monk-councillor; it came to have a central role in the monastic reform as the official model of Benedictine observance for all the imperial abbeys – a kind of ascetical staff college, where abbots and monks would be sent to learn the approved practices, so that they could return home and instruct their communities. Benedict was given the authority of abbot-general over all the monasteries of Francia, situated in the lands between the Loire and the Meuse. The programme of reform and standardisation was explained to two assemblies of abbots which met in the imperial chapel of Aachen, the first in August 816, the second in July 817. In the course of debate these two synods, which were steered by Benedict, produced a series of decrees which received the assent of the emperor, and which were subsequently conflated into an imperial edict that became known as the Monastic Capitulary.[17]

The general spirit of the Aachen ordinances is encapsulated in the opening decrees of the first synod: it was to be the literal observance of the Benedictine Rule, to the exclusion of all else. Every abbot present, on returning home, was to read and expound the Rule to his monks, and to take pains to implement it meticulously. Those monks who were able, were to learn the Rule by heart. All present at the synod agreed to celebrate the divine office according to its instructions. The rest of the ordinances range over various other details of the regular life. Some dealt with trivialities, such as not shaving in Lent; others with more fundamental matters, such as the duty of abbots to share the life of the brethren. The object was to draw up a common custumal that all would follow. On some minor points the decrees of the second synod were less restrictive than those of the first. The Rule forbade the eating of flesh-meat, except by the sick; did this prohibition include the flesh of birds? The first synod insisted that it did: monks were not to eat fowl, unless it was prescribed for the sick. But the second synod relaxed the prohibition for the Christmas and Easter seasons. The first synod followed the Rule in restricting the use of baths, though allowing bathing at Christmas and Easter; the second left the ordering of baths to the discretion of the prior. These minor emendations apparently reflect pressure by a more liberal group at the synod that wished to modify the rigorism of Benedict of Aniane.

There were dissenting voices. Some muffled echoes of the debate can be heard in the comments that Haito of Basel wrote for his monks of Reichenau. The synods decreed that abbots should share the life of their monks in table and dormitory; but 'in this matter', wrote Haito, 'I wish to avail myself of the authority of the Rule, which is not to be prejudiced by any new constitution'. As for forbidding abbots to eat with guests by the monastery gate, he had eaten with guests from time to time, but in the abbot's auditorium, and 'this practice we wish to keep, unless it be more clearly forbidden'. The synod had forbidden the eating of fowl, 'though', he observes tartly, 'it is not forbidden by the authority of the Rule'.[18] Haito was not the only one who had reservations. The plan for the rebuilding of Saint-Gall, drafted for Abbot Gozbert shortly after the synods, included a separate house and kitchen for the abbot, and a bath-house for the monks.[19] Probably the strait-jacket Benedict of Aniane sought to impose was not accepted by many establishments without some modification.

All the same, the Aachen decrees were not just an expression of pious hopes. Active steps were taken to enforce them. Special *missi* were appointed by the emperor to visit monasteries and inquire whether the decrees were being observed. Each house was required to send representatives to reside at Inde for a period to learn the observance, so that they could return home and instruct their own communities. The primitive and cumbersome apparatus of the state was now harnessed to the task of imposing a uniform pattern of life on all the imperial monasteries. The outcome of this effort was that throughout Northern Europe the Rule of St Benedict became for the first time the sole norm of observance for monks. But paradoxically, in bringing this standardisation about, Benedict of Aniane set Western monasticism on a new path which increasingly diverged from the Rule. For one thing the autonomy of each community in the management of its internal affairs was now curtailed by the over-riding authority of the abbot-general, which was backed by the power of the secular government. Also the interpretation that Benedict of Aniane placed upon the Rule was coloured by Gallic practices of the early ninth century which departed in significant ways from the intentions of St Benedict and upset the symmetry of his original model. The most obvious of these changes were the large number of additions to the divine office set out in the Rule. 'It is not to be believed', wrote Theodemar of Cassino to Charlemagne, 'that it would displease the blessed father Benedict, rather would it gratify him, if anyone cared to add anything over and above what he ordained for the divine praises'.[20] And Angilbert evidently agreed with him: his Order for Saint-Riquier provided for 3 monastic choirs, each of 100 monks and 34 boys, litanies, solemn processions, and the celebration of at least 30 masses daily at the different altars.[21]

These and other ritual developments of the time were accepted by Benedict of Aniane and were prescribed by the Aachen decrees. In addition to the sevenfold office of the day, monks were now required to chant additional psalms before the night office and visit the numerous altars in procession, and to recite the Office of the Dead daily. Besides these services, the community or chapter mass was now celebrated daily, and it was a growing practice for individual monks to celebrate 'private' masses on the numerous altars that were coming to be a feature of monastic building. This elaboration of liturgical activity meant that a lengthening part of the monk's day was spent in choir. And the pace set by Benedict of Aniane was quickened in the tenth and eleventh centuries by the musical elaboration of the chant. In this way the old equilibrium between prayer, work, and study, that the Rule advocated, was destroyed. The divine office, which had always been a central point in the life of the monk, now became almost his exclusive occupation. There was little time left for manual work. The monastery employed servants for that purpose. The skills of the monk were more properly used in singing the divine praises. The idea that the perfect execution of the liturgy was the characteristic function of a Benedictine community originated in the ninth-century reform. It accorded well with the notions of lay benefactors. This was the unceasing stream of prayer which, it was hoped, would bear them and their relatives into heaven. It was primarily to maintain this vital service that they gave landed endowments and offered their children as reinforcements for the ranks of the spiritual militia.

One of the major objects of the Aachen decrees had been to enforce stricter rules of enclosure. St Benedict had warned of the dangers that beset the souls of the brethren when business took them beyond the walls of the monastery. The ideal monk was Brother Ratpert, the historian of Saint-Gall, who rarely put a foot outside the cloister and feared going out like death, so that he only needed two pairs of shoes a year.[22] The other side of the problem was how to keep the outside world from filtering into the cloister. It was with this in mind that the assembly at Aachen decreed that there should be no school in the cloister except for the child-oblates. Secular clerks and lay people were excluded. The intention of the prohibition was to preserve the peace and segregation of the monastic enclosure. It did not stop a monastery from acting as the proprietor and director of an external school outside its walls. We know from Ekkehard that Saint-Gall had both a claustral school and an external school in the ninth century and that monks taught in both of them.[23] But the more austere spirits were opposed to this kind of arrangement; it was safer to leave the conduct of the external school in the hands of a secular master.

Although Benedict of Aniane wanted monks to disengage from secular education, he was eager to promote study in the cloister. But the learning he wanted was confined to what was implied by the *lectio divina* of the Benedictine Rule: the Scriptures, Origen, Augustine, and Jerome and, above all, Gregory the Great – this was the syllabus he prescribed for his disciple Garnier. It was a programme designed to enlarge understanding of the dogmas of faith, and so to lead to contemplation.[24] 'All progress comes from reading and meditation', wrote Abbot Smaragdus in the *Monks' Diadem*[25]; but the only reading he recommends is that of Scripture. It was a narrower and more exclusively monastic culture than Alcuin had purveyed at the palace school of Charlemagne or that Einhard had acquired at Fulda before the reformers got into the saddle. The change is reflected in the literary product of the ninth-century monasteries. Rhabanus Maurus at Fulda and Walafrid Strabo at Reichenau stand out like lone peaks among their contemporaries as learned abbots who retained an interest in the classics and wrote live poetry, as well as Scriptural commentaries and treatises of ascetical theology. As a whole, the chief monastic contribution to the Carolingian Renaissance took the form of commentaries on the books of the Bible, derived largely from the Latin Fathers, and anthologies of patristic texts. The ninth century also saw the production of the earliest commentaries on the Benedictine Rule, those of Smaragdus and Hildemar, which became classics of monastic literature. The *florilegia*, the anthologies of the Fathers, were the most characteristic work that emerged from the scriptoria of the Carolingian abbeys. It was unoriginal work, but in the end it served a wider purpose than its authors could have foreseen: the patristic anthologies of the ninth century provided a compost in which the Schoolmen of a later age were able to grow strange plants as yet undreamed of.

Benedict of Aniane died in 821 and the organisation he had brought into existence did not outlive him for very long. Italy had never been brought within the orbit of his reform programme. In the Germanic lands of the Empire, there is evidence of the *missi* conducting monastic visitations in the 830s, but the system collapsed with the disintegration of imperial authority. It was not just the problem of enforcement that caused the plan to wither in the opening bud; the conditions of the ninth century blighted monastic life. Monasteries, unlike other wealthy landowners, were unarmed and defenceless communities. They could only survive in a violent society so long as they had the patronage and effective protection of strong rulers; and in the dominions of the later Carolingians this condition ceased to exist. The civil war between the sons of Louis the Pious, and the troubled period that followed the partition of the empire in 843, led to the widespread secularisation of abbeys. The reformers had never succeeded in eliminating the practice of appointing lay abbots, and during the years of upheaval the contestants distributed abbeys freely among their aristocratic followers as a way of rewarding service. The resulting exploitation of monastic buildings and lands disrupted regular observance and impoverished the monks, who either dispersed or adopted the easier-going life of individual canons and joined in dividing the spoils.

Political instability and lay exploitation were not the only enemies of organised monastic life. The monks had to face more fearsome foes in the heathen Vikings and the Saracens. In the ninth century Christian Europe was under siege. Ireland, England, and the north of Gaul, were ravaged by the Northmen. Abbeys situated near the coasts or on the inland waterways of these areas were sitting targets. Lindisfarne, Clonfert, and Clonmacnoise, were among the first to be sacked. The more accessible abbeys near the coast of northern Gaul and along the valley of the Seine, the Meuse, and the Loire, fell victims to the onslaught. The monasteries of the Rhône valley and central Italy suffered the same fate at hands of the Saracens, who established themselves in the Maritime Alps as well as in Sicily and the Campania. In 883 they burned Cassino and slaughtered the monks, leaving it deserted for the next sixty years. The communities of some of the ravaged abbeys escaped the raiders and dispersed; others maintained a precarious existence as refugees, like the monks of Noirmoutier, who fled from the Danes in 836, and were sheltered in five successive monasteries, before finding a permanent home at Tournus thirty-nine years later. Their saga was paralleled by that of the monks of Lindisfarne, who fled to the mainland from a second Danish attack, taking the body of St Cuthbert with them, and wandered in Northumbria with their precious freight for seven years until they found a residence at Chester-le-Street. Such enforced migrations were commonplace at this period.

Before the end of the century, regular monastic observance had almost disappeared from Western Gaul and England. Alfred of Wessex lamented over the destruction of the Anglo-Saxon abbeys and their libraries. He made an attempt to restore the Benedictine life with his new foundations at Athelney and Shaftesbury, but the enterprise made small progress; a full-scale revival had to await more settled times. In the east German lands, religious observance and scholarship survived at Fulda and Saint-Gall; and Reichenau was an island of peace and learning under the gentle abbacy of Walafrid Strabo. The situation in other parts of Gaul is indicated by the biographer of St Odo. As a young man, the son of a Frankish knight, he was comfortably installed in a canonry at Tours, when a reading of the Rule of St Benedict convinced him he should become a monk. With a like-minded friend he set out in search of a monastery where the Rule was observed, but they traversed most of Francia without finding one. Odo returned home frustrated; but his friend travelled further afield and eventually discovered what they had been looking for in the remote abbey of Beaume, on the west side of the Jura – a monastery where the observance of St Benedict of Aniane had survived. Its abbot was Berno, a Burgundian, who had been called in to restore regular life there in accordance with the Aachen decrees. The friend sent back the news, and both he and Odo took the habit there. A few years later, when Duke William of Aquitaine decided to found a monastery on his Burgundian estates, he sought the advice of Abbot Berno. Duke and abbot set off together to reconnoitre a suitable spot, and Berno selected the richly wooded valley of Cluny. William protested that the site was his favourite hunting ground, but Berno was inexorable: 'which will serve you better at the judgement, O Duke, the prayers of monks or the baying of hounds?' William yielded, and Berno became the first abbot of the new foundation. He was thus a link between the reform of St Benedict of Aniane and the monasticism of Cluny, which was to dominate the religious life of the next two hundred years.

NOTES

1. *Die Urkunden der Karolinger*, ed. E. Mühlbacher, *MGH* (1906), I, pp. 75–6.
2. *Ibid.* 86–7.

3. *Poenitentiale Theodori*, ed. A. W. Haddan and W. Stubbs, *Councils and Ecclesiastical Documents* (1871) iii, pp. 173–203.
4. Text in A. Bruel, *Receuil des chartes de l'abbaye de Cluny* (Paris 1876) i, pp. 124–8.
5. *Chronique de l'abbaye de Saint-Riquier*, ed. F. Lot (Paris 1894), pp. 118–19.
6. A. Schulte, *Der Adel und die deutsche Kirche im Mittelalter*, 2nd edn. (Stuttgart 1922), p. 3 & n.
7. *Ibid.* p. 114.
8. *Vita Sancti Sturmi*, MGH SS II, 366–77.
9. J. Semmler, 'Karl der Grosse und das Fränkische Mönchtum' in *Karl der Grosse*, ii, *Das Geistige Leben*, ed. B. Bischoff (1965), pp. 255–89. This is the best modern account of Charlemagne's monastic policy.
10. From the general capitulary for the missi of 802: *MGH Leges* II: *Capitularia Regum Francorum*, ed. A. Boretius (1881) i, p. 94.
11. *MGH Concilia*, ed. A Werminghoff (1906) II, 290.
12. E. Lesne, *Histoire de la propriété ecclésiastique en France* (Lille 1926), ii, *passim*; P. Schmitz, *Hist. de l'ordre de Saint Benoit* i, (Maredsous 1942) pp. 80–90.
13. *MGH Epistolae* IV, 94.
14. *Chronique de Saint-Riquier,* p. 53.
15. *Vita Benedicti Abbatis Anianensis*, MGH SS XV, 202.
16. O. G. Oexle in *Forschungen zu monastischen u. geistlichen Gemeinschaften im Westfränkischen Bereich* (Munich 1978) p. 151, argues that the abbey of Ile-Barbe was organised according to the Benedictine Rule by Archbishop Leidrad of Lyons in *c.* 802 and that, contrary to the statements of Ardo, Benedict of Aniane had no part in it. In Oexle's view the importance of Benedict of Aniane has been exaggerated.
17. The original texts of the Aachen decrees have now been clarified and newly edited by Semmler in *CCM* I (1963), pp. 451–68, 471–81. Semmler has shown that the so-called *Capitulare Monasticum*, ed. A. Boretius in *MGH Capitularia* (1883) I, 343–9, is a document produced in *c.* 818/19 by conflating the capitularies containing the decrees of both the first and second synods: J. Semmler, 'Zur Uberlieferung der monastischen Gesetzgebung Ludwigs des Frommen', *Deutsches Archiv zur Erforschung des Mittelalters* **16** (1960), 309–88.
18. Haito's commentary is contained in the so-called 'Statutes of Murbach', *CCM* I (1963), 443–8.
19. W. Horn and E. Born, *The Plan of St Gall* (1979) i, pp. 24.
20. *MGH Epistolae* IV, 511.
21. *Chronique de Saint-Riquier*, pp. 70–1; see the discussion by J. Hubert, 'Saint-Riquier et le monachisme bénédictin en Gaulle à l'époque carolingienne' in *Il Monachesimo nell' alto medioevo* (Spoleto 1957), pp. 293–309.
22. *Casus S. Galli*, MGH SS II, 94, 97.
23. Cited in *The Plan of St Gall* i, p. 24 & n.
24. Cf. J. Leclercq, in J. Leclercq, F. Vandenbroucke and L. Bouyer, *The Spirituality of the Middle Ages* (1968), pp. 77–8.
25. PL 102, 597.

Chapter 6

The Age of Cluny

THE RISE OF CLUNY

It would have needed a prophetic vision to discern in Duke William's plantation of the year 909 the grain of seed that was to grow into such a mighty tree. At the height of its magnificence at the end of the eleventh century, Cluny was the head of a huge monastic empire containing many hundreds of dependencies and associated houses spread throughout Western Europe. It was a nursery of zealous prelates and the mentor of pious princes. Its holy and learned abbots were prominent counsellors at the courts of popes and emperors. Before Leo IX ascended the papal chair at the end of 1048 and made Rome the headquarters of the so-called Gregorian Reform Movement, it was to Cluny that men looked for spiritual leadership and religious inspiration. Even after its heyday was past and its creativity and confidence had begun to ebb, it remained a powerful force in the ecclesiastical and political establishment of the twelfth century. But all this lay in the future. Cluny stands in the tenth century for the restoration of Benedictine monastic life, largely as it had been understood by Benedict of Aniane a hundred years earlier.

As a house that was dedicated to reviving strict observance of the Rule, Cluny was not unique. It had spiritual parentage in Beaume and St Martin of Autun; it also had important contemporaries. Within a few years of its foundation, a monastic revival was sponsored in Flanders by the count, Arnulf I. He found an enthusiastic collaborator for his purpose in Gerard of Brogne, a young nobleman who had adopted the ascetical life and created a monastery on his own patrimony at Brogne. Under the count's active patronage, he restored Benedictine observance, first at St Bavo of Ghent and St Peter's on Mount Blandin, and then at the other Flemish abbeys of St Bertin, Saint-Amand, and Saint-Omer. A similar revival of even wider dimensions began in Lorraine in the year 933, when the abbey of Gorze was reformed by John of Gorze and Archdeacon Einold, acting under the authority of the bishop of Metz. Gorze in turn became the head of a large federation of reformed abbeys in Germany. The striking thing about the promoters of the monastic revival of the tenth century is that they worked independently of each other in the different areas, apparently expressing a common need felt by individual ascetics and by lay patrons and that, despite differences of organisation, all three groups owed their inspiration and formative ideas to the work of St Benedict of Aniane.

Cluny received the basic organisation of its internal regime from Berno, its first abbot. It was also to him and Duke William that it owed a feature of its constitution that enabled it to preserve its identity and provided the base on which its later greatness was built: it was given a degree of autonomy that was still uncommon for a monastic establishment. William's foundation charter expressly authorised the monks to choose their own abbot after Berno's death, without interference by any outside persons either lay or ecclesiastical. The abbot and community were to have sole and undivided control over their properties, free from intrusion by any secular power, including William's own. In order to guarantee this immunity he resorted to a device which a number of other founders had adopted in the previous fifty years: he vested the proprietorship of the establishment in the Apostles Peter and Paul and placed it under the immediate protection of the Apostolic See. In recognition of this special relationship, the abbey was to pay a *census* or tribute of 10 s. every five years to maintain lights burning round the shrine of St Peter in Rome. Recent work has shown that this arrangement was not as original as was once believed.[1] Other benefactors had donated their monastic foundations to St Peter. In any case, the invocation of the bishop of Rome as protector of the monastery can have been an act of little more than symbolic significance at this time, for the tenth-century popes, immersed in the dynastic politics of Rome, appeared to lack either the will or the means to defend their distant protégés. What made the case of Cluny different was that the bond with Rome later developed into a special relationship of mutual advantage, which enabled the abbey to achieve its unique position of independence, privilege, and power. This development was largely the work of a series of exceptionally gifted men who ruled Cluny for the next 140 years.

In this respect, Duke William's self-denying ordinance in granting the monks complete freedom to elect their abbot was a provision of crucial importance. In fact, this freedom, which the earlier reformers had struggled for in vain, was not exercised in the way specified by the Rule; for Berno and the three abbots who followed him designated their successors. But it was a primary factor in establishing the Cluniac ascendancy. It produced in St Odo (926–44), St Mayeul

(965–94), St Odilo (994–1048), and St Hugh (1049–1109), four spiritual leaders of genius, each of whom in his own way stamped his imprint not only upon the regime of Cluny but upon the religious life of his age.

Much that was characteristic of the Cluniac ideal was the creation of Odo, who was brought from training the oblates at Beaume to succeed Abbot Berno. He gave the monastic vocation a new theology and a new sense of mission. The vision of the world he communicated in his *Occupation of the Mind* – a prolonged meditation written in hexameters – was unrelievedly sombre. The evils of society were convincing evidence that the end of the world and the Day of Judgement were at hand. For the great mass of mankind which was enslaved by concupiscence there seemed to be little hope. The only safe way to salvation lay through repentance and conversion and entry into the monastic life. The monks were the Pentecostal Church created and renewed by the Holy Spirit. If they utterly renounced the world and were faithful to their calling, they were already living in paradise: the great silence that engulfed the cloister was a participation in the eternal silence of God; and the monk was united to God through the practice of unbroken prayer.[2] This conviction that the restored Benedictine life was the only authentic fulfilment of the Christian vocation was at the heart of the appeal Cluny made to the society of its time.

To his disciples and admirers Odo himself seemed a living embodiment of the Benedictine ideal. He taught the message of renunciation with an evangelical fervour: 'He found me at Rome', wrote Brother John, his biographer, 'trapped in the toils of earthly desires, and in his compassion he landed me in his net like a fish.'[3] He observed the Rule meticulously. Some wag in the cloister nicknamed him 'Ditcher' because he went about keeping constant custody of his eyes, with his head bowed and his eyes fixed on the ground. Two of the practices he inculcated in his monks came to be regarded as distinctive marks of early Cluniac observance: the keeping of silence, and the continual use of vocal prayer. Not only in choir, but wherever he went and whatever he was doing, the monk was to recite the Psalms. Brother John recalled·an incident that occurred during one of their many journeys across the Alps. A gang of robbers was lying in wait for travellers. But the leader of the gang was astounded at the unusual spectacle of a cortège moving with bowed heads and ceaselessly chanting psalms: 'I never remember seeing men like these before.' And he would not let his men attack them.[4] Another of Odo's disciples, Brother Godfrey, had learned the lesson of silence so well that he lost the community one of its horses. While the party was in Rome, he had been set to guard the horses, which had been put to grass overnight. Rather than shouting to the sleeping

watchmen during the hours of the Greater Silence, he allowed a thief
to mount one of the animals and ride off with it.[5]

In terms of buildings and material goods Cluny was still poor in
Odo's time. He saw the first church completed, but when the bishop
of Mâcon came to consecrate it, the monks were embarrassed by his
large entourage, as they had not got the wherewithal to feed everybody. Their dilemma was solved, according to Brother John, by a
wild boar which came and banged on the door with his trotters and,
having failed to gain admittance, lay across the entrance and oblig-
ingly offered himself to the episcopal spears. Yet despite these
humble circumstances, the reputation of Cluny as a model of Benedictine observance was already spreading, and Odo was invited by
princes and bishops to undertake the reform of other monasteries.
Fleury and Romanmôtier were among the first of a whole series of
French abbeys on which he imposed the customs of Cluny. It was to
promote his mission of monastic reform that in 931 he obtained from
Pope John XI a most significant privilege. By this Cluny was authorised to accept a refugee from any other monastery who was in search
of a stricter observance. He got the same privilege for Déols, and a
few years later for Fleury as well. These bulls in effect conferred
official recognition on the Cluniac reform and authorised its
expansion.

It was Odo's regime and his own charismatic personality that set
Cluny on the path to European status. He was a figure on the European stage himself. By constantly seeking papal approval for his work
of monastic renewal he developed the special relationship with Rome
at a time when papal influence in the churches of Northern Europe
was at low tide. His reputation outside France was strikingly
demonstrated by the fact that only twenty-five years after the foundation of Cluny he was invited by a secular ruler to undertake the
reform of monasteries at Rome and in the Roman duchy. Rome at
this time (c. 930) was ruled by the Senator Alberic, son of the notorious Lady Marozia and head of the dynasty of Theophylact. Most
of the Roman monasteries had been secularised by this period. The
establishments which served the patriarchal basilicas of the city and
the imperial abbey of Farfa in the Sabina were occupied by married
secular canons. Alberic has not had a kindly press from ecclesiastical
historians. And it has been argued that he sponsored the monastic
revival for very worldly reasons: the resumption and reallocation of
ecclesiastical lands which had fallen into the hands of rival families
would serve to strengthen the hold of his own dynasty upon the
duchy. Certainly he was not above foisting his own son, the profligate
and half-illiterate John XII, upon the papacy in order to perpetuate
the family's fortunes. Whatever his motives, he placed his authority
behind Odo, who embarked on his task in 936. Odo made six

prolonged stays in the city during the following years and introduced Cluniac observance to St Paul's-without-the-walls and to Farfa, and presided over the newly founded abbey of St Mary's on the Aventine, constructed out of one of Alberic's palaces which he donated for the purpose.[6] None of the Roman monasteries were placed in a relationship of dependence upon Cluny at this date, and Odo's reforming work was not long-lasting; but it impressed upon the capital of Christendom the fact that Cluny was the recognised standard-bearer of regular Benedictine life.

The expansion of the Cluniac family that Odo had begun was continued by Mayeul, whose life-history resembled Odo's in many ways. He too had come to the monastic life as an adult. He was already an archdeacon when he knocked on the doors of Cluny. He had been to the schools and acquired a love of the philosophers and the poets which he afterwards renounced so fiercely that he would neither read them nor suffer others to read them: 'the divine poets are sufficient for you; what need to pollute yourselves with the voluptuous eloquence of Virgil?'[7] But the reading habit never left him, and even in the saddle he rode with an open book in his hand. As abbot he was constantly in demand to reform other monasteries, which involved him in frequent and prolonged absences from Cluny, and his Life, written by Brother Syrus, is filled with anecdotes of his journeys to and from Italy. On one occasion he was seized by Saracens while crossing the Alps and had to be ransomed. He was a familiar figure at Rome and a welcome guest at the imperial court, where he won the admiration of the dowager Empress Adelaide. She got him to introduce the Cluniac observance to the new foundation of San Salvatore at Pavia; and when the Roman see fell vacant, she and her son, Otto II, urged him to accept the papacy. But he refused the distinction of being the first Cluniac pope, saying he did not relish the ways of the Romans and, in any case, he was not willing to desert the monastic life and the monks under his care.

THE CLUNIAC EMPIRE

The missionary zeal and energy of Odo and Mayeul placed Cluny at the centre of the monastic map of Europe. But it was the regime of Odilo and Hugh that gave it a great spiritual empire. The extraordinary reign of these two men, both of whom were long-lived, lasted for 115 years. Slight in build and ascetical, always gentle and perceptive in his relations with his monks, to Fulbert of Chartres 'the archangel of monks', Odilo had a capacious mind and humane sympathies which make him one of the most attractive figures in the gallery of Cluniac saints.[8] Like his predecessor a constant traveller in the cause of monastic revival and reform, he was friend and counsellor to popes and kings and moved with assurance in the courts of Europe. It was through his tireless efforts that the first outlines of Cluny's monastic empire began to emerge. Besides the abbeys in France, Italy, and Spain which accepted Cluniac customs, a growing number of monasteries were donated to Cluny by their patrons, and these remained direct dependencies in the sense that the abbot of Cluny was their head. The process of forging a Cluniac order was taken a stage further by the privilege of exemption which Odilo obtained from the papacy. Like the previous abbots, he assiduously courted papal support for the monastic reform. And he used his influence at Rome to extricate Cluny from diocesan authority. In 998 he procured a privilege from Pope Gregory V to the effect that no bishop might celebrate mass or ordain at the abbey except by the abbot's invitation. The final step towards autonomy was taken in 1024 when Odilo secured from John XIX a grant of complete exemption from the jurisdiction of the bishop of Mâcon, which placed Cluny under the direct authority of the Roman see. And this exemption extended to monks of Cluny wherever they resided. This effectively freed all the dependencies of Cluny from episcopal oversight and left them under the sole supervision of the abbot of Cluny.

The need to supervise the dependent houses kept Odilo continually on his travels in the later years. But Cluny was where his heart lay and he always tried to get back there for the major festivals. He revelled in its triumphs, as he happily contemplated the growing numbers of novices and the monks from elsewhere who had come to learn the observance. 'How festively he would stand', wrote Jotsaldus his pupil and biographer, 'in the middle of that holy choir, looking to left and to right at the new plantation which was his crown.'[9] Success had brought the abbey a flood of endowments. The stringency of the early days was forgotten and the exalted grandeur of the Cluniac ideal was beginning to take palpable shape in magnificent buildings. In order to accommodate increasing numbers, Mayeul had replaced the church of Odo's time with a new and grander building. Odilo set about reconstructing the community's domestic premises. He was a great builder; he renewed everything, wrote Jotsaldus, except the walls of the church. A new dormitory and refectory were built and a guest-house in two sections with beds for forty men and thirty women. But the major source of his pride was the cloister, which he had rebuilt with piers of marble procured from Provence and shipped up the Rhône and Saône. 'He used to boast', says Jotsaldus, 'that he had found it wood and was leaving it marble, following the example of Octavius Caesar who, the historians say, found Rome brick and left it marble.'[10]

With the assumption of the abbacy by Hugh, Cluny entered on its last and greatest period of expansion. The year 1049, when his reign began, was also a milestone in the history of the secular Church. It saw the arrival in Rome of the emperor's cousin, Bruno of Toul, who, as Leo IX, inaugurated a new style of papal government. The first year of Leo's pontificate proved in fact to be an *annus mirabilis* for the growing party of high-minded churchmen who were pressing for the reform of abuses and an end to the secularisation of ecclesiastical offices. Following a brisk drive to restore clerical discipline in Rome, he set out to make his presence felt north of the Alps. Assemblies of bishops and abbots were summoned to meet him at Reims and Mainz. The prelates who attended were examined on the circumstances of their appointments and were asked whether they had paid money for their offices; those who admitted having done so were disciplined; absentees were declared suspended; the disobedient were excommunicated; and new canons were promulgated. This burst of activity indicated that the pope had stepped into the leadership of the reform movement. It inaugurated a new phase in which the papacy demanded an ever more active and interventionist role in the affairs of local churches and called in question the domination of the Church by secular rulers. It was significant that Leo's synod at Reims was cold-shouldered by the king of France. The pope's attack on simony had thrown down the first challenge to lay control of ecclesiastical offices that was to lead to the Investiture Contest.

Cluny, by its idealism, its assertion of spiritual autonomy, and its constant appeal to papal protection, had helped create the necessary spiritual climate in which the reform movement could flourish, and it could hardly avoid being drawn into the ensuing conflict between the papacy and secular rulers. Thanks to the status won by his predecessors, Abbot Hugh entered at once into a European role. And his birth and his own talents equipped him well for the part. He was born to the purple. He was the son of a count of the Brionnnais, with family connections among the higher aristocracy of Aquitaine and Burgundy.[11] He had entered the noviciate of Cluny in his early teens. Odilo, who was no respecter of persons but a good judge of managerial capacity, appointed him prior at the age of twenty-two. His wholly unpriggish devotion to the Rule and his successful management of the abbey's external affairs during Odilo's later years marked him out as the obvious successor. He was a tall, well-built man, with an impressive physical presence. His shrewd judgement was combined with an urbanity and perceptiveness that attracted confidences from others. He had all the mental and personal gifts of the successful executive, which contended in his soul with the deeply ingrained humility of the monk: 'the flesh wanted it', he answered with utter candour, when with other abbots he was asked at the Council of Reims how he had obtained the abbacy, 'but the mind and rational part refused it'.[12] He read much, but he seems to have felt no urge to authorship; his talents lay elsewhere – in planning, directing, and building. Intense bodily mortification and constant prayer had enabled him to sublimate personal ambition into an unflagging will to promote the monastic ideal and enhance the grandeur of Cluny. His zeal in supervising the dependent houses of the order made him a constant traveller and he was a familiar figure to many of the French and Italian bishops as well as a welcome visitor to the courts of the emperor and the king of France. While he was prior, he had already met and won the confidence of the Emperor Henry III, and he later accepted the invitation to be godfather to Henry IV. It was this long-established association of the leaders of Cluny with the imperial family, as well as their carefully cultivated links with the papacy, that obliged them to assume a role in the investiture struggle.

For many of the aims and ideals of the Gregorian Reform Movement the Cluniacs were bound to feel a profound empathy. They whole-heartedly endorsed that part of the reform programme that aimed at purifying the Church from abuses and rescuing it from exploitation by secular rulers. And the fact that they owed their own freedom from lay interference and episcopal jurisdiction to the favour of St Peter and his vicar made them natural allies of the papacy in its struggle to assert its spiritual authority over Christendom. On the other hand, the spread of Cluniac monasticism owed much to the enthusiasm of pious princes; and their long history of collaboration with lay rulers, especially with the German imperial family, disposed the leaders of Cluny to adopt a cautious attitude to the more radical of the hierocratic claims made by Gregory VII.[13] Their dilemma is clear from the part played by Abbot Hugh in the bitter struggle between Gregory and Henry IV of Germany.

Gregory had been a monk himself, possibly at St Mary's on the Aventine which had links with Cluny, and he admired the Cluniac ideal. Hugh was a friend, to whom he looked for moral support in the darkest days of his struggle. In 1075 he poured out his heart to him in a long letter written in a mood of deep depression and discouragement at the violent opposition to his decrees on clerical celibacy and lay investiture. But Hugh was also godfather and counsellor to Henry. And this made it impossible for him to remain aloof from the contest. So he bent all his efforts to bring about a reconciliation. He was in fact one of the chief architects of the dramatic meeting between the pope and emperor-elect at Canossa in 1077; he was present at the negotiations, and attested the oath Henry swore to implement the terms of the concordat. Six years later, when the German army was investing Rome and Gregory was trapped in the Castel Sant' Angelo, Hugh was allowed to cross the lines in a last but unsuccessful attempt to mediate between Henry and the pope.

The fact that he managed to retain the trust and affection of both the contestants throughout the struggle is a tribute to his detachment and diplomatic skill. But ultimately, of course, the interests as well as the ideals of Cluny were bound to align it with the Gregorian papacy. If Hugh felt a painful division of personal loyalties, he never wavered in his support for the papal programme of reform; and he served Gregory well as papal legate in France. Other Cluniac monks also served at the papal Curia; and the old alliance was consummated in 1088, when a former grand prior of Cluny, Odo the cardinal bishop of Ostia, was elected pope as Urban II.

In the course of Hugh's abbacy, which lasted for sixty years, Cluny touched the peak of its power and social esteem. Urban II was only the most conspicuous of a stream of Cluniac monks who were recruited to the ranks of the episcopate. It was during Hugh's regime, too, that a vast and complex network of relationships began to emerge between Cluny and its dependencies which has baffled the descriptive powers of modern historians. New foundations that were colonised by monks from Cluny were organised as priories immediately dependent upon the mother-house, which appointed the superior of each house, who was often drawn from Cluny itself. Hugh also brought pressure to bear upon abbeys reformed by Cluny to accept reduction to the status of priories. Those old and wealthy abbeys, such as Vézelay and Moissac, that were allowed to keep their abbatial status, were subject to the control of the abbot of Cluny, who either appointed their heads or supervised the election of their abbots. Some of the subject abbeys and priories were themselves the parents and overseers of a large family of dependent monasteries. Moissac, in the Toulousain, acquired a cluster of houses in Catalonia. And the priory of La Charité, situated in the upper valley of the Loire, had a far-flung family of some seventy dependencies, which included five foundations in post-Conquest England. Besides the host of monasteries that stood in a relationship of direct or indirect subordination to Cluny, there was a shifting circle of satellite establishments which were drawn into the organisation after accepting Cluniac observance, but subsequently regained their independence. Others again adopted Cluniac practice without ever surrendering their autonomy.

These differing degrees of association were to be seen in most parts of Europe by the end of the eleventh century. In the duchy of Rome, the ancient abbey of Farfa was restored to Cluniac observance with the help of Odilo, but it never became constitutionally subordinated to Cluny. By contrast, during the regime of Hugh a whole series of dependent priories were founded in North Italy at Lodi, Pontida, and in the region of Milan. The major focus of Cluniac influence in Germany was the Swabian abbey of Hirsau, which adopted Cluniac observance after 1079 under the leadership of Abbot

William of Hirsau, who got Ulrich the prior of Zell to compile a custumal for him; but Hirsau itself was never directly affiliated to Cluny. In Spain, Cluny acquired a group of subject monasteries after 1072 thanks to the enthusiastic patronage of Alfonso VI of Leon-Castile. Cluniac penetration of the Spanish kingdoms began in the time of Odilo, when Sancho the Great sent monks to Cluny to learn the observance and introduce it to the abbey of San Juan de la Peña in Aragon. The personal links with the royal dynasty forged by Odilo were strengthened in Hugh's time by the marriage of his niece to Alfonso VI. Alfonso gave several monasteries to Cluny, but its ethos was disseminated in Spain not so much through its subject priories as through the abbeys which adopted its customs without becoming dependencies. Chief among these was the royal abbey of Sahagun in Leon, which Alfonso forced to accept the customs of Cluny in 1080, together with a Cluniac monk as abbot. Sahagun became in fact the major agency through which Cluniac observance was introduced to the monasteries of Leon-Castile.

This ramshackle spiritual empire was not an order in the proper sense of the term. It was a vast spatial extension of St Benedict's idea of a monastery as a family community living under the personal direction of a father-abbot. All Cluniac monks, wherever they lived, were in theory members of the community of Cluny itself. When they visited the mother-house, they were entitled to take their place in chapter. Postulants who had been admitted to any house of the congregation, once they had completed their noviciate, were sent to make their profession to the abbot of Cluny or alternatively awaited his visitation of their own monastery. He was the spiritual father of all Cluniac monks everywhere. It was a theory that stretched St Benedict's model to breaking-point. For although Odilo and Hugh were indefatigable travellers and visitors of the daughter-houses, any real supervision of such a huge congregation was obviously beyond the capacity of one man. As time went on, the relationship between the mother-house and the dependencies lost the intimacy of a filial bond and assumed some of the colour of feudal lordship that existed in the secular world. The role of the abbot of Cluny became that of a distant potentate, to whom every house of the congregation owed obedience and to whom it looked for protection. The outward sign of this subjection was the annual tax or *census* paid to Cluny by each of its daughter-houses.

The Cluniac empire lacked an effective organisation because it was not the outcome of any clearly formulated design. Its colonies were acquired piecemeal in the course of two centuries through unsolicited donations and requests for help. It owed its existence chiefly to the enthusiasm of lay magnates who either sponsored new foundations or donated abbeys in their possession with an appeal, not always happily endorsed by their monks, for the introduction of Cluniac observance. Two cases illustrate the different ways in which additions were made to the Cluniac family. One of these was the case of Fleury which came into the hands of Abbot Odo about the year 930. It was an acquisition of special and symbolic significance as it contained the body of St Benedict. It was a royal abbey, but Odo's biographer tells us that the Robertian King Rudolf I gave it as a reward for service to Count Elisiard. Elisiard was an admirer of Cluny and gave the abbey to Odo to be reformed. But the community did not share the count's enthusiasm. When Odo arrived with a heavy escort of two counts and two bishops, he found the doors barred against him. The monks waved royal privileges which promised they should never be ruled by a person from another congregation; and some retreated to the roof of the cloister from which they pelted the visitors with brickbats. Odo, who was a peaceable but persistent man, allowed the siege to continue for three days; then, unescorted and unnoticed, placed a ladder against an inconspicuous corner of the wall and quietly let himself into the enclosure. He was received without violence, and his gentle persuasiveness prevailed on the monks to accept him as their abbot. According to Brother John, their change of heart was prompted by a threat from a personage more exalted than either count or bishop: one of the brethren, returning from duties outside the cloister, was confronted by the Blessed Benedict himself who gave him a frightening message for the community: 'Since they will allow me no rest, I am departing from this house, and know that I shall not return to this place until I bring from Aquitaine a man after my own heart.'[14] Thus Fleury passed into the Cluniac family through the collaboration of St Odo with the wishes of a lay proprietor.

A different case was that of Lewes in Sussex, which was a new foundation. Cluny began to penetrate England after the Norman Conquest, but the initiative came from the king and the Anglo-Norman nobility and not from Abbot Hugh, who showed no great eagerness to extend his monastic family across the Channel. In fact he declined a request from King William to supply him with monks for English abbeys in return for an annual payment to Cluny. The foundation of Lewes priory, the first of the English Cluniac houses, was the result of an initiative by William de Warenne, the first Norman earl of Surrey. After the turmoil of the Conquest and settlement, William and his English wife, Gundrada, set out on a pilgrimage to St Peter in Rome. They made a leisurely progress through France and stopped at Cluny, where they were royally received and entertained in the palatial building Odilo had designed for noble guests.[15] The warmth of the hospitality and the splendour of the liturgical life made a deep impression on them, and they sought and obtained the privilege of confraternity. And on returning home, they determined to create a Cluniac priory at Lewes, close to the castle which was the head of their lordship. They petitioned Abbot

Hugh to send monks, promising to donate the newly built stone church of Lewes and an endowment big enough to support a community of twelve. But Hugh at first demurred. As he had told King William, he was disinclined to send monks to an alien country across the sea, where supervision would be impossible. The earl and countess persisted and in the end they got Cluny to send a small party consisting of a prior and three monks, and the work of erecting the priory could begin. Lewes in fact came to have a privileged position as one of the five major priories of the Cluniac congregation. The circumstances of its foundation are only remarkable in that they typify the way in which the unsolicited efforts of lay magnates added fresh colonies to the empire of Cluny.

THE CLUNIAC IDEAL

What was it about the Cluniac life that evoked such an eager response from the leaders of eleventh-century society? The Cluniac teaching that the secular world was irremediably sinful and that the life of the monk was the only sure way to salvation struck a deeply responsive chord in the minds of men oppressed by the need to make satisfaction for their sins and fearful of the impending Day of Judgement. Cluny, as St Hugh wrote to King Philip of France, was the refuge of the penitent; let the king therefore resign his earthly kingdom while there was still time and lay hold on the eternal kingdom by ending his days as a monk.[16] 'Acknowledging the enormity of my sins', runs the charter of a benefactor, 'and at the same time fearing the dread condemnation of the reprobate, and mindful of the greatness of God's mercies, I fly to the harbour of safety.'[17] Arnaldus, the author of the charter, donated both himself and his church to the abbey, where he purposed to take the habit. To those who could not commit themselves in this way (and King Philip was one of them), the best hope lay in winning the remission of sins by sharing in the merits of Cluny through association. This could be achieved by the gift of property or of children. A child-oblate provided a kind of living investment in the monastic community from which a family hoped to reap rich spiritual rewards. At Cluny the children, the *nutriti* reared in the cloister, were trained up to sing the elaborate services with a professional expertise that was hard for an adult convert to master.

The repetitious formulas alluding to the burden of sins and the terror of the Last Judgement, which recur again and again in the hundreds of charters of donation written during the abbacies of Odilo and Hugh, reveal the mind and handiwork of the monk draftsman; but there can be no doubt that they echoed the sentiments of the donors themselves; they hoped to make satisfaction for their offences by sharing in the observances of the monks. The surest and most coveted means of obtaining this was to be received into confraternity. This was a form of association that was conferred on monks of other congregations who requested it and on more privileged lay benefactors. An application for confraternity was considered by the community in chapter, and if it was granted, the applicant was brought into the chapter and inducted by a special form of words. In effect, he was made a participant in all the spiritual benefits of the monastery, and on his death the community celebrated the full Office of the Dead as it did for its own monks. The names of confraters and benefactors were written in a *Liber Vitae*, or Book of Life, which was placed on the high altar during the celebration of mass. These books, in which fresh names were constantly being inserted, are eloquent witnesses to people's belief in the efficacy of the intercessory prayer of the Cluniac monks. One of them, compiled during the abbacy of Hugh for the small dependent priory of Villars-les-Moines at Murten in the diocese of Lausanne, contains as many as 10,000 names.[18]

The observance with which benefactors were so eager to associate themselves was the unending round of vocal prayer. It was this that averted the anger of God from sinful men and made reparation on behalf of the living and dead. The liturgical life of Cluny satisfied this deeply felt need to a degree that had never been achieved before. Our knowledge of the liturgical practices of medieval monasteries is chiefly derived from custumals. These, which survive in increasing numbers from the end of the tenth century onwards, were treatises setting out detailed regulations for every part of the monastic day. They filled out and supplemented the more general instructions contained in the Rule. Custumals were widely circulated and copied and were the primary means of preserving uniformity of practice among different houses of the same congregation. In fact one of the earliest custumals of Cluny is a copy that was made in the time of Abbot Odilo for the abbey of Farfa.[19] It reveals a timetable in which choir duties occupy the greater part of the monk's day – perhaps as much as eight hours on festival days. This was much longer than the time allocated to the divine office in the Rule of St Benedict.

In much of its liturgical practice Cluny had simply adopted and developed the legislation of St Benedict of Aniane. Additions to the canonical hours, such as the recitation of the Matins of the Dead and the Office of All Saints following the night office, were already established practice in the ninth century; so too was the custom of celebrating two community masses every day. The prolongation of services was a trend that had been going on for centuries. At Cluny it was given a further push by the constant addition of Psalms for benefactors and the lengthening of the lessons recited at the night office – in the two weeks preceding Lent, the entire books of Genesis and Exodus were chanted at Matins. Another factor was the multiplication of saints' days on which the longer night office of twelve lessons was recited. 'In Lent', observes the custumal of Ulrich grimly, 'the psalmody is extremely prolix.' On some days it must have been almost continuous. On Good Friday, after the office of Prime, the community retired barefooted to the cloister and recited the entire Psalter. Besides this, the custumals lay down elaborate rules for processions to the altars, with cross, candles, incense, and reliquaries.

For this endless solemn celebration of the liturgy the efforts of Odilo and Hugh had provided an architectural setting of incomparable magnificence. Odilo had reconstructed the abbey's domestic buildings on a grand scale. Hugh set about replacing Mayeul's church with a third and still bigger building, a huge basilica 531 feet in length, constructed on the plan of a patriarchal cross, with four transepts, fifteen towers, and five chapels radiating from the ambulatory of the choir. The grandeur of Hugh's design caught the imagination of Europe; subventions were received from Henry I of England and Alfonso VI of Leon-Castile, who exacted the money from his newly conquered Muslim subjects; the Empress Matilda presented the bells. The work was begun in 1088. By October 1095 the altars of the chevet were ready to be consecrated by the Cluniac pope, Urban II, who had come to France to preach the First Crusade; and in 1130 Innocent II dedicated the whole church. All but a fragment of Hugh's church has gone, but something of the harmonious masses of the design and the richness of its historiated capitals can be seen from its imitators at Paray-le-monial and Vézelay, and from the debris housed in the Musée de Cluny at Paris. The marble sculptures of Odilo's cloister have vanished, but they live on, for ever encapsulated in the vivid denunciation of St Bernard[20]:

> in the sight of the brethren reading in the cloister, what is that ridiculous monstrosity doing? what is that deformed beauty and that beautiful deformity? those unclean monkeys? those ferocious lions? those battling knights? those monstrous centaurs? those huntsmen sounding their horns? Here are several bodies under a single head; there a quadruped with the head of a serpent; there a fish with the head of a quadruped . . . on all sides one sees such a rich and amazing variety of forms that it is more pleasing to read the marbles than the manuscripts.

It was all a disgraceful aberration from the austere simplicity of the Rule. But Bernard was the spokesman of a new monastic age which was in the process of rejecting the Cluniac model. In Hugh's day, the great choir with its high altar hung with orphreys and lit by a forest of candelabra, and the splendour of the liturgy it housed, seemed to most people to be a symbol of the glory of heaven, expressing in palpable form the highest realisation of the monastic ideal.

Cluny was the spiritual Everest in a landscape containing many peaks. Its far-flung network was only one of several monastic associations which derived their inspiration from the revival of St Benedict of Aniane and the Aachen decrees. In the course of the tenth and early eleventh centuries many ruined abbeys were repeopled with monks, new foundations were made, and fresh congregations sprang into existence. Some of these took their pattern of monastic life from Cluny while remaining outside the Cluniac empire; others followed a distinct, if not very different, type of observance, given them by the mother-house of their own congregation.

Among the groups that were influenced by Cluny, but not of it in any constitutional sense, was the large constellation of reformed monasteries which received their customs from St Benigne of Dijon. Its animator was an Italian, William of Volpiano, who ranks among the greatest ascetical revivalists of the age. It is observable but perfectly understandable that most of the reformers were men who had come to the monastic life as adults; often they were clerks, who had absorbed the best of the learning the schools of the time had to offer. The oblate, educated in the cloister and trained from childhood in the habits of obedience and conformity, was less likely to question the accepted norms of his establishment than was a recruit from the outside world, who had formed his ideals independently. But William of Volpiano was the exception. He had been placed as a child in the monastery of Lucedio near Vercelli. The stimulus that made him a reformer came from a meeting with Mayeul, which drew him to Cluny. In 989 he was sent to reform St Benigne at Dijon, where he introduced the customs of Cluny. For the next forty years, as abbot of St Benigne, he worked to extend the Benedictine revival in northern Italy, where he founded the Piedmontese abbey of Fruttuaria. But the area of his most impressive achievement was Normandy. In 1001, at the invitation of Duke Richard II, he took a party of monks from Dijon to Fécamp, where he restored regular observance. In the following years the reform was extended to the Norman abbeys of St Ouen, Jumièges, and Mont-Saint-Michel; and the duchy became famous for the quality of its monastic life.

In Catalonia Cluny had little direct influence. There the monastic revival of the early eleventh century, which followed the ravages of the Muslim conqueror al-Mansur, stemmed from the abbeys of Cuxa and Ripoll. They were ruled jointly by the famous Abbot Oliva, who founded a dependent priory of Ripoll to serve the sanctuary of the Blessed Virgin at Montserrat. Later in the century, Ripoll was absorbed into the spiritual empire of St Victor of Marseilles, which formed a large congregation of subject abbeys extending from the Midi into northern Spain.

GORZE AND THE GERMAN REVIVAL

Apart from a few outposts across the English Channel, the Cluniac empire was largely confined to the Romance-speaking lands. In the East Frankish lands which were gradually welded into the medieval kingdom of Germany, the monastic revival of the tenth century was led from the abbey of Gorze, near Metz. Gorze had been founded in the eighth century by St Chrodegang of Metz, but monastic life had ceased there, and it was much dilapidated when in 933 Adalbero of Metz gave it to John of Gorze and the Archdeacon Einold of Toul, so that they could restore Benedictine observance. Helped by the enthusiastic patronage of bishops and German princes, the reform of Gorze was imported into St Maximin of Trier, St Vanne of Verdun, and other abbeys of Lorraine. And from Lorraine it was transmitted to both revived monasteries and new foundations in Hesse, Swabia, and Bavaria. The major role in spreading the Gorzer observance in Bavaria was played by St Wolfgang of Regensburg. He had abandoned his post as *scholasticus* to the cathedral school of Trier in order to take the habit at Einsiedeln, but the cloister could not hold him for long. In 971 he set off to evangelise Hungary. The following year his friendship with members of the Bavarian ducal house brought him to the see of Regensburg. His first step was to introduce the custumal of Gorze to the monastery of St Emmeram, which he separated from the bishopric; and from this base, he restored Benedictine life to a series of Bavarian abbeys and founded several monasteries for women.

In Germany and the Empire Gorze played a role in the Benedictine revival similar to that of Cluny in France, but with a difference.[21] The monks of Gorze followed an elaborate liturgical routine derived, like that of Cluny, from the reform of St Benedict of Aniane, but Gorze had developed a tradition of its own quite independently from Cluny. Its lectionary was different, and so were some of its liturgical ceremonies. It is in the custumals of the Gorzer group that we encounter for the first time the Easter play of the Sepulchre, the birth-point of medieval drama, played out during the night office. It was unknown to Cluny; but the common custumal of the English monks, which was compiled in 970 and drew upon the experience of Gorze, has a vivid description of the ritual performed during the night of the Resurrection: three monks in albs, and carrying incense, advance slowly up the church towards the place of the sepulchre, step by step, as though searching for something; and when they draw near 'he that is seated there shall begin to sing softly and sweetly'

'Whom is it you seek in the sepulchre, O worshippers of Christ?'[22]

Organisationally, the family of monasteries that sprang from the

Gorzer reform had little in common with the centralised patriarchal structure of the Cluniac empire. The Lotharingian and German reformers owed much to the patronage of the imperial house and to the active sponsorship of bishops. Unlike Cluny they did not seek large-scale exemptions from episcopal jurisdiction. Nor did they attempt to reduce newly reformed abbeys and daughter foundations to dependent status. The German abbeys that received the customs of Gorze retained their autonomy. No abbot east of the Meuse claimed the kind of suzerainty exercised by the abbots of Cluny. Instead the monasteries of the Gorzer tradition developed 'filiations' or associations of houses grouped round the abbeys from which they had received their common custumal. These groups were not linked to their mother-house by juridical bonds; they were primarily associations of prayer, which provided full services at death for each and every monk of the congregation. So besides Gorze itself, St Maximin of Trier, Fulda, which had the customs of Gorze imposed on it by the Emperor Henry II, Einsiedeln, and the Bavarian abbeys of St Emmeram and Niederaltaich, all became the nuclei of congregations of coequal monasteries.

THE ENGLISH REVIVAL OF THE TENTH CENTURY

Cluny and Gorze represented two distinct traditions which both derived their interpretation of the Benedictine life from the reform of Benedict of Aniane and the Aachen decrees. Both traditions played a part in shaping the form taken by the monastic revival in tenth-century England. Social pressure and foreign invasion had combined to cut short the first spring of monasticism in the Anglo-Saxon kingdoms. Practically no organised monastic life survived the Danish invasions of the ninth century. Monastic lands had been appropriated, and those monastic buildings that were not deserted and ruinous were occupied by groups of married secular clerks. The way for the revival was prepared by individual ascetics who had found it necessary to go to the Continent to fulfil their vocation. One of these was Archbishop Oda who came to the see of Canterbury in 942. He had previously taken the monastic habit at Fleury, and he sent his nephew Oswald there to become a monk, and so initiated a connection with the Cluniac abbey on the Loire that influenced the whole course of the English movement. On being recalled to take up the bishopric of Worcester in 961, Oswald became one of the three leading promoters of the monastic revival, and it was from Fleury that he summoned Germanus, another English monk, to be the first abbot of his new foundation at Westbury-on-Trym. There were also personal links with the Lotharingian reform. St Dunstan, the chief architect of the revival, spent an instructive period of exile at Blandinium of Ghent, which had accepted the customs of Gorze. This process of cross-fertilisation later bore fruit in the common custumal agreed by all the English abbots in 970.

The English revival was mainly the work of three determined men, St Dunstan, St Ethelwold, and St Oswald. But it could not have been accomplished without the active support of the Wessex kings. The movement began when King Edmund gave Dunstan, the son of a Somerset thegn and a relative of the royal family, the old abbey of Glastonbury where he had been educated. Dunstan repaired the monastic buildings and recruited a community following the Benedictine Rule. His disciples included Ethelwold, the most austere and dynamic of the reformers. Dissatisfied with the observance at Glastonbury, Ethelwold hankered to search out his ideal abroad, but King Eadred diverted him by giving him the derelict monastery of Abingdon to restore. The movement suffered a setback during the crisis of Eadwig's short reign, when Dunstan was forced into exile. But the accession of the young King Edgar in 959 gave the reformers the enthusiastic patron they needed to pursue their work. Dunstan was recalled to be bishop of Worcester, and from there was quickly translated, first to London, and then in 960, to Canterbury. Ethelwold, who had been the king's mentor, was appointed to Winchester, where he took the drastic step of expelling the married secular canons from the Old Minster and installing a community of monks brought from Abingdon. And, at Dunstan's suggestion, Oswald was summoned home to take up the see of Worcester.

With the force of the king behind it the monastic revival now made rapid progress. The two restored abbeys at Glastonbury and Abingdon, and Oswald's foundation at Westbury-on-Trym became the power-houses of the movement, each of them sending out groups of monks to people and restore ruined houses or to found new ones. The community of Abingdon supplied monks for a group of new foundations made by Ethelwold in East Anglia, including Medehamstede (the later Peterborough), Ely, Thorney, and Croyland. Westbury colonised a group of houses in the West Midlands including Worcester, Pershore, Ramsey, and at one remove, Winchcombe. Glastonbury supplied monks for Bath, Malmesbury, Sherborne, and at a later stage for Westminster. Besides the monasteries for men, several abbeys of nuns were either restored or newly founded, including the large and richly endowed establishments at Romsey, Shaftesbury, Wilton, and the Nunnaminster at Winchester. All the English monasteries followed the Benedictine Rule, but within this common framework there was much variation of practice stemming from the differing background and experience of the founders. It was therefore thought desirable to compile a single uniform custumal which all would observe. So an assembly of abbots and abbesses was convened at Winchester under the presidency of the king in 970, and an agreed code of observance was drawn up called the *Regularis Concordia*.

According to Aelfric, the *Concordia* was the work of Ethelwold. We know in fact very little about the circumstances which produced it or why it was thought necessary. The desire for a nation-wide uniformity of monastic observance and the idea that the king should be its patron and guardian, a notion quite foreign to the Rule of St Benedict, was a product of the Carolingian reform of the ninth century and a society that assigned a sacral role to kingship. The programme of monastic life set out in the *Concordia* is that of the Aachen decrees, derived from the traditions of Cluny and Gorze. As was to be expected, the leaders of the English movement looked to the Continent for guidance in interpreting the Rule. The preface to the document, in fact, acknowledges the help given by monks who had been summoned from Fleury and Ghent to advise the council. The timetable of the monastic day as set out conforms to the Continental practice of the tenth century in making the chief task of the monk the execution of the liturgy. The additions to the divine office adopted at Cluny are included in the instructions of the *Concordia*, but at some points the document follows the Lotharingian tradition: the order for the last three days of Holy Week and the week following Easter is that used by the Gorzer congregation. The Easter Play of the Sepulchre is apparently derived from the same source. A special feature of the custumal is the emphasis upon the role of the king as patron and protector: it was agreed that Psalms and prayers for the king and queen should be recited after all the liturgical offices except Prime. In this way the abbots acknowledged the bond of mutual service that existed between the English monasteries and the monarchy.

The English monastic renaissance could not, in fact, have been accomplished without the constant support and collaboration of the Wessex kings. The endowment of minsters restored to monastic use involved the resumption of Church lands which had been secularised or appropriated by secular canons, and this could only be done by acts of royal power. Besides the forcible bestowal of lands and churches, the king in many cases endowed the abbeys with important franchisal privileges which gave them seignorial jurisdiction over the population of large areas. The abbots of Medehamstede, for instance, were given jurisdiction over eight of the hundreds of Northamptonshire, and in this area the hundred courts were presided over by the steward of the abbey. Not all the nobility shared Edgar's enthusiasm for the monastic revival, and after his death there was a brief insurrection by a group of families which had suffered loss through the king's largess. But the gains made in his reign could not now be reversed. New foundations were sponsored by Aethelred and Cnut, the greatest and richest of which was the foundation of St Edmund's abbey at Bury in Suffolk – Cnut's reparation for the murder of the last king of the East Angles by his countrymen in the ninth century. By the eve of the Norman Conquest, though something of the initial zeal had cooled, the intoxicating sense of pioneering a great revival had been lost, the Benedictine abbeys had struck long and deep roots in the social landscape of southern England.

The English revival had drawn much of its inspiration from Cluny. Yet before the end of the eleventh century new kinds of religious organisation were rising to challenge the Cluniac ascendancy. Some of the best minds of the time were turning away from a life dominated by corporate ritual in search of a simpler form of ascetical life which allowed more opportunity for private prayer and reflection and which was less involved with the secular world. Behind the imposing façade, there were signs of malaise, which became plain for all to see following the death of St Hugh. His successor, Pons of Melgueil, proved a disaster. Having been induced to resign, he reappeared three years later, during the abbacy of Peter the Venerable, at the head of a mob of runaway monks and, with the help of malcontents in the community, seized the abbey, which was subjected to an orgy of plunder and violence before Peter regained possession. The fact that Pons found helpers within the cloister indicates that the success of St Hugh had been bought at a dangerously high price. Cluniac propaganda had attracted large numbers of adult converts, many of whom had no real aptitude for the monastic life and who lacked the education necessary to take part in the elaborate liturgy. The rebellion was the nemesis of a propaganda that represented Cluniac monasticism as the universal vocation of all Christians.

NOTES

1. For a modern discussion of the charter and its precedents see H. E. J. Cowdrey, *The Cluniacs and the Gregorian Reform* (1970), pp. 8–15.
2. For Odo's doctrine of the monastic life see R. Morghen in *Cluniac Monasticism in the Central Middle Ages*, ed. Noreen Hunt (1971), pp. 11–28; and K. Hallinger, *ibid.* pp. 29–55.
3. *Vita S. Odonis, PL* 133, 45.
4. *Ibid.* 71.
5. *Ibid.* 66.
6. On Odo's work at Rome see E. Sackur, *Die Cluniacenser in ihrer Kirchlichen u. allgemeingeschichtlichen Wirksamkeit* (1892–94) i,

pp. 99–114; and B. Hamilton, 'Monastic revival in tenth-century Rome', *Studia Monastica* iv (1962), 35–68.

7. *Vita S. Maioli, PL* 137, 752.

8. See the *Vita S. Odilonis* by his pupil Jotsaldus in *PL* 142, 897–940. For a striking modern prtrait see R. W. Southern, *The Making of the Middle Ages* (1953), pp. 158–9.

9. *PL* 142, 906.

10. *Ibid.* 908. For buildings of Cluny see J. Hourlier, 'Le monastère de Saint Odilon', *Studia Anselmiana* **50** (1962), 5–21; the authoritative monograph is that of K. J. Conant, *Cluny: Les Églises et la maison du Chef d'Ordre* (Mâcon 1968).

11. On Hugh and his regime see Noreen Hunt, *Cluny under St Hugh 1049–1109* (1967).

12. *S. Hugonis Vita, PL* 159,

13. The question of the relationship of Cluny to the Gregorian Reform has been investigated by Cowdrey, *op. cit.*

14. *Vita S. Odonis, PL* 133, 80.

15. According to a thirteenth-century tradition, they were warned to proceed no further as the war between the pope and the emperor had made the passage of the Alps unsafe. This, and other details are derived from the spurious foundation charter of Lewes, printed in W. Dugdale, *Monasticon* (1825) v, pp. 12–13. This was shown to be a forgery by C. T. Clay in *Early Yorkshire Charters* viii, *The Honour of Warenne* (Yorks. Archaeo. Soc. Record Series vi, 1949), pp. 59–62; but the historical material is apparently derived from an earlier and genuine narrative.

16. *Epistolae, PL* 159, 9302.

17. A. Bruel, *Receuil des chartes de l'abbaye de Cluny* (Paris 1876) iv, No. 3063.

18. J. Wollasch, 'Ein Cluniacensiches Totenbuch aus der Zeit Abt Hugos von Cluny' in *Frühmittelalterliche Studien*, ed. K. Hauck (Berlin 1967) i, pp. 406–43.

19. *Liber Tramitis Aevi Odilonis Abbatis*, ed. P. Dinter in *CCM* x (1980). This supersedes the earlier edition of Bruno Albers. On the liturgical practice of Cluny see G. de Valous, *Le Monachisme clunisien des origines au xve siècle* (Ligugé-Paris 1935) i, pp. 327–72.

20. From Bernard's Apologia to William of Saint-Thierry: *S. Bernardi Opera*, ed. J. Leclercq, C. H. Talbot, and H. Rochais (Rome 1959) III, p. 106.

21. The distinctive liturgical tradition of Gorze and its independence of Cluny were vindicated in K. Hallinger's monumental study *Gorze-Kluny* 2 vols (*Studia Anselmiana* **22–25**, 1950–51); on the organisational differences see particularly vol. ii, 765–80.

22. *The Regularis Concordia*, ed. T. Symons (1953), p. 50.

Chapter 7

THE CLOISTER AND THE WORLD

THE DAILY ROUND

Bare ruined choirs and empty cloisters kindle the imagination of the modern visitor but cannot satisfy it. Standing on the floor of the dormitory at Fontenay and glancing down the night-stairs into the transept of the great church, one easily visualises the cowled figures scurrying down for the night office. From the pulpit of the roofless refectory of Fountains one can look down upon a ghostly multitude of bowed heads. But it is much harder to recapture the experience and atmosphere of daily life in a medieval cloister. How exactly did monks spend their day? Here at once we have to make distinctions. Although the Rule of St Benedict constituted a thread of continuity through the centuries, the domestic arrangements and assumptions of a monastic community were no more static than those of the society which surrounded it. The experience and mental furniture of a Benedictine monk living in the fifteenth century would have been different from those of a monk of the twelfth century, and the life-style and expectations of both would have differed from those of a monk living in a Carolingian abbey of the eighth century. Let us try to reconstruct the daily round in a Benedictine establishment towards the close of the eleventh century.

Letters and monastic chronicles provide us with occasional glimpses through the walls of the enclosure; but the most systematic information about the occupations of the monk's day comes from the custumals. These were treatises recording the customary practices of particular monasteries. They were compiled to supplement the general instructions of the Rule and contained detailed regulations for the celebration of the divine office and for every activity that filled the monastic day. One of the primary objects of these compilations, which survive in substantial numbers from the two centuries between 1050 and 1250, was to secure uniformity of observance within houses belonging to the same congregation, and so they were widely circulated. Uniformity of practice was the avowed motive for the composition of the *Regularis Concordia* in tenth-century England; and a similar intention must have underlain the regulations or so-called statutes that Archbishop Lanfranc gave to the cathedral priory of Christ Church Canterbury soon after 1070, for they were copied in other cathedral monasteries of Norman England.

Some of the fullest of these rule-books are those written in the eleventh century as a guide to the customs of Cluny. One of them was compiled by a monk of the Italian abbey of Farfa, who had been sent to Cluny by his abbot to learn the usages and report back home.[1] Another was compiled by Ulrich, himself a monk of Cluny. He had been on a visit to the Swabian abbey of Hirsau about the year 1075, and during his stay his host, Abbot William, had plied him with questions about Cluniac practice. So on returning home Ulrich wrote up the customs of his abbey for William's benefit and also, unforeseeably, for ours.[2] Together these two treatises provide us with a fairly detailed guide to the pattern of life at Cluny under the regime of Odilo and St Hugh. We have already drawn upon them in describing some of the features of Cluniac observance. All the custumals give elaborate instructions for the celebration of the divine office at the various seasons of the year and omit much else that we should like to know. Nevertheless they do enable us to reconstruct in some detail the routine of daily life in a Benedictine abbey of the eleventh century.

Both the brethren and the children slept in the common dormitory fully clothed in their habits except for cowl and scapular. This may have been no hardship on winter nights in an unheated stone building, but it must have been uncomfortable in summer. It was the rule at Cluny that even on the hottest nights no more than feet or arms might be uncovered. At some time between 2 and 3 a.m., depending upon the time of year, the community was roused by the bell. They rose, pulled the covers over their beds, put on night-shoes and cowl – a monk, explains Ulrich, must not enter the lavatory (which connected with the far end of the dormitory) with head uncovered, for the cowl conferred anonymity – and then, while the bell continued to ring, they made their way down the stairs which led directly into the church and assembled in choir to sing the night offices of Nocturns (now called Matins) and Lauds. A monk who is not in choir in time for the preliminary prayers, which are said when the bell ceases to ring, must confess his fault and ask pardon in chapter. The adult monks were followed into the choir by the boys, shepherded by their master. And after them came the novices, who slept in their own quarters. When they had arrived the service could start. Engulfed in a cavern of darkness that was only intermittently broken by the pools of light shed by lanterns and candelabra, the cantors began the chant.

Staying awake during the lengthy readings of Nocturns was evidently a problem. The Cluny custumal provides for a lantern-bearer to perambulate the choir to make sure that everybody is awake. If he comes upon a monk who has fallen asleep during the lessons, he does not speak, but gently moves the lantern to and fro close to his face until he wakes. Although the day began in the early hours of the morning, it was not unduly long as the community retired for the night at dusk. The longer summer days were punc-tuated by a siesta that was allowed in the afternoon. At some periods of the year the community would go back to bed after singing the Lauds of the Dead and rest until the bell woke them again at first light. They then returned to the church to sing Prime – the first service of the day. After this there was an interval, which in summer might last a couple of hours or more, before the bell rang for the short office of Terce, the service of the third hour sung towards 9 a.m. During this period the monks changed into their day-shoes and washed hands and face at the lavabo, which was situated in the cloister, and occupied themselves with reading or tasks about the house.

As St Benedict had intended, vocal prayer at the canonical hours formed the framework of the monastic day. There were the three short services of Terce, Sext, and None, the last two sung respectively at about midday and three in the afternoon, and the rather longer evening office of Vespers. And the day concluded at dusk with the brief service of Compline. But as we have seen, by the eleventh century the relatively simple liturgical scheme of the Rule had been greatly enlarged by the addition of further services – the offices of the Dead and of All Saints – and by additional Psalms. The community now attended two masses daily, the 'morning mass' celebrated immediately after Terce, and the high mass that followed the office of Sext at about midday. Besides these, there were the private masses murmured at the many side-altars in the early hours before daybreak, for by this period it had become the practice to ordain a high proportion of monks to the priesthood.

At major festivals the rituals of the liturgy were enriched with added magnificence. On the vigils of Christmas, Easter, and Pente-cost, the church and cloister were decorated, and the brethren were woken for the night office by the pealing of all the bells. The high altar was illuminated by hundreds of candles, the cantors wore gorgeous copes, and during the Nocturns two priests circulated incen-sing the altars and the members of the community. When Matins was finished, the solemn mass of the feast was celebrated, heralded by a peal of bells, and following this the night services were completed by the singing of Lauds. The brethren could then return to bed to snatch what sleep they could before daybreak. It is impossible for the modern student to assess the psychological impact upon the individual of these interminable hours spent daily in vocal prayer and liturgical rituals. How much of the participation was simply mechanical? It is significant that some of the most reflective minds of the period rejected the Cluniac pattern of observance and that the new orders of the twelfth century drastically pruned the traditional monastic liturgy.

Outside choir, the most important assembly point of the day was the chapter. Following the morning mass, the community processed out of the church into the chapter-house. The brethren sat on the gradines – the tiered seats round the walls – and the abbot or prior presided. After the reading of a lesson and a chapter of the Rule the head of the house delivered a conference or sermon. Business matters concerning the community might then be discussed. This was also the occasion when individuals who had committed breaches of the Rule confessed their faults or were accused by others, and were assigned penances. The boys met in a chapter of their own. There, Ulrich explains, those who have blundered in singing the psalmody, misbehaved in any way, or simply fallen asleep during the services, are stripped of cowl and frock and beaten by their master with willow rods. Harsh, but no harsher than the treatment children expected to receive in the outside world. It was a general conviction in medieval society that constant beating was indispensable for the proper education of the young.

After chapter, which would have ended towards 10 a.m., there was a clear period that could be devoted to work or study, lasting until the bell rang for Sext, about midday. Work was a part of the monk's routine expressly enjoined by St Benedict. There were always tasks to be performed in the offices and workshops of the monastery. But the abbeys of the eleventh century employed servants for the menial jobs. In a major establishment such as Cluny, or the cathedral priory of Canterbury, which contained perhaps upwards of 100 monks, as much as half of the community might be occupied with administrative duties either inside or outside the enclosure. Those who were not involved in administration spent the hours outside choir in reading, copying books in the scriptorium, or in artistic work. The manual labour prescribed by the Rule had by now become largely ritualised. 'To tell the truth', says the maestro in Ulrich's custumal, 'it amounts to nothing more than shelling the new beans or rooting out weeds that choke the good plants in the garden; sometimes making loaves in the bakery. On the days when it is done, after holding a shorter chapter than usual, the abbot says, 'Let us proceed to manual labour.'All then process out, the boys leading, to the spot.'³ Psalms are sung, and after a spell of weeding the procession re-forms and returns to the cloister.

The virtual elimination of manual work in favour of intellectual activities was partly the result of the great elaboration of the monk's liturgical duties. Far more of his day was spent in choir than St Benedict had envisaged; and choir duties were physically exhausting as well as time-consuming. The change also reflected changing social assumptions. Tilling and hewing were work for peasants. Peter the Venerable argued that the delicate hands of his monks, who came from a social milieu unfamiliar with toil, were more suitably employed furrowing parchment with pens than ploughing furrows in fields. It was one of the objects of the Cistercian reform to reinstate manual labour and assert its spiritual value. But it was a reversal of the prevailing trend, in which the Benedictine houses did not follow the reformers.

The importance of reading in the life of the monk was underlined by the generous amount of time allocated to it in the Rule; and it was symbolised by the annual issue of books for private reading at the beginning of Lent. At Cluny, the keeper of the book store, in accordance with the Rule, had the books laid out on a carpet spread on the floor of the chapter-house. A list of the books issued the previous year and their recipients is read out. Each monk, on hearing his name, hands back his book and receives another. Anyone who has not finished his book confesses his fault and asks pardon. Lanfranc's constitutions describe an identical ritual at Canterbury. A chance survival in the Farfa abbey custumal of a list of sixty-three books issued to the monks one Lent in the mid-eleventh century gives us a momentary glimpse of the reading tastes of one community.⁴ Most of the books fall into the expected categories of works of devotion and ascetical theology – Cassian, Smaragdus's commentary on the Rule, Lives of the saints, and the Scriptural commentaries of the Fathers from Jerome to Gregory the Great, as well as the later commentators like Bede, Alcuin, and Rhabanus Maurus. But the list also contains an interesting selection of historical works – the *History* of Josephus, the *Ecclesiastical History* of Eusebius, an anonymous *History of the English*, which must be Bede, and, more surprisingly, the secular Roman history of Livy, not a work that was widely known at this period. The reading of history was regarded as an improving spiritual exercise. As John of Salisbury observed in the twelfth century, through studying the chronicles of the past men came to perceive the invisible working of God.

A significant part of the book-holdings in a Benedictine library was likely to come from donations. When Odo became a monk at Beaume he took with him 100 books, which were probably transported in due course to Cluny. Medieval library catalogues, like the great catalogue of Canterbury cathedral priory which was compiled in the thirteenth century, sometimes list the books under the names of donors. Nevertheless, a proportion of the librarian's stock had to be supplied by the monastery's own scriptorium.

The work that went on in the scriptorium or writing-room was vital to the internal life of the monastery and it also provided an important service to the outside world. At any given time several monks were likely to be copying texts or composing books of their own. Sometimes they worked in the northern walk of the cloister alongside the church, but often a separate room off the cloister was allocated to the task. The ninth-century plan of Saint Gall provides for a spacious scriptorium above the library with seven writing-desks. The first charge on the workers in the scriptorium was the reproduction of the books needed for the services in choir and the readings in the refectory – the antiphonals, tropers, missals and lectionaries. An equally important task was the provision of grammars for the education of the boys in the cloister and the multiplication of books to stock the library. Most of the energies of the monks engaged in writing would be devoted to making copies of approved texts. If exemplars were needed, they could be borrowed from other monasteries. Since pen, ink, and parchment were the sole materials of production, books took long to make and they were rare and costly objects in the medieval world. Men used them as security for loans, and they were often passed on by pious bequest. A complete Old Testament might cost more than the total annual stipend of a country curate. Understandably, therefore, some abbeys demanded a deposit before lending books. 'Send by the bearer of these present letters', writes Peter the Venerable to the monks of the Grande Chartreuse, 'or by some other trustworthy person securities for the books I have sent – not as a pledge for their better preservation, but so that the orders of our father St Hugh relating to such loans may be observed.'[5]

It was not only the humble copyists of texts who worked in the scriptorium of course. The regulated leisure of the cloister provided the ideal conditions for authorship. The evidence lies in the product. The monastic writing-office was the factory that, until the twelfth century, produced the great bulk of the literary works, secular as well as sacred, that filled the libraries of the Middle Ages. Abbo of Fleury (d. 1004), grammarian, mathematician, historian, and hagiographer, to Fulbert of Chartres 'the most famous master of all France', held that, after prayer and fasting, the practice of literary composition did most to bridle the lusts of the flesh.[6]

Although the community itself had first call upon the resources of its scriptorium, monastic scribes also provided important services to the outside world. Both in France and pre-Conquest England, early rulers who possessed no organised chanceries of their own, made use of the scriptoria of the abbeys to write their letters and diplomas. Abbot Hilduin of Saint-Denis was arch-chancellor to Louis the Pious, and the abbey supplied the emperor with a writing-office. But besides such periodic help to princes the monasteries performed an essential service for the world of letters by reproducing books to order for scholars or secular patrons. Some houses acquired a reputation for the technical excellence of their calligraphy and the beauty of the illumination and miniature painting with which they decorated their manuscripts. It was of course a source of income to the monastery. The person who ordered the book paid for the labour, and it was quite common for him to supply the necessary parchment. Canon Hillin of Cologne, when he commissioned a text of the four Gospels from the tenth-century workshop of Reichenau, apparently sent the monks the parchment already cut and made up into quires.[7] Reichenau in the tenth-century, like St Augustine's Canterbury in the twelfth, was famous for the sumptuous quality of its painted manuscripts. But the monks produced utilitarian copies of texts as well as display books. In fact, until the rise of the university stationers in the thirteenth century, who specialised in the rapid reproduction of cheap scholastic texts, the monasteries had a virtual monopoly of book production. As time went on, however, the pressure of demand made it necessary to supplement the efforts of the monk copyists by employing professional scribes, who were paid a salary out of the monastic coffers.

The monastic timetable allocated two periods of the day to reading or writing, one in the morning before the midday office, and the second between the main meal of the day and Vespers. The hour of dinner – the main meal – varied according to the season. In the summer months, beginning with Easter, it was eaten soon after midday following the high mass; and there was a second meal in the evening after Vespers. In the shorter days of winter the timetable allowed for only a single meal, which was taken rather later in the afternoon, but some other form of solid refreshment or a drink of wine was given before Compline and departure to bed. Meals, like other activities, had their ritual. After washing their hands, all entered the refectory, where places were allocated by strict rules of seniority, and remained standing until the arrival of the abbot or prior, who pronounced the blessing. The meal was served and eaten in silence except for the voice of the lector who read to the community from a lectern or pulpit.

The preservation of silence in which prayer and reflection could flourish was one of the primary aims of all strict monastic observance. After the morning chapter and after dinner in the afternoon there were periods of the day when conversation was permitted in the cloister. But in church, refectory, and dormitory, silence was perpetually observed, save for the chant and the public readings of the lectors. Some latitude was allowed to individual officers engaged in business or to the head of the house who might be entertaining guests in his own quarters, but with Compline all talking had to cease. The silence of Cluny in the early days was proverbial. An elaborate sign language was developed so that the monk could express his needs without speaking. 'The novice must needs learn the signs with diligence', explains Ulrich, 'for after he has joined the community he is very rarely allowed to speak.' A request for bread was indicated by a circular motion made with the thumbs and first two fingers of both hands; fish was signified by a motion of the hand simulating the tail of a fish moving through water; trout was the same, but in addition the finger was drawn from eyebrow to eyebrow – a sign indicating that even if no flesh-meat was eaten at Cluny, the table did not lack some variety; for milk, the lips were touched with the little finger, 'because thus does an infant suck'.[8] A monk who wanted to make confession approached a priest of his choice and standing before him indicated his wish by drawing his right hand from his scapular and placing it on his chest; whereupon the priest rose and led him into the chapter-house to hear his confession.

The rules of silence did something to mitigate what strikes a modern student as one of the most oppressive aspects of life in a medieval monastery – the total lack of privacy. It was not only that the individual slept, ate, and moved about in the constant company of others; even such humdrum personal activities as shaving and taking baths were closely supervised communal exercises. Shaving was reserved for the eve of major festivals, so that by the end of Lent the community must have presented an exceedingly shaggy appearance. At Cluny the razors were locked away in a cupboard beside the entrance to the dormitory, to be produced when a general shave took place. The brethren sat in lines along the cloister wall and passed round the razors and bowls. The operation was preceded by the recitation of Psalms and collects. The Benedictine Rule urged that bathing was a practice to be discouraged except for those who were sick; and the custumals commonly ordained baths three times a year, before the festivals of Christmas, Easter, and Pentecost, but always with the proviso that those who did not wish to participate need not do so. Lanfranc's constitutions for Canterbury lay down an elaborate procedure for the provision of baths before Christmas. The brethren assemble in the cloister and wait until the senior monk in charge of the operation calls them in groups to the bath-house. There each monk undresses and enters a cubicle shielded by a curtain and takes his bath in silence. And even this moment of solitude was not to be prolonged: 'when he has sufficiently washed, he shall not stay for pleasure, but shall rise, dress, and return to the cloister'.[9] An unmistakable air of anxiety hangs over the whole proceeding.

It would be a mistake, of course, to suppose that the monks themselves felt oppressed by the lack of solitude. Medieval society did not afford the individual much opportunity to be alone, unless he retreated to the desert. Peasant families occupied one-room dwellings separated, in many cases, from their livestock by only a partition; townsmen lived in small congested houses; and rural knights lived and ate in halls surrounded by family, bailiffs, neighbours, and servants. Continuous company was the normal lot. The privacy we take for granted is the product of a more affluent society. As Héloise reminded Abelard when she was trying to dissuade him from marriage, only the very rich had houses with many rooms, and scholars were not usually wealthy.

The custumals set out an orderly routine covering every hour of the day and night. They make it clear what everyone has to do and when he is required to do it. What they cannot tell us, however, is the extent to which the rules were observed at any given time. The history of most monasteries that were long-lived reveals alternating periods of strict observance and relaxation. Much depended upon the quality of the superior. Under an easy-going or senile abbot discipline tended to disintegrate. There were always those in a community who were ready to take advantage of such a situation. For, so long as the practice of child-oblation continued, a fair proportion of monks in the Benedictine houses had been drafted. Some, when they reached adulthood, were able to rise to the ideal that had been wished upon them; others obviously sought to create a comfortable life for themselves in a predicament from which medieval society offered no escape. Nor were all adult postulants motivated by a simple enthusiasm for the ascetical life. Many sought admission because the monastic habit offered them the best prospect of status and security.

Apart from the question of lax observance, the custumals by their very nature convey a deceptive impression of peaceful and undisturbed routine. But this was a condition few communities can have enjoyed for very long. The erection of monastic buildings, which look homogeneous to the casual eye of the modern visitor, often took several generations. And in a thriving establishment there was a constant process of rebuilding and enlargement. During the eleventh century there can have been few periods when the claustral peace of Cluny was not disturbed by the sound of hammer and chisel, the creaking of hoists and the clatter of workmen. The even tenor of monastic life was often disrupted, too, by natural mishaps and by the violent intrusion of the outside world. A wealthy landed corporation could not hope to insulate itself entirely from the turmoils of war and political upheaval. Canterbury cathedral priory, like other English monasteries, suffered disturbance of its internal harmony after the Norman Conquest by the forcible importation of an alien prior and a group of Norman monks; and for some years racial animosity kept the two sections of the community apart. The life of the priory was also disrupted by the wholesale building operations that followed the Conquest. Its church was twice rebuilt in the course of the next sixty years, only to be devastated in 1174 by a fire which left the monks without a usable choir for more than a decade. Such mishaps were almost commonplace. But the quiet erosion of community life was less the consequence of catastrophes like this than of forces that sprang from the internal administration of the monastery itself.

MONASTIC OFFICIALDOM

As St Benedict had envisaged, the abbot found it necessary to appoint a number of subordinate officers from among the brethren to assist in the management of the monastery's affairs. By the eleventh century a fairly elaborate chain of officialdom had been evolved in the greater Benedictine houses. The special task to which each official was assigned was called an 'obedience' and he himself was referred to as an 'obedientiary'. In the first place there was the prior. Although the abbot appointed all his subordinates, the head of a great abbey was a prominent person with public responsibilities that frequently took him away from the monastery. He might be absent for long periods in the service of king or pope or on the business of his own congregation. When he was at home, he was expected to entertain important visitors at his table. All this tended to separate him from the routine life of his monks; and during the twelfth century it became normal practice for the abbot to have his own house, with hall, kitchen, and chapel, within the enclosure. This development meant that the responsibility for maintaining regular life and discipline in the cloister fell increasingly to the abbot's second-in-command, the claustral prior. The bigger houses had more than one prior. At Cluny, where the abbot was constantly on his travels visiting his far-flung dependencies, there was a grand prior, charged with the general management of the abbey's properties and its relations with the external world, a claustral prior to oversee the internal life of the community, and second and third priors to help him. There were also roundsmen, called *circatores*, whose role was to tour the premises during periods of work and reading and ensure that there was no disorder or idle gossiping.

The various administrative departments of the establishment were entrusted to a lengthening chain of obedientiaries. The precentor, or cantor, was responsible for training the monks in the chant and the proper celebration of the liturgy and also, since he had to ensure a supply of service books, for supervision of the scriptorium. The sacrist had the duty of looking after the fabric of the church, the altars, and sacred vessels, and he had care of the shrines – a heavy duty in abbeys that boasted famous relics and attracted a large number of pilgrims. The novice-master had the care and training of the novices. The almoner was entrusted with the task of dispensing food and other forms of relief to the poor. It was an evangelical obligation that was reiterated in the Rule, and most monasteries took it seriously. Monastic alms-giving was in fact the only regular form of poor relief that existed in medieval society. The almoner of Cluny was assigned a portion of the tithes from the churches in the abbey's possession to enable him to meet the demands on his charity. There was a daily distribution of bread and wine and twelve pies, weighing three pounds each, from the monks' kitchen. On Quinquagesima Sunday all the poor who cared to come were fed with a meal of salt pork. Besides giving food to those who begged at the abbey gates, the almoner also provided hospitality for the poorer pilgrims and clerks who arrived on foot. And his charity was not confined to callers. According to Ulrich, he was expected to make a weekly tour of the township to seek out any who were sick and in need of food or medicaments. It was a practice that Lanfranc enjoined upon the almoner of Canterbury.

The monk-chamberlain saw to the provision and laundering of clothing for the brethren. The supply of food, drink, and fuel for the community and its guests was the business of the cellarer. 'He should be sober and no great eater', urges St Benedict with understandable anxiety. Much of his time was taken up with the transport, checking, and storage of provisions from the abbey's estates. It was common practice to allocate to his use the buildings off the west range of the cloister for storage purposes.

Another sensitive appointment was that of the infirmarian. He had charge of what was in effect a parallel establishment, usually situated a little to the east of the main complex, containing its own dormitory, hall, chapel, and suites of private rooms. It was a monastery in cameo. This was because it not only had to house and nurse monks who were sick, but also to provide a permanent rest-home for those who were too old and infirm to take full part in the routine of the monastery. It might also be called upon sometimes to furnish quarters for the head of the house if he retired on account of age or bad health. As the Rule restricted the eating of meat to the sick, in times of strict observance the refectory in the infirmary was the only place in the monastery where meat was served.

In a great abbey like Cluny one of the heaviest tasks was that of the guest-master. He was in fact running what, by eleventh-century standards, was a first-class hotel, providing accommodation, meals, and stabling facilities, for a continual stream of visitors which included prelates and princes and members of the higher nobility. The guest-house built by Odilo was a palace with a frontage of 135 feet, containing forty-five beds for male guests and, in another wing, thirty beds for their ladies; but it was reserved for visitors who came on horses; those arriving on foot were assigned to a less grand establishment under the infirmarian's jurisdiction.[10] As time went on, the senior obedientiaries, who had the heaviest responsibilities, delegated part of their task to subordinate officers, so that it came about that an ever larger proportion of the community was involved in administrative or supervisory duties. Thus the sacrist was assisted by a sub-sacrist and in some cases by a separate warden of the shrine, and some of the cellarer's duties were distributed among a kitchener in charge of the catering, a refectorer, a gardener, and a woodward.

Although all the obedientiaries owed their appointment to the abbot, in practice they acquired a large degree of independence in the administration of their offices. This was the outcome of a growing tendency to divide the properties of the abbey in such a way that a proportion of lands, tithes, and offerings was allocated to maintaining each of the offices. This subdivision was encouraged by the habits of benefactors, who often made pious bequests expressly earmarked to support specific departments such as the almonry – a favourite object for charitable bequests – the infirmary, or the guest-house. It gave each of the major obedientiaries control over a portion of the monastery's income and over the property from which the income came. It was a practice fraught with dangerous implications both for regular observance and for financial stability. It meant that a group of monks were not only preoccupied with internal administration but were also involved in managerial responsibilities which frequently took them away from the monastery, for estate management necessitated inspecting distant properties, interviewing bailiffs, hearing accounts, and attending courts. It was thus necessary to exonerate obedientiaries from regular attendance in choir, a duty that St Benedict had insisted was the first priority in the life of a monk: 'Let nothing take precedence over the Divine Office'.[11]

The devolution of authority and economic decision-making could also have damaging financial consequences. In the course of the twelfth century bad housekeeping or financial adventurism by individual monastic officers got some abbeys into serious debt. Cluny, whose estates were under the control of twenty-three monk-deans, was in financial difficulties when Peter the Venerable was elected abbot in 1122. Excessive expenditure and mismanagement of the demesne manors had made it difficult to keep the abbey supplied with regular provisions. It had to be rescued from this predicament by a reorganisation of the abbey's farms and by generous financial help from one of its former monks, Henry of Blois, the brother of King Stephen and now bishop of Winchester.[12] Crises like this were common among the Benedictine houses. In the thirteenth century there was a general move by ecclesiastical authorities to improve the situation by re-establishing central control over monastic finances. This was done by pressing each house to appoint a monk-treasurer and to set up a central exchequer, through which all income and disbursements had to pass, and by requiring an annual audit of accounts.

THE CLOISTER AND THE WORLD: RECRUITMENT

Although monks had in principle withdrawn from the world, the monastery was an organism whose roots were deeply embedded in the social landscape. Many of the older Benedictine houses were situated in, or on the fringe of towns, and were intimately involved in civic life. At Bologna the ancient abbey of San Stefano still carries on its twelfth-century façade an open-air brick pulpit, the outward and visible sign of the pastoral role it discharged towards the surrounding city. Those richly endowed abbeys that were founded in the countryside usually became the nuclei of new townships, created by the need of a large monastic community for goods and services.

The most obvious and immediate link between the cloister and the world outside it lay in its sources of recruitment. Throughout the eleventh and twelfth centuries new monasteries were founded and the monastic population continued to increase. The rising number of monks and nuns was a dimension of the general population increase that most parts of Western Europe experienced during this period. In the latter end of the period, growth was most conspicuous among the new orders, particularly the Cistercians. Firm figures for the Benedictines are hard to come by before the thirteenth century and have been variously interpreted.[13] Some abbeys suffered a marked decline in numbers after the eleventh century; others, after a phase of rapid expansion which was often the result of local circumstances, settled down to a steady level of recruitment which continued with little change for the next 200 years. Canterbury cathedral priory, for instance, experienced a boom in applicants in the two generations that followed the Norman Conquest, which can be explained by the dispossession of many English landed families and the destruction of their worldly prospects. Thus by 1120 the number of monks at the priory had risen from about 60 in Lanfranc's time to something like 120. Thereafter numbers declined to about eighty and remained at about this level during the thirteenth century. Here, as elsewhere, the relative constancy of numbers over a long period of time indicates not so much a shortage of recruits as a determination of monastic chapters to match numbers to material resources. Numbers at Cluny touched their maximum of about 300 by the death of St Hugh. He seems to have admitted all who applied, without much regard to their character or suitability; but his successors found it necessary to adopt a more discriminating policy over admissions. By 1250 the community contained 200 monks, and it seems to have remained at roughly that level for the next 100 years.[14]

Who were these people and where did they come from? As we have seen, the children donated by their parents formed one section of the monastic population. But the new orders generally declined to accept child-oblates, and although the Benedictines continued to take them, the children formed a declining proportion of black-monk communities in the twelfth century. Peter the Venerable regarded them as a potential source of trouble and he reduced the number of boys at Cluny to six. The surge of new recruits to the cloister thus consisted largely of adult postulants, both clerical and lay.

The scarcity of systematic records makes it difficult to generalise about their social origins. Some establishments, like the Swabian abbey of Reichenau, boasted of their social exclusiveness, but this was far from being the general situation. The requirement of noble birth as a qualification for entry was commoner in the monasteries and cathedral chapters of Germany than it was elsewhere. The leading figures in the Cluniac empire were men of aristocratic birth, but the rank and file were trawled from a more varied background. Most Benedictine houses appear to have recruited from their own locality and to have admitted men without distinction of birth, provided they could bring some form of endowment with them. The only class debarred was that of the unfree. But the property requirement, even if it was small, obviously meant that most recruits came from the ranks of middling landowners and better-off townspeople. One reservoir of recruits, about which we know too little in this early period, may have been provided by the local schools in monastic ownership. The chronicler of Bury St Edmund's tells us that his hero, Abbot Samson of Bury, got his early education at the abbey's school in the borough, where he was taught by Master William of Diss, a secular clerk.[15] We have no means of telling how many others made their first and most decisive contacts with the cloister through this channel.

Canterbury Cathedral Priory provides an illuminating case history of a large and wealthy Benedictine establishment which drew a significant number of recruits from the local township. The surviving rent-rolls reveal that in the twelfth century many Canterbury families gave a relative to the cathedral monastery.[16] Those monks who can be identified, including some of the senior obedientiaries, were children of the more substantial families – those of the borough reeves and the wealthier tradespeople, such as goldsmiths and mercers. The endowment they brought with them when they took the habit consisted in many cases of quite modest properties – a house or a plot of land within the city walls. Some of these recruits were evidently late converts to the monastic life. One of them, a monk named Henry, was the father of Hamo, the reeve of Canterbury. Another late convert, a leading citizen named John Calderun, retired to the cloister about the year 1176, while his wife was still living: he arranged for her maintenance by contracting the priory to supply her with a daily corrody or pension of food from the monastic kitchen and a periodic provision of clothes. Thus many of the monks had relatives among the townspeople including, in some cases, sons as well as brothers and sisters.

THE SOCIAL AND ECONOMIC ROLE

The Canterbury muniments give us some insight into the close economic ties that existed between a large monastery and a medieval township. By the twelfth century the priory had acquired through gift or purchase the lordship of nearly half the houses in the town and its suburbs, and the rent from these properties constituted a steady though minor element in its income. The economic converse of the priory's role as landlord was its function as employer. It provided a livelihood for a large number of the city's residents. For on its payroll there were, besides a hundred or so domestic servants employed in the precincts, a multitude of professional people and craftsmen who provided it with specialist services, such as attorneys, physicians, masons, goldsmiths, and plumbers. There were, too, a group of residents who derived support from the priory in the form of a corrody or pension. At a later period corrodies came to be a serious drain on monastic resources. Kings and other patrons adopted the practice of requiring the monks to provide a pension, or often board and lodging on the premises for retired clerks and soldiers. But there also existed corrodies of a different sort. In twelfth-century Canterbury we find a number of townspeople who have granted the priory a house or a rent in return for an undertaking to provide them with daily food from the monks' kitchen and a cash allowance for the duration of their lives; sometimes the contract will include the spiritual privileges of confraternity and burial within the precincts. In effect, these corrodians were purchasing an annuity, and the monastery was discharging the role of an insurance company.

The town of Canterbury predated the foundation of the cathedral priory. As it was a royal borough, the monastery had no governmental responsibilities towards it. In this respect it differed from

111

many of the satellite towns that grew up round the Benedictine abbeys in England and on the Continent. Population centres like these had been created by the needs of the monastery for servants, craftsmen, and retailers, and the land they occupied had formed part of the original endowment of the monks. Where an abbey possessed famous relics, the original nucleus of the settlement was augmented by pilgrim traffic, which in turn attracted trade. In such cases, where the abbey had given birth to the settlement, it was landlord of the entire town and acquired all the advantages and responsibilities that went with medieval landlordship. It not only collected the rents and managed the leasing of urban properties; like secular landlords, it had seignorial jurisdiction over the tenants, held the borough court, and took the profits of justice. This was the situation at Bury St Edmund's, where a township had sprung up round the abbey founded by King Cnut before the Norman Conquest. The monastery had sole and undivided jurisdiction over the borough. Though several of the obedientiaries drew rents from properties within the town, the lion's share of the spoils was divided between the cellarer and the sacrist. The cellarer held the lordship of the manor of Bury, which included receipts from mills and the sale of pasture rights as well as the right to the proceeds of the manorial court. The sacrist had control over the borough; he received rents from urban houses, dues from the market and tolls levied upon all merchandise passing in and out of the town, and the profits of the portman moot or borough court. He also had the appointing of the reeves or bailiffs who administered the township on his behalf.

Rent from urban properties constituted part of the income of most Benedictine houses, but the primary form of endowment from which they derived their income was land. In the early Middle Ages, the abbeys were richly endowed with estates by their princely founders, and these initial grants were augmented by gifts from kings and members of the higher nobility. But by the twelfth century the heyday of monastic endowment was past. Small gifts and bequests continued to be made; but as population growth pressed upon natural resources, the area of cultivable land available for charitable use diminished; and the lay aristocracy were more concerned with preserving their family inheritance, and more cautions about giving parts of it away.

Nevertheless, the estates of the more ancient abbeys were vast in extent and, as a result of piecemeal acquisition, they were often situated in widely scattered areas. Generally these properties were managed in much the same way as the great estates belonging to secular lords. The land was worked by the servile labour of serfs or villeins – peasant smallholders whose labour and bodies were at the disposal of the landlord. A proportion of the manors that made up the estate were leased to tenants, who exercised all the powers of manorial lords, and paid the monastery a fixed rent in cash or kind; the remaining manors were retained in demesne – in other words, instead of installing tenants, the monastery exploited them directly and consumed the produce, selling any of it that was surplus to its needs. The primary purpose of the demesne manors of a great abbey was to supply the table of the monks and to feed the army of servants and guests. In order to ensure more regular supplies, Peter the Venerable reorganised the demesne manors of Cluny so that each group specialised in a particular product – some supplied wheat for the white bread, some rye for the bread of the lower orders, others specialised in cheese, beans, or wine. Each manor was made the sole supplier of its particular produce for a given period of time. Lourdon supplied bread-corn for February and March; Mazille had to supply all the oats required for the horses at Cluny for a single night. Jully and Saint-Hippolyte had to supply the abbey with wine.[17]

As landlords, monasteries were subject to the same economic forces as secular lords and responded in much the same way. After about the year 1180, population growth and the corresponding growth of demand, caused a continuing rise in the price of agricultural produce and in land values throughout Northern Europe. Most landlords responded by recovering leases and adding to their demesne lands so as to produce large surpluses for sale. 'Yesterday I would have given sixty marks to recover that manor', shouted Abbot Samson of Bury St Edmund's gleefully, when they reported the death of one of the abbey's tenants, 'but now the Lord has freed it.'[18] The raising of a cash crop was becoming a major preoccupation. In the thirteenth century Christ Church Canterbury organised its demesne manors into groups round a number of centres where the corn crop could be concentrated for bulk sale and shipment round the coast or abroad. The historian of its estates has described them in this period as 'a federated grain-factory producing for the market'.[19]

The remarkable thing is that as money and exchange came to play an ever greater role in the agrarian economy, increasing numbers of landowners got into a chronic condition of debt. And the monasteries were no exception. Cluny was in almost constant debt after 1140; and monastic indebtedness is a recurrent theme of the chronicles and visitation records of the thirteenth century. The scarcity of financial records, and the complexity of those that do survive, make it difficult to unravel the causes of the problem. It does not admit of any single explanation. Lavish expenditure on building, and the incessant drain of hospitality, were obviously contributory factors. Some houses got into financial difficulties by raising loans on the security of a future grain harvest or wool crop, which subsequently failed to come up to expectations. But the malaise was more persistent and deep-seated than this. Grain prices – a fairly accurate barometer for the state of an undeveloped economy – reveal that the period 1180–1300 was a time of prolonged inflation. This underlying trend was responsible for many of the political problems of thirteenth-century governments, whose efforts to meet rising costs by taxing the property of their subjects encountered stiffening resistance. Monasteries were among the big spenders most affected by fluctuations in prices. A great abbey, containing upwards of 200 monks and as many servants, and feeding a continuous stream of guests, was a major consumer of goods and purchaser of services. Its attempts to keep up with contemporary standards of living in an age of persistent inflation meant a steadily widening gap between expenditure and income. It was this chronic financial problem, rather than any shortage of applicants, that imposed limits upon the number of recruits entering the greater Benedictine establishments.

FEUDAL OBLIGATIONS

The possession of land conferred both privileges and public responsibilities. The kings who endowed the ancient Benedictine abbeys with great estates expected temporal returns as well as spiritual dividends from their investment. Abbots were enfeoffed with their lands in return for services. Like the king's lay vassals, they owed their lord suit of court – the obligation of attendance at the royal court and council – and military service. They could also expect to be used from time to time as royal judges, ambassadors, or inspectors-general. Charlemagne and his successors constantly used abbots as imperial *missi*, charged with the duty of visiting counties and investigating the conduct of the counts and the emperor's other agents.

It was the Carolingians, too, who began the practice of requiring abbots to supply contingents of mounted soldiers for the royal army. These contingents were raised from the tenants who had been enfeoffed on the abbey's estates. Early in the ninth century, the abbey of Saint-Riquier was supplying the imperial army with a force of 100 knights. The contingents provided by the German abbeys, together with those raised by the bishops, constituted the mainstay of the armies that the Saxon and Salian emperors led across the Alps in the tenth and eleventh centuries. In the same way, a group of royal abbeys in north-eastern France supplied the Capetian kings with troops. There are traces of this kind of military obligation in late Anglo-Saxon England; but it was only after the Norman Conquest that the English Benedictine abbeys were subjected to the full impact of the feudal customs that had developed on the Continent. The

Conqueror assessed their lands for a specified quota of armed knights. The abbots of Abingdon had to supply thirty, and the abbots of Peterborough sixty knights, for the royal host. The abbots of Bury St Edmund's had to provide forty knights to garrison the royal castle at Norwich, ten at a time, throughout the year. A few privileged establishments, like the Conqueror's foundation at Battle, were exempted from military service; otherwise, only monasteries that were not in the king's patronage, and the houses of the new orders, escaped the obligation. It was one of the strengths of Cluny that Duke William, its founder, had freed it from all secular ownership or patronage, and so from the burdens of knight service.

In the train of military service came the other incidents of feudal tenure. There were gifts or financial aids, demanded by the king to defray the cost of war or to meet some other crisis; scutage – a cash commutation of military service – was sometimes exacted instead of knights; and, most serious of all for monastic finances, on the death of an abbot the estates of his abbey were liable to be treated like those of a lay vassal who had died without an adult heir, and occupied by the king's bailiffs, who diverted their income into the royal treasury, until such time as a new abbot had been appointed. In order to protect themselves against this threat to their livelihood and against the depredations of lay abbots, monastic bodies created a legal division between the property of the abbot and that of the monks. This device, which appears in the Carolingian period, had been adopted by most of the Benedictine abbeys by the end of the eleventh century. That portion of the estates that fed the community and supported the various offices of the monastery was separated from the lands of the abbot; and it was the abbot's portion alone that bore the burdens attached to military service and that was liable to be taken into the king's hands while the abbot's office was vacant.

If the abbot was a tenant-in-chief, holding his land immediately of the king and owing knight service for it, he was himself an overlord in relation to the knights enfeoffed on his estates. And lordship in a feudal society involved mustering troops, holding courts, litigating over property and services, exacting financial aids, and much else. It was a position manifestly at variance with the role assigned to an abbot by the Rule of St Benedict. In order to free abbots and monks from these distracting burdens, the abbeys of the Carolingian age appointed lay agents called advocates. Originally the lay advocate was the abbot's representative in legal and business matters. He acted as general manager of his lord's estates, presided over the manorial and feudal courts in place of the abbot, and mustered and led the abbey's contingent of knights when they were called out on active service. Such functions could only be discharged by a man of some social standing, and advocates were commonly appointed from the ranks of substantial landowners or the lesser nobility of the area.

The English counterpart of the advocate was the lay steward of the estates, who figures in the chronicles and records of the Benedictine houses from the eleventh century onwards. It was clearly a position of influence and patronage, which afforded opportunities for personal enrichment; and many aristocratic families regarded it as a worthwhile prize. But the stewards of the English monasteries never achieved the kind of power and independence that was gained by the lay advocates of the Continent. In France particularly, in the troubled political conditions of the ninth century, the advocate's role became primarily a military one – that of defending his abbey and its property against predators – and the office was converted into a hereditary fief.

LAY PATRONS

The religious and social motives that prompted kings and members of the nobility to found and endow monasteries have already been examined.[20] The special rights and privileges that a founder acquired in the religious establishment he had nurtured did not die with him; they were transmitted to his descendants. This was how the position of lay patron originated: the patron was the descendant of the founder unless, as was not uncommon, the patronage had been taken over by the king. Princes and magnates tended to adopt a proprietary attitude towards the abbeys and priories they or their families had founded. They regarded the property of their monasteries as being at their disposal, and took it for granted that they would designate the abbot in each case. But in the course of the eleventh and twelfth centuries, the movement of Gregorian Reform and the growth of canon law did much to erode the notion that lay lords could be proprietors of abbeys and churches. In the new climate of opinion, it was recognised that a layman could not own a monastery, and founder's kindred had to be content with the role of patrons. This position, though less exploitive than that of proprietor, still conferred important privileges and provided possibilities of interference in the life of the monastery. The patron retained the right to consultation when a new abbot was to be elected; he could claim hospitality in the establishment for himself and his household; he might require the monastery to provide corrodies, in the form of board and lodging or an annuity, for his dependants or retired servants; and, of course, he had a right to the spiritual privileges of burial in the precinct and to have the monks sing the Office of the Dead for his soul.

Not all patrons were princes, nor were all monasteries large establishments. In the twelfth century many of the lesser nobility and members of the knightly class, and also royal ministers, founded religious houses of modest size. And the relationship between the patron and the community of such a foundation was often one of mutual respect and even intimacy. This was how it was between the small Cambridgeshire priory of Barnwell and the Pecche family, who were its patrons in the thirteenth century. The monks were regarded as friends and country neighbours. The annalist of the priory displayed a lively interest in the family's affairs, faithfully recording marriages, births, and deaths; and when Gilbert de Pecche died in the East while on crusade, two of the monks went out to bring his body home to the cloister for burial.[21]

The most powerful and demanding patron a monastery could have was the king. In Germany and England kings had been the chief promoters of the tenth-century monastic revival, and so they assumed patronage of most of the older Benedictine abbeys. The Capetian kings who ruled in France from 987 brought with them to the crown a cluster of abbeys of which their family had been patrons, including the prestigious establishment of St Martin at Tours; and as the monarchy slowly extended the territorial range of its power, more monasteries were brought under its patronage. The relationship cut both ways of course. In a violent age, kings were potent and desirable protectors; and they often made princely gifts. But conversely royal abbeys were subjected to heavy demands. One of these was the provision of knights for the royal host and, as we have seen, the occupation of the abbot's estates to the financial benefit of the crown during a vacancy. Another was royal control over the appointment of abbots. When their abbot died, the monks had to seek a licence from the king to proceed to an election; and although the formalities of election by the monks in chapter might be observed, until the thirteenth century they were often instructed whom to elect.

One of the most onerous obligations was that of offering hospitality to the royal patron. The life of a medieval ruler was spent in a constant itinerary about his kingdom, and the greater abbeys situated on the habitual routes of the royal progress were frequently called upon to provide lodging for the king, his household, and his numerous retinue. Saint-Denis, Saint-Vaast at Arras, and Saint-Médard at Soissons, were the most favoured residences of the later Carolingians; and the Capetian kings maintained the tradition. It was the same in England in the Norman and Angevin period. When the court was not residing at one of the king's rural palaces, it was to be found at one of the abbeys that lay on his usual route across the southern counties and the Midlands – St Alban's, Bury St Edmund's, Waltham, Hyde abbey at Winchester, Reading, and St Peter's abbey at Gloucester. The abbeys not only served as convenient hostels for the royal household on its travels; they were also used as centres for national assemblies. Few secular palaces, even those of the king, were spacious enough to accommodate a gathering of all the baronial tenants of the crown. A large abbey, with its church, chapter-house, and refectory, could provide just the kind of accommodation that was needed. Thus St Peter's Gloucester was a favourite venue for the annual assembly of magnates that the Norman kings summoned to meet the court at Christmas. The impact of such enforced hospitality upon monastic finances could be catastrophic; but there were usually compensations. The presence of the royal visitor offered a heaven-sent opportunity to secure new privileges or the confirmation of old ones, and gifts could be expected. Henry III was a frequent visitor to St Alban's, but he never left without proffering jewels or precious fabrics for the shrine of the martyr.

RELATIONS WITH BISHOPS AND THE SECULAR CLERGY

Lay patrons and guests were not the only channel of communication between the cloister and the world outside it. As an ecclesiastical institution the monastery was subject to the spiritual jurisdiction of the bishop within whose diocese it lay. In some cases, the bishop was the founder of the establishment and his successors continued to be its patrons. But apart from such a special relationship, the bishop had the right and the duty of supervising all the religious houses in his diocese. He discharged this duty by overseeing and confirming the election of abbots or priors, by consecrating monastic churches, and, if he was conscientious, by making periodic visitations. When he visited, he was entitled to receive procuration, maintenance that is, for himself and his entourage of clerks and servants. This was the canonical position as it was outlined in the imperial decrees of Charlemagne and his son: the monastery was under the jurisdiction of the diocesan. It continued to be normal in the centuries that followed. But in the course of time a number of Benedictine abbeys succeeded in obtaining special privileges which exempted them from episcopal supervision and placed them directly under the authority of the pope.

The process by which some monasteries passed from enjoying the special protection of the apostolic see to a state of total independence in relation to diocesan authority is a tangled story. The privilege was always a rare one before the twelfth century. Bobbio and Fulda had it from early times. Odilo secured it for Cluny by a gradual process which terminated in 1024. In England, it was gained by a handful of Benedictine abbeys – St Albans, St Augustine's Canterbury, Malmesbury, Evesham, and the two royal nurselings of Westminster and Battle. In the twelfth century claims to exemption multiplied.

The Cistercian Order gradually negotiated it for all its members. The effect of the privilege was to emancipate an abbey from the bishop's visitation and disciplinary supervision; it could only be inspected by visitors appointed by Rome; its abbot, when newly elected, sought confirmation from the pope, not from the bishop; the abbot could have his monks ordained by any bishop of his choosing; and he was freed from the duty of attending diocesan synods.

Naturally, exemption was not popular with bishops. It deprived them of any power to control or discipline important religious communities within the boundaries of their jurisdiction. Sometimes they fought back. Thus the twelfth and early thirteenth centuries are littered with lawsuits pursued both locally and at the papal Curia between bishops and self-assertive monasteries. And the monks involved in these litigious duels were not over-scrupulous in their choice of weapons. Forged papal letters were freely used to vindicate claims to exemption, and in the absence of any scientific documentary criticism, they often carried the day. In the famous case between Evesham abbey and the bishop of Worcester, which was finally determined by the pope himself in 1205, the monks produced forged privileges which deceived even the sharp legal mind of Innocent III.[22]

Bishops were the more inclined to look askance at claims to exemption from diocesan authority because monasteries were the possessors of parish churches, which involved them in pastoral responsibilities. A monastery acquired churches in a variety of ways, through the ownership of land, through direct donation, and through appropriation. In the early Middle Ages most rural churches were 'proprietary churches' (*Eigenkirchen*) – the property of landlords who built and endowed them for the use of their tenants and themselves, and appointed clergy to serve them. Thus when an abbey was endowed with estates, it became the proprietor of the churches that went with the land and like other landlords, it often erected and endowed new churches on its properties. Monasteries also received churches as gifts; for under the influence of the Gregorian Reform Movement many lay landlords were persuaded to relinquish their rights over churches to monks or bishops. Monasteries continued to acquire churches, but from the later years of the twelfth century, under the stimulus of the reforming councils, bishops began to impose conditions upon such appropriations. An abbey that wanted to appropriate a church was required to make a legal division between the portion of the parish endowments that would be assigned to the monks and the portion needed to support a priest to serve the people of the parish. A fixed proportion of the income from glebe land, tithes, and offerings, was thus allocated to maintaining a perpetual vicar, who would reside in the parish and who, once instituted, would enjoy security of tenure.

As a rule, monks did not serve parish churches in their possession themselves. They installed secular clergy to perform the pastoral duties. The effect of appropriations was simply to divert income from the parish clergy to the monasteries. The system had its critics, even among monks. St Bernard challenged Peter the Venerable to justify Cluny's possession of parish churches and tithes, since these had been assigned to the secular clergy to support the pastoral care: 'theirs is the office of baptizing and preaching and carrying out the other duties that concern the salvation of souls. Why do you usurp it, as you ought to do none of these things?'[23] But the exploitation of parochial endowments for a variety of ends, which included the support of royal bureaucrats and university teachers as well as monks, was too deeply rooted in the structure of medieval society to be eradicated by facile moralisation. An appropriated church was a source of both income and patronage. An abbot could use his ecclesiastical patronage to present relatives or protégés to the benefices in his gift; or he could use it to secure influence with members of the aristocracy, who often petitioned him to provide livings for kinsmen and clients.

To most monasteries, which had not obtained exempt status, the bishop was an ecclesiastical superior with whom they came into only occasional contact. They might apply to him to ordain their monks or to license the appropriation of a parish church. More rarely, he might stay under their roof as guest of the abbot or, more rarely still, he might come and inspect them in his capacity as their official visitor. But there was one group of establishments that stood in more constant and immediate relationship to their bishops. These were the cathedral monasteries. Normally a cathedral church was served by secular clergy who, by the end of the eleventh century, were organised as a chapter of canons, with a dean at their head. But in some cases the place of this capitular body was taken by a community of monks. It was an extremely rare arrangement outside England. The English monastic cathedrals were the outcome of the monastic revival of the tenth century. They came about at the behest of the leaders of the revival, who were monk-bishops and sought to improve their cathedral clergy by forcing them to adopt the monastic life. Thus by the time of the Norman Conquest, the cathedrals of Canterbury, Sherborne, Winchester, and Worcester, had chapters consisting of Benedictine monks.

It was a model that appealed to some of the newly imported prelates, like Lanfranc of Canterbury and William of St Carilef of Durham, who were monks themselves; and following the Norman settlement it was extended to the cathedrals of Rochester, Durham, Norwich, and Ely. Last of all it was adopted at Carlisle, which was given a community of Augustinian canons regular in 1133. The bishops of Wells and Lichfield, each of whom had a cathedral with a secular chapter, created second cathedrals served by monks by taking over the abbeys of Bath and Coventry. Theoretically the bishop discharged the role of abbot towards the monks of his cathedral monastery. But in practice the demands of diocesan business, and his need to surround himself with a corps of clerical assistants and canonists, took him away from the monastic community, and the effective headship of the monastery fell to the prior.

The relationship between cathedral priory and bishop worked fairly well so long as the bishop was himself a monk. But after the middle of the twelfth century, when bishops were mostly recruited from the ranks of the secular clergy, tensions developed. Sometimes these escalated into bitter confrontations. A common cause of dispute was the bishop's insistence on exercising his abbatial rights by appointing the prior and the senior obedientiaries. The monks resented this intrusion into their affairs by secular clergy, who had no experience of life in the cloister and often showed scant regard for it. Monastic chapters reacted to heavy-handed episcopal paternalism by resisting visitation and asserting their independence in various other ways. Squabbles over the endowments of the see and conflicts over jurisdictional rights were endemic. In the course of time the monks, like the chapters of the secular cathedrals, won for themselves a large measure of corporate autonomy. They secured the right to elect their own priors and to govern their own affairs with the minimum of episcopal interference. But the path to this victory was long and it was charted by many sharp skirmishes and litigious battles.

There is a striking sameness about these struggles between cathedral monasteries and their spiritual overlords. The scene varies and the cast changes, but the plot remains the same. Hugh du Puiset, the son of an aggressive baronial dynasty of northern France, after his election to the see of Durham in 1153, engaged in forty years of strife with the monks of his cathedral over his claims to appoint their prior and his right to custody of the priory's parish churches.[24] And the contest was resumed intermittently under his successors. One of the issues in dispute was du Puiset's restoration of a collegiate church of secular canons at Darlington, which the monks opposed because they saw it as potentially a rival chapter. It was a similar project that brought several archbishops of Canterbury into collision with the monks of Christ Church cathedral priory.

Archbishop Baldwin embarked on a plan in 1186 to found a college of secular canons at Hackington and appropriated the income of some of the priory's churches for the purpose. After a prolonged struggle, in the course of which the archbishop placed the cathedral under interdict and barricaded the monks in their enclosure, they forced him to abandon his plan. Archbishop Hubert Walter transferred the project to the manor of Lambeth, which he had acquired from Rochester cathedral priory, and set about building a large collegiate church there with fifty prebends, but the Canterbury monks thwarted this enterprise as well by successfully appealing to Rome. What the archbishops sought was a foundation that would provide canonries for the clerks and canonists they employed in diocesan administration. They were at a disadvantage in having a chapter of monks, which provided them with no means of patronage. But the monks saw the plan for a large collegiate church, endowed out of the properties of the archbishopric and peopled by learned clerks, as a threat to their position; it might prove to be the first step in transferring the chapter's electoral rights, and even the see itself, to the new foundation. And possibly their fears were not entirely groundless. In 1189 they had seen Hugh de Nonant, the bishop of Lichfield, drive his monks out of Coventry by armed force and replace them by secular canons. 'In a couple of months, believe me', he was reported to have told the king, 'there shall be no monk in any bishop's church in your kingdom, for it isn't right. The monks', he added with characteristic vehemence, 'can go to the devil.'[25]

One of the functions which the monastic chapters had in common with their secular counterparts was that of electing the bishop. It was a dangerous privilege, which intermittently placed the monks at the centre of contending political forces. For although by the twelfth century canon law vested the election of a bishop in the clergy of his cathedral church, in practice the chapter's right to elect was circumscribed by the customary claims of the king to make a nomination. A chapter that attempted to ignore or pre-empt the royal choice did so at its peril. It was one such attempt by the monks of Canterbury that precipitated the most famous conflict between the Church and the English monarchy in the Middle Ages. Following the death of Hubert Walter in July 1205, King John intended the archbishopric for John de Gray, the bishop of Norwich, a former royal minister. But the monks endeavoured to pre-empt the decision by secretly electing their own sub-prior, Reginald, and hastily packing him off to Rome for confirmation. The stages of the ensuing struggle – the rejection of both candidates by Pope Innocent III, the king's refusal to accept the pope's approved candidate, Stephen Langton, and the pope's imposition upon England of the Great Interdict which lasted from 1208 until 1213 – are too well known to need repeating here. The point is that the episode was triggered off by the understandable if myopic desire of the monks of Christ Church to have a monk as their bishop, preferably one of their own brethren. And they paid heavily for their rash attempt to thwart the royal will. They became the primary target of the king's fury. His agents hounded them from the monastery and seized the property of the priory. Those that were fit enough to travel were driven into exile and took refuge in the abbey of St Bertin in Flanders, where they remained until King John made his peace with the Church.

The calamity that overtook the monks of Christ Church, and the recurrence of violent conflicts between monastic chapters and their bishops, illustrate the paradoxical character of the cathedral monastery. Although the monks had the public responsibilities of electing the bishop, and in some cases exercised part of the bishop's spiritual jurisdiction when the see was vacant, they could not provide the administrative services a bishop expected to obtain from members of a secular chapter. And their relationship with a titular abbot who was not a monk was at best ambivalent, and at worst actively hostile. The Benedictine chapters were not of course the only capitular bodies that quarrelled with bishops. Conflicts sometimes occurred between bishops and secular chapters bent on asserting their corporate powers. But the special title of the bishop to the pastoral direction of his monks gave their disputes the wounding intensity and destructive hatreds of a family feud.

NOTES

1. *Liber Tramitis Aevi Odilonis Abbatis*, ed. P. Dinter in *CCM* X (1980).
2. *Udalrici Consuetudines Cluniacenses*, *PL* 149, 633–778; modern edition by B. Albers, *Consuetudines Monasticae* II (Montecassino 1945); for the text of an eleventh-century English custumal, with translation, see M. D. Knowles, ed. *The Monastic Constitutions of Lanfranc* (1951). For modern reconstructions of the monastic day see Joan Evans, *Monastic Life at Cluny 910–1157* (1931); Knowles, *op. cit.*, pp. xxxv–vii, and *The Monastic Order in England* (1940), pp. 448–71; G. de Valous, *Le Monachisme clunisien* (Ligugé-Paris 1935), i, pp. 228–93; Noreen Hunt, *Cluny under St Hugh* 1049–1109 (1967) pp. 99–123.
3. *PL* 149, 675–77.
4. *CCM* X, pp. 261–4.
5. *The Letters of Peter the Venerable*, ed. G. Constable (Cambridge, Mass. 1967), I, p. 334.
6. *Abbonis Vita*, *PL* 139, col. 393; cited by E. Lesne, *Histoire de la propriété ecclésiastique en France* iv (Lille 1938), p. 135 n.
7. Lesne, *op. cit.*, iv, pp. 298, 330.
8. *PL* 149, col. 703.
9. Knowles, *Monastic Constitutions of Lanfranc*, p. 10.
10. *CCM* X (1980), pp. 304–6. On the duties of the obedientiaries at Cluny see Valous, *op. cit.*, i, pp. 123–86.
11. *The Rule*, C. 43.
12. G. Duby, 'Un inventaire des profits de la seigneurie clunisienne à la mort de Pierre le Vénérable' in *Petrus Venerabilis 1156–1956*, ed. G. Constable and J. Kritzeck (*Studia Anselmiana* **40**, Rome 1956), 128–40.
13. U. Berlière, 'Le nombre des moines dans les anciens monastères,

Revue bénédictine XLI(1929), 231–61; XLII (1930), 31–42; and 'Le recrutement des moines bénédictins aux xiie et xiiie siècles', *Académie royale de Belgique Mémoires* 2nd series, II (1924), fasc. 6, gives examples of numerical decline after the eleventh century. R. W. Southern in an interesting and informative discussion in *Western Society and the Church in the Middle Ages* (1970), pp. 233–5, takes these as symptoms of a universal decline. Although I have profited from his discussion, my conclusions are somewhat different. The problem is that in most cases the base-line from which we have to work is extremely uncertain, since the figures for the earlier period are mainly derived from the notoriously unreliable general statements of hagiographers. The figures compiled by Valous, *op. cit.*, i, pp. 211–12 and notes, do not indicate any general decline in recruitment to the Cluniac houses; cf. the figures given for English Benedictine houses by Knowles, *Monastic Order*, pp. 713–14.

14. Valous. *op. cit.*, i, p. 212 n. He queries the alleged number of 400 monks in the time of St Hugh. Noreen Hunt, *op. cit.*, suggests a figure of about 300.

15. *The Chronicle of Jocelin of Brakelond*, ed. H. E. Butler (1949), p. 44.

16. For the following two paragraphs see W. Urry, *Canterbury under the Angevin Kings* (1967), pp. 153–68.

17. G. Duby, *op. cit.*

18. *The Chronicle of Jocelin*, p. 33.

19. R. A. L. Smith, *Canterbury Cathedral Priory* (1943), p. 142.

20. Above, pp. 61–5.

21. *Liber Memorandorum Ecclesie de Bernewell*, ed. J. W. Clark (1907), p. 48. On monastic patrons in general see Susan Wood, *English Monasteries and their Patrons in the Thirteenth Century* (1955).

22. See the exhaustive account of the Evesham case in C. R. Cheney, *Innocent III and England* (1976), pp. 196–9.

23. *Letters* I, p. 56.

24. G. V. Scammell, *Hugh du Puiset, bishop of Durham* (1956), pp. 128–67. On the general problem of relations between secular bishops and their monastic chapters see Knowles, *Monastic Order*, pp. 313–30.

25. *Gervase of Canterbury, Opera*, ed, W. Stubbs (RS 1880), I, pp. 488–9. For the phases of the Canterbury dispute see Cheney, *op. cit.*, and the present author's *St Edmund of Abingdon* (1960), pp. 165–7.

Chapter 8

THE QUEST FOR THE PRIMITIVE

'We appeal to the life of the primitive Church', wrote Peter the Venerable, 'for what is the monastic life except what was then called the apostolic life?' Peter was defending the practices of Cluny against the onslaught of St Bernard. About the year 1130, when this exchange took place, Peter's sentiments were echoed by Abbot Rupert of Deutz: 'If you will consult the evidences of the Scriptures, you will find that they all seem to say plainly that the Church had its beginning in the monastic life.'[2] The theme had long been a common-place of monastic literature. Smaragdus stated it in the ninth century: the apostles were monks and the true authors of the coenobitic life.[3] What is new in the twelfth century is not the myth, but the apologetic use made of it by both defenders and critics of established practice. The controversial appeal to the model of the primitive Church sprang from the sharpened historical consciousness of a century that was in the process of rediscovering the lost philosophy and science of the ancient world. By 1080 the law doctors were lecturing on the Digest and Code of Justinian in the Bologna schools; and the whole corpus of Aristotle's logic was known and taught at Chartres by 1140. The revival of intellectual and literary life that occurred in Western Europe between 1050 and 1200 took many forms and flowed into many channels; but the common source was the flood of Latin translations which was making Greco-Arabic philosophical and scientific works available to Western scholars. The remote past had come alive again, and seemed to offer an inexhaustible fund of lessons for those who knew how to interpret it.

The appeal from the present to the remote past was central to the strategy of the Gregorian Reform. It was the avowed aim of the Gregorian party to restore what they conceived to be the discipline and order of the primitive Church. To this end the papal Curia set scholars to work to search libraries and archives for early sources of canon law, and new collections were produced containing 'the ancient law' – the law that governed the Church of the early centuries. At the Roman Council of 1059, Hildebrand, then deacon of the Roman Church, invoked the image of the primitive Church to support his argument that the secular clergy ought to forgo private property and embrace 'a communal life, after the example of the primitive Church'.[4] His history may have been dubious, but the logic could hardly be faulted: if the apostles were monks, then the clergy, who exercised the apostolic ministry, ought also to live like monks. This conviction helped to fuel the drive for clerical celibacy which formed an important part of the Gregorian programme; it also provided the theoretical basis and inspiration for the Canons Regular – the new hybrid orders of clerical monks that began to appear before the end of the eleventh century.

This search for the order of the primitive Church was at the heart of the ferment that troubled the monastic world of the twelfth century. New ascetical movements and new orders sprang into existence, all in one way or another expressing discontent with the traditional forms of monastic life. The Benedictine tradition as it was interpreted by Cluny and Gorze no longer satisfied many of those who wanted to become monks. The reaction was partly a protest against the corporate wealth and worldly involvements of the great abbeys; it was also a rejection of a type of community life that imposed a crushing burden of vocal prayer and external ritual and made no concession to the need of the individual for solitude, private prayer, or reflection. In fact the common theme that runs through all the new experiments in religious life at this period is a quest for disengagement, solitude, poverty, and simplicity. The thinking of the reformers focused upon three models which seemed to be offered by Christian antiquity. One of these was the eremitical life of the Desert Fathers, an obvious model for individuals who had read the early classics of monastic literature. The Benedictine tradition had never in fact wholly lost sight of the anchoritic ideal, which was enshrined in the opening chapter of the Rule. Even Cluny had its hermits, who had been allowed to withdraw from the community to remote spots in the Jura and the Pyrenees. In the eleventh century the pull of the desert was felt again and became a major force in Western religious experience.

Another antique model that provided inspiration for many new kinds of monasticism was what men called 'the apostolic life'. This was a fertile idea with a vigorous future before it. It meant different things to different people, but its common source was the life-style of the apostolic community at Jerusalem as it is briefly described in the Acts of the Apostles: 'And they continued steadfastly in the apostles' doctrine and fellowship, and in the breaking of bread, and in prayers. And all who believed were together and had all things in common. And sold their possessions and goods and parted them to all men as every man had need.' (Acts ii. 41–5): This was the passage invoked by the apologists of the monastic tradition to justify the conventional forms of coenobitic life. To them, the essence of the apostolic life was life in community, organised for corporate prayer, and based upon the renunciation of personal property. 'What am I to say about these canons or monks, the Apostles?' asks Peter of Celle: 'Jesus taught the discipline of the cloister to the Apostles and the seventy-two disciples. They had no property of their own, but all things in common.'[5] Peter was a Benedictine monk and a bishop. He was writing in 1179, in old age, from his abbey of Saint-Remi, where he had retreated to nurse his sciatica. He expounded the traditional monastic virtues, and he defended them with the conventional arguments. His inclusion of the canons regular in the apostolic troop was a courteous concession to his correspondent, who was a canon of Merton priory. But long before he wrote his book on *The Claustral Discipline*, the appeal to the practice of the apostolic Church had been wrested from the hands of those who were defending existing institutions and was being used to justify new forms of religious life. The apostles may have been poor, but their primary role, after all, was to preach the Gospel. Evangelisation was coming to be seen as an essential part of the apostolic life. Before the end of the eleventh century, religious movements sprang up in Italy and France which sought to realise this idea by combining poverty with itinerant preaching.

The other model that inspired critics of existing observance was the Benedictine Rule itself. It was the perennial appeal from present practice to the primitive document which was normative. The elaborate ritual life and the secular involvements of Cluny were contrasted with the relatively simple observance outlined in the Rule, and were found wanting. This was the central thrust of St Bernard's famous attack upon Cluny, which drew a detailed defence from Peter the Venerable[6]:

How do they keep the Rule who wear furs, who feed the healthy on meat and meat-fats, who allow three or four dishes daily with their bread, who do not perform the manual labour the Rule commands? Your hands are grown delicate with leisure. What right has conferred on you the possession of parish churches and tithes, since by canon law all these things pertain not to monks but to clerks?

The point of Bernard's quill was sharpened by wounded *amour-propre* over a cousin who had defected from Clairvaux to seek a less austere home at Cluny. But his argument expressed the mind of growing numbers of dissidents who wanted to discard the developments of Carolingian monasticism and get back to the literal observance of the Rule. This was the major theme of the Cistercian reform.

THE ORDERS OF HERMITS

The first in time was the eremitical movement – the search for solitude. 'O lovely desert, filled with lilies and scattered with flowers, the refreshment of the poor of Christ, the dwelling place of the lovers of God, O chaste and pure solitude, long sought-for and found at last, who has stolen you from me, my beloved?'[7] John of Fécamp's lament for his lost peace voiced the sentiment of a whole generation of ascetics who had gathered new inspiration from reading the Lives and Sayings of the early Egyptian monks. By nature a contemplative, John was a hermit *manqué*, condemned to end his days in Normandy as abbot of Fécamp. But another from his native Ravenna, the fervent restless Romuald, succeeded in translating his vision into reality. A hermitage was not necessarily in a remote and secluded place. Many a parish church of the twelfth and thirteenth centuries supported an anchorite, who lived in a cell attached to the chancel of the building. The individual anchorite was a figure well known to, and respected by, medieval society at all times. But in the eleventh century, ascetics who rejected the conventional versions of monastic life began to congregate in groups, in the secluded mountain regions of central Italy and the forests of northern France. The founding fathers of the Italian eremitical movement were the Greek-speaking Calabrian monk St Nilus, who founded a monastery of the Basilian type at Grottaferrata in the Alban hills, and St Romuald.

Important though he was as the patriarch of the movement, Romuald left nothing of his own in writing; and what we know of him comes from the glowing encomium written a generation later by Peter Damian. An adult convert to the ascetical life, he had taken the habit at the Cluniac monastery of Sant' Apollinare in Classe; but the life at Sant' Apollinare failed to satisfy his fervent quest for self-renunciation, and he left the community in search of solitude. He read the *Lives of the Fathers*, and under their inspiration adopted the life of a hermit, settling first in the Veneto, then in the Pyrenees within the orbit of the abbey of Cuxa; and finally in the hills of Tuscany at Camaldoli, where he organised a monastery soon after the year 1010. Camaldoli became the mother-house of the first eremitical order to be founded in the West. Its distinctive character lay in the fact that it brought together two modes of ascetical life – the coenobitical and the eremitical – and co-ordinated them in the same institution. At the foot of the slopes was a coenobitical community following the Rule of St Benedict with an austere simplicity. But the *raison d'être* of the monastery was the congregation of hermits living, each in his own hut, higher up among the forested crags. The community provided the nursery, the essential training place, for the solitaries who were to embark on their lonely spiritual conflict.

Although it was an arrangement St Benedict had expressly envisaged, the ethos of Camaldoli, with its severe regime of fasting, flagellation, and perpetual silence, was more in tune with the desert tradition than with the gentle spirit of the Benedictine Rule. Its attraction was only for a contemplative élite, and, although the order endured, Camaldolese monasteries were never very numerous. Some were founded in France and Spain, but Italy remained the chosen land of the congregation.

The same unrest and discontent with Cluniac observance produced a foundation of a different type at Vallombrosa. This was the work of John Gualberto of Florence, another spiritual refugee, in this case from the abbey of San Miniato above Florence. Like Romuald, Gualberto had fled to the cloister in revulsion from a family feud. After leaving San Miniato, he tried his vocation at Camaldoli for a time, but decided in favour of a fuller kind of coenobitical life, and his perturbed spirit finally found rest in the community he gathered at Vallombrosa – Milton's autumnal forest – on the western slope of the Pratomagno hills. It was a completely coenobitical monastery governed by the Benedictine Rule. What distanced it from the practice of older abbeys like San Miniato was the way in which the Rule was scrupulously followed in every detail and the strict seclusion from the outside world. This isolation was preserved by the use of lay brothers who were fully professed monks, but who did not share the choral duties of the community; their job was to manage the administrative side of the monastery, to do the necessary buying and selling, and to act as an insulation between the monks and secular society. Vallombrosa, like Camaldoli, became the head of a small monastic congregation which had only a few colonies outside Italy. Its main contribution to the Western monastic tradition was the idea of a reversion to a literal observance of the original Rule, and the specialised use of *conversi* or lay brothers, both practices that were adopted by the Cistercians with great success.

The most compelling and influential figure in the Italian eremitical movement of the eleventh century was St Peter Damian. He was a child of Romuald's Ravenna. Through the patronage of a clerical relative, he acquired an education in the city schools of northern Italy that made him one of the foremost Latin writers of his generation. Like many great ascetics, Damian is a figure of contradictions. Later, after he had abandoned the schools for the life of the desert, he reacted violently against his early classical education. With that queer intellectual dualism we see in Jerome, he castigates monks 'who join the crowd of grammarians, and forsaking spiritual studies, desire to learn the follies of worldly knowledge, who think little of the Rule of St Benedict and find their pleasure in the rules of Donatus'.[8] It is a curious invective from a man who himself wrote not only a powerful and elegant Latin prose, showing all the traces of grounding in the classical poets, but also some of the best lyrical poetry of the century. He was in fact making a promising career for himself as a teacher of grammar and rhetoric when he gave it all up to join the solitaries living at Fonte Avellana in the Apennines. It was one of the foundations inspired by St Romuald; and Damian, who had never known him, was to become Romuald's most illustrious disciple and his biographer.

His evocative strophes on the Song of Songs expose the motor nerve of his personality. Behind the fierce asceticism and the intense vision of the mystic lay the tortured sensibility of the poet. His ceaseless macerations and his ferocious denunciations of the flesh reflect the long struggle of his own soul. He became the major prophet of the eremitical movement, a teacher and confessor of hermits and mystics – in the *Paradiso* Dante saw him as a figure of blinding light, standing in the seventh sphere of the contemplatives. He attracted disciples and founded new establishments for them on the model of Fonte Avellana. The way of life at Fonte Avellana under his direction is described for us by his biographer, John of Lodi, and by his own *Institutes for the Order of Hermits*. It was a regime of great severity which made small concession to human weakness. In the house of the community, the brothers occupied cells in pairs; in winter and summer alike they remained barefoot; fasting was almost perpetual; on four days of the week there was only a single meal consisting of bread, salt, and water. Higher up the slopes, among the caves and crags, were the eyries of the strict solitaries, who had completed their apprenticeship in the monastery below. They passed the day in reciting the divine office, which was done in solitude at the appropriate hours, reciting the Psalter, manual work, and reading. Great austerities were demanded. Damian was a particular enthusiast for the practice of self-flagellation for the purpose of taming the flesh, and he promoted it among his followers. When any of the brethren died, each of the community is enjoined to fast for seven days on his behalf, to receive the whip seven times, and to recite the Psalter for him in entirety thirty times.[9]

Damian's reputation and powerful pen found him friends among the party of reform at the papal court. He became the friend and correspondent of Cardinal Humbert, Archdeacon Hildebrand, and Hugh of Cluny, and although he recoiled from the hierocratic political doctrine of Hildebrand, he played an active part in the campaign against simony and clerical marriage. His *Book of Gomorrah*, which he wrote in 1051 and dedicated to Pope Leo IX, was a savage indictment of the sexual vices of the Italian clergy and one of the classics of early Gregorian literature. In 1057 he was made Cardinal-bishop of Ostia and began to occupy a central place on the stage of public events. But he remained all his life a passionate ascetic and contemplative, and even as cardinal he continued to preach a return to the desert as the surest means of salvation from the corruption of the secular Church.

In Italy at least, the movement Damian so fervently promoted seems to have recruited mainly among the aristocracy and urban patriciate. He himself came of a poor family, but in this he was the exception. Both Romuald and John Gualberto were of patrician origin; and Damian's observations on the hermits of Camaldoli point in the same direction: 'Who would not be astounded at seeing men previously dressed in silken and golden robes, escorted by cohorts of servants, and accustomed to all the pleasures of affluence, now content with a single cloak, enclosed, barefooted, unkempt, and so parched and wasted by abstinence?[10] Naturally the ideal of renunciation and voluntary poverty appealed primarily to the children of the rich; it could have little meaning for people to whom poverty and deprivation were the normal condition. Women also played only a small and inconspicuous part in the Italian religious movement of the eleventh century, though Romuald founded a few houses for women. Significant though it was for the monastic tradition, the revival of the eremitical ideal affected only a small élite within the monastic world. Fonte Avellana in Damian's time contained only twenty monks and fifteen lay servants. All the hermits of the Apennines together must have been vastly outnumbered by the monks of Italy who were following the conventional Benedictine observance.

THE LETTER OF THE RULE

North of the Alps, the same restless spirit was abroad seeking an outlet in new forms of religious organisation. Eremitical movements appeared in Brittany, Maine, and Burgundy, some of which originated new monastic orders. All these displayed a common desire to break away from existing forms of monastic and clerical life and to restore the practice and ideals of an earlier age. In some cases, the aspiration was for a simpler kind of claustral life based upon a literal observance of the Benedictine Rule, a desire to reinstate manual labour and private meditation, and recover seclusion from the outside world. These were the ideals that prompted Robert of Molesme and a group of hermits in the Burgundian forest to found the abbey of Molesme, and later, in 1098, to secede from it in search of a wilder and more remote spot at Cîteaux. The same objectives were at the basis of the Order of Tiron, founded by Bernard of Poitiers in 1109, and the Order of Savigny, the mother-house of which was founded by Vitalis, a Norman clerk turned itinerant preacher, some twenty years earlier. In its austere spirit and its literal devotion to the Rule, Savigny resembled the Cistercian Order in many respects. Planted in a secluded valley on the borders of Normandy and Maine, it enjoyed the patronage of the Norman kings, and it rapidly put out colonies in northern France and England until, in 1147, it formally merged with the Cistercians.

Tiron and Savigny both represented an attempt to re-create the coenobitical life in accordance with the primitive model of the Benedictine Rule. But in France, as in Italy, the Rule contended in men's minds with those other traditions derived from the literature of the desert and the current understanding of the apostolic life. Before they founded coenobitical communities, both Bernard and Vitalis had experienced the pull of the desert and taken part in the eremitical movement which had found a habitat in the forests of Maine and Brittany. The most conspicuous leader of the movement was Robert of Abrissel, a Breton by birth, who had taught in the schools and acquired an archdeaconry before he abandoned his clerical career to retire to a hermitage. Robert is the harbinger of a new spring, which came to full flower in the Mendicant Movement of the early thirteenth century: to him the apostolic life meant the total destitution of the hermit combined with the life of the wandering preacher, calling his fellow men to penance. He was a powerful preacher and his message stirred a strange ferment in his hearers. His call to repentance and renunciation was enthusiastically taken up by a throng of devout people which included both clergy and laity of both sexes. And the forest became peopled with groups of hermits living under his direction. It was to provide for one of these groups that shortly before 1100 he founded in the county of Maine the monastery of Fontevrault.

Fontevrault, which became in time the head of a small order, was a significant innovation. It was a mixed monastery, of men and women. In many ways Robert of Abrissel's ascetical career resembled that of Damian, but he differed from him in this: whether prompted by his devotion to Our Lady for which he was famous, or by greater psychological security, he appreciated the religious aspirations of women converts and welcomed their participation in the penitential movement. The community at Fontevrault consisted of nuns dedicated to the contemplative life and following the Benedictine Rule. To provide for their material needs, protect their seclusion, and perform sacramental functions, Robert settled alongside of them a community of monks, containing both clerics and lay brothers. At the outset, the settlement at Fontevrault contained a social omnium gatherum of the penitents Robert had brought in from the woods, including reclaimed prostitutes[11]. He appointed a prioress to rule both communities; but under the first prioress, the Lady Petronilla, the priory attracted the interest of the ducal family of Anjou, and soon became a handsomely endowed and aristocratic establishment. In 1189 Eleanor of Aquitaine chose it as the burial place for Henry II, and in so doing made it the recognised mausoleum of the Angevin dynasty. The rapid spread of the order and the influx of recruits indicates that Robert of Abrissel's revival of the mixed monastery for the benefit of women answered a substantial social demand.

Fontevrault was a by-product of the eremitical movement in north-western France. A more thorough-going attempt to institutionalise the solitary life gave birth to the Order of Grandmont. The originator of this was Stephen of Muret, the son of a viscount of the Auvergne. As a young man he had been taken by his father on a pilgrimage to the shrines of southern Italy and had encountered groups of hermits living in the mountains of Calabria. It was this encounter that inspired him to create a group hermitage back home in the Limousin. After his death in 1124 the site of the settlement at Muret was claimed by the Benedictines of St Martial, and the community he had gathered retreated to a new site at Grandmont among the mountains of La Marche.

Although Grandmont provided a community life of shared church, refectory, and dormitory, the spirit of the order was that of the desert hermitage. Its aim was solitude as a means to contemplative prayer. And to this end the community was divided into clerical monks, who devoted themselves exclusively to prayer, and lay brothers or *conversi*, who ran the business side of the monastery. The Rule of St Stephen, compiled some years after his death from the reminiscences of his disciples, outlines a harsh regime with much stress on simplicity, poverty in clothes and artefacts, perpetual seclusion, and detachment from managerial tasks or from anything else which could disturb the isolation of the cloister.

La Marche was part of the Angevin inheritance that came to Henry II from his marriage to Eleanor of Aquitaine, and he showed great interest in Grandmont and subsidised the building of its monastic church. Under royal patronage the order spread rapidly in France, mainly within the Angevin dominions. The Grandmontines – the *bonshommes*, as they were known to their rural neighbours – were imported into England by the wife of the seneschal of Anjou, the Lady Joanna Fossard, who endowed then with a modest estate in Eskdale. But although a few other foundations followed, the order never attracted wide support in England as it had done in France.

THE CARTHUSIANS

It was the Carthusians who really succeeded in translating the ideal of the desert into a fortress of stone. It did not happen all at once.

The prime mover was Bruno of Cologne, the chancellor and master of the cathedral school of Reims. Haunted, according to his later hagiographer, by the example of the desert hermits, somewhere about the year 1080 he decided to quit the schools and joined the hermits living in the forest of Colan. A few years later, he obtained from Bishop Hugh of Grenoble the gift of a more remote spot high up in a valley of the Alps, where he was installed with a group of companions. But though Bruno was the patriarch of the Carthusian Order, he was not properly speaking its founder. In 1090 Pope Urban II, who had once been his pupil, summoned him to Rome, and he left for Italy never to return. He died in Calabria, where he found a new retreat after escaping from the distractions of the Roman Curia.

Like many of the eremitical movements of eleventh-century France, the humble hermitage in the Alps seemed bound for extinction when it was joined by a new and dynamic convert from the ecclesiastical fleshpots – Guigo, or Guigues du Pin, the dean of Grenoble. In 1109, three years after his arrival, the brethren elected him their prior. It was Guigo who was the architect of the order. He was a man with a wide circle of influential friends and correspondents, which included St Bernard and Peter the Venerable, and through him the hermitage got known, recruits were attracted, and new colonies were planted. In 1132 an avalanche which killed several of the brethren forced them to move to the site of the Grande Chartreuse lower down the valley. By this time the endless trickle of friends, pious pilgrims, and curious tourists, had begun. Peter the Venerable, who was a great admirer, made an annual visit, though the year of the avalanche defeated him: 'as it was the opinion of everyone that no horseman could reach you on account of the vast mounds of snow, I despaired of being able to do it on foot'.[12] The creation of colonies elsewhere made it urgent to compile some sort of written rule or custumal, and before 1130 Guigo committed the customs of the Chartreuse to writing.

In many ways the Carthusians were eclectic. Their customs drew upon a wide range of monastic experience. Their practice of mitigating the trials of solitude with some degree of community life had some affinities with Camaldoli; many of Guigo's customs, including the liturgical instructions, were taken from the Benedictine Rule; also, as the order developed, it took some constitutional features from the Cistercians, most importantly the annual general chapter which was attended by all the priors, a valuable device for maintaining uniform standards. This practice was begun by Prior Anthelm of the Grande Chartreuse when he summoned a meeting of all the heads in 1141. It remains, though, that the Chartreuse was unique in having successfully domesticated the ideal of the desert in the form of a permanent institution, which never relaxed or compromised its distinctive pattern of life, so that to the end of the Middle Ages it never required the attention of reformers.

The regime differed from other experiments of this kind by creating a group hermitage in which the individual pursued the solitary life within the context of a community. Each monk lived and slept in the solitude of his own cell: 'as water is needful for fish and folds for the sheep'. wrote Guigo, 'let him regard his cell as necessary for his life and salvation'.[13] Originally the settlement had consisted of separate huts, but by the middle of the twelfth century the distinctive Carthusian building plan had evolved, which remained unchanged in essentials down to modern times. It comprised a series of independent stone cells, like terraced houses, ranged round a covered cloister walk; at the back of each cell was a small walled-in plot of garden and a private latrine. Adjacent to the cloister was the monastic church, the kitchen, refectory, and other offices. The monks met in community daily in the church for the common celebration of Vespers and the night office; the remaining services of the day were recited by each individual in his own cell. Similarly, the single meal of the day that was taken in winter, and the two meals in the summer were prepared and eaten by each monk in solitude. Community occasions happened only on Sundays and major festivals, when mass was celebrated, a chapter was held, and the brethren sat down together to eat dinner in the refectory. In the afternoon of these days a period of conversation was allowed. This was the only time in the week when the rule of absolute silence was relaxed. The physical austerity of the observance matched the wild desolation of the natural surroundings: the diet was sparser than St Benedict had allowed – meat was excluded, and on Mondays, Wednesdays, and Fridays, bread and water was the rule, though wine was permitted with food; clothes and bedding were of the coarsest materials. And this spirit of poverty was extended to the monastic church: the customs forbade the use of golden or silver ornaments and vessels, excepting for the chalice.

Obviously a totally enclosed hermitage could only survive provided others serviced it. And for this purpose the Carthusians adopted the practice of Vallombrosa in using *conversi* or lay brothers. It was they who performed the manual tasks, did the necessary buying and selling, and dealt with visitors and guests. The procurator in charge of them, who was an ordained monk, was in effect the business manager of the whole community. Their function was primarily to act as a buffer between the inhabitants of the cloister and the outside world. They lived in a separate establishment called the lower house, because at the Grande Chartreuse it was situated further down the hill. Guigo assumes they will be illiterate: when the bell rings for the night office they proceed to **their** own oratory, and their procurator chants the office for them while they remain silent, bowing at the appropriate places; for the remaining offices, they recite pater nosters in place of the psalms.

The life of the solitary in his cell was organised round the fundamental purpose of the Charterhouse, which was contemplation. Manual work was encouraged, but as it had to be done within the confines of each cell and its adjoining garden plot, its object must have been therapeutic rather than economic. Apart from meditation and vocal prayer, the task that was especially recommended was the making of books. On this subject Guigo, usually laconic in his instructions, is stirred to a glow of enthusiasm: 'let the brethren take care the books they receive from the cupboard don't get soiled with smoke or dirt; 'books are as it were the everlasting food of our souls; we wish them to be most carefully kept and to be zealously made'.[14] Monks who could not write when they joined the community were to be taught to do so. Each cell of the Charterhouse was a scriptorium, equipped with parchment, quills, ink-well, and ruler. It was not only that the founders, being refugee Schoolmen, regarded intellectual pursuits as an integral part of the contemplative life; for Guigo, books had a missionary purpose – they disseminated the word of God. And in fact the copying, illumination, and binding of books, was an important service the Carthusians rendered to the ecclesiastical community. We get a glimpse of the process in the letters of Peter the Venerable, who supplied them with codices to copy from the library of Cluny: 'I have sent you the booklet or Epistle of the Blessed Ambrose against the Proposition of Symmachus. The treatise of St Hilary on the Psalms I have not sent, because I found that our copy has the same textual corruption as yours.'[15] 'The letter you sent', he grumbles, 'talked only about books, and was silent about those to whom the books are to be sent.' But the traffic was not all one way: 'Send us, if you please, the larger volume of St Augustine's Letters, for a large part of ours has been accidentally eaten by a bear.' This pleasing literary correspondence reminds us that the physical solitude of the Charterhouse did not involve spiritual isolation.

In the nature of the case, it was not a vocation that attracted large numbers. As Bruno wrote from his Calabrian hermitage, 'the sons of contemplation are fewer than the sons of action'.[16] Numbers at the Grande Chartreuse remained small. In Guigo's time there were only thirteen monks and the number of lay brothers was fixed at sixteen, though 'now there are more, for some of them are old and infirm and not able to work, so that on that account we were obliged to take others'.[17] It was a deliberate policy designed to obviate the need for large-scale endowments. Charterhouses elsewhere remained similarly small. The growth of the order itself was slow, but remarkably persistent over the centuries. The earliest English foundation was at Witham, in Selwood on the border of Wiltshire and Somerset, which owed its existence to an initiative by King Henry II in 1178. A small and struggling community to begin with, it acquired a new lease of life and some fame from its third prior, Hugh of Avalon, who was elected to the see of Lincoln in 1186. But it was forty-seven years before a second English Charterhouse was founded at Hinton. By the eve of the Dissolution there were only nine Carthusian houses in England.

THE CANONS REGULAR

The Chartreuse embodied the spiritual experience of the desert in permanent form. That other model of the ascetical life drawn from Christian antiquity, the life of the Apostles or *vita apostolica*, which the Benedictines had long claimed to be the source and origin of monasticism, acquired a new shade of meaning after the middle of the eleventh century, when it was invoked to justify the new religious institute of the canons regular. The canons regular were really a hybrid order of clerical monks. They represented an effort to give practical effect to the conviction of the Gregorian papacy that the Apostles were monks and that the secular clergy, who had inherited their office, should model their lives upon them. As Hildebrand had said, the proper life for clerks was one in common, based upon the renunciation of personal property 'after the example of the primitive Church'. Damian argued in a tract on *The Common Life of Canons*, addressed to the canons of Fano cathedral, that the call to embrace a fully communal life was evangelical and therefore obligatory upon all clergy serving cathedral and collegiate churches, as opposed to the rural clergy for whom it was obviously impracticable. This campaign to impose a monastic type of life on an important section of the clergy was closely connected with the Gregorian Reform programme. The reformers sought to put an end to the secularisation of ecclesiastical offices, to separate the clergy from worldly entanglements and impress upon them the superior character of their sacred calling; and the drive for clerical celibacy was an integral part of this programme. It was perceived that the discipline of community life offered the best hope of achieving these ends: the rejection of personal ownership severed the root of worldly ambition, and membership of a collegiate society made marriage impossible. And it would be a faithful imitation of the life of the apostolic Church as it was described in the Acts. In response to this propaganda, houses of canons regular began to appear about the middle of the eleventh century; groups of clergy, that is, who had renounced private property, and lived a fully communal life, observing a monastic timetable and sharing a common refectory and dormitory.

These establishments varied in their origin and recruitment. The movement began in northern Italy and southern France where it was actively promoted by bishops of the reforming tendency. In some cases the clergy of a cathedral chapter took a spontaneous decision to turn themselves into a community of canons regular; rather more often, they resisted the proposal that they should forgo their private houses and relinquish their wives, and had the canonical regime imposed upon them by an enthusiastic bishop. This was what happened at Lucca, where the objections of the cathedral clergy were overcome by Bishop Anselm, the canonist and future Pope Alexander II. Bishop Altmann of Passau encountered similar resistance when he introduced the new regime in Germany. In other cases, groups of clergy who had experimented with an eremitical type of life, organised themselves into a canonical community with the help of a sympathetic bishop. The important abbeys of Saint-Ruf – an early foundation made in 1039 on the outskirts of Avignon – and Arrouaise, on the frontier of Flanders and Vermandois, both originated in this way.

What the movement lacked was a rule to provide an authoritative foundation for the apostolic life. There was an eighth-century formula in the *Rule for Canons* which St Chrodegang had compiled for the clergy of his cathedral church of Metz. This had been given the sanction of imperial approval by the Synod of Aachen in 816. It prescribed for canons a mitigated regime of communal life based upon a cloister and common refectory. This code was widely copied, and in the eleventh century it still provided the model of observance for a great many collegiate bodies of clergy in all parts of Europe. But it did not fully answer the requirements of the reformers of the eleventh century because it allowed the canons to own personal property and occupy their own private houses. It was this need that was met by the so-called Rule of St Augustine. The Rule of St Augustine was one of the great discoveries of the late eleventh century. In the Western monastic tradition its impact was rather like that of the discovery of America on the people of a later age: it had been there all the time, and though it was not precisely what they had been looking for, the world never looked quite the same afterwards; but its implications were only gradually absorbed. The Augustinian Rule influenced all subsequent thinking about the monastic life. It provided, in fact, the formal basis for three major institutions – the canons regular, the Order of Prémontré, and the Dominicans or Order of Friars Preachers; it also provided the rule for those groups of canons who constituted the male side of mixed institutions, like the English Order of Sempringham. What was the Rule of St Augustine? Here is a tangled story, which it has taken modern scholars some pains to unravel.[18]

After his conversion and baptism in 385, St Augustine lived a communal life with a group of fellow-converts on his estate at Tagaste. On his ordination to the priesthood, he had taken up residence at Hippo, but he continued to follow a monastic life-style; and when he was consecrated bishop, he turned his episcopal household into a monastery, requiring his clergy to renounce private property and live a community life. His sister also entered a religious community, and it was for them that Augustine wrote his famous letter, No. 211, which is a treatise on the virtues of chastity, charity, and concord, here seen as the foundation of a religious community. The Rule of St Augustine as it was known at the beginning of the twelfth century consisted of this brief exhortatory treatise, in which an unknown hand had made some interpolations and had changed the gender of the recipients into the masculine, together with a more specific *ordo* for a monastery, containing instructions on the subject of liturgical prayer, poverty, reading, and silence, which if not the work of Augustine himself, is apparently a document of the fifth century. But the liturgical instructions of the *ordo* were archaic, so in 1118 the canons of Springiersbach sought and obtained from Pope Gelasius II the authority to dispense with that part of it. Thereafter, for the rest of the twelfth century, what passed as the Rule of St Augustine was the doctored version of letter No. 211 – the so-called *Regula Tertia* – together with the shortened *ordo*, known as the *Regula Secunda*.

Here was apparently first-rate authority for the organisation of the apostolic life as it had been lived by the greatest of the Western Fathers at the end of the patristic age. And it suggested that the very essence of the *vita apostolica* was the life of clerks living in a community based upon the renunciation of personal property. Early privileges and charters of endowment in favour of houses of canons regular refer to the canons living there 'in community according to the apostolic life'; but the actual adoption of the Rule of St Augustine by these establishments is an obscure process. References to it occur here and there in the last thirty years of the eleventh century; but it was in the twelfth century that it was gradually accepted as the identity card of the regular canonical life. One of the curious things about it was its generality. In the attenuated form which gained universal acceptance it gave little practical guidance on how to organise a community or construct a timetable. For this the various houses of canons regular compiled their own custumals, which drew upon the traditional monastic sources, including the Benedictine Rule and the Synod of Aachen.

In essentials the canonical observance was monastic. In fact, for practical purposes, the difference between a house of canons regular and a Benedictine monastery is sometimes hard to define, the more so as by the eleventh century it was the practice for most Benedictine monks to be ordained. The observance of the canons regular varied from one house to another. All the custumals stress the evangelical ideals of poverty, simplicity, and submission to the will of a superior. Generally the emphasis was upon moderation, a virtue for which Peter Comestor commended them: 'You have discovered honey, that is the life of moderation, which the Philosopher calls golden.'[19] There was the full liturgical round of choral offices, but the office used was that of the secular clergy, which was shorter than the monastic office. The diet was rather more generous than the Rule of St Benedict allowed, and study and intellectual pursuits were commended in place of manual labour.

It might be expected that, being an order of clergy vowed to imitate the examples of the Apostles, the canons regular would be committed to active pastoral work. In some cases they were. Those communities that were attached to a cathedral were inevitably involved in helping the bishop with the government of his diocese. Houses of canons were often given parish churches as part of their endowment by lay proprietors, and occasionally they would perform the pastoral duties themselves rather than delegating the task to secular clergy. But the cure of souls was not invariably regarded as a concomitant of the apostolic life in the twelfth century; many still regarded personal poverty and community living as the authentic hallmarks of apostolicity. And in fact a substantial element in the canons regular refused to be directly involved in the cure of souls, and opted for a more austere life of strict enclosure and separation from the world. This was the pattern of life adopted by the abbey of Arrouaise, whose abbot, Gervase (1121–47), modelled the practice of the community on the more severe customs of the Cistercians. And the same type of austere monastic observance was adopted by the famous abbey of St Victor at Paris, founded by the retired dialectician William of Champeaux. The canons regular tended to attract and produce both scholars and contemplatives, and the Victorines represented the best in this tradition, though few houses could boast such a constellation of ascetical theologians as Hugh of St Victor, Richard of St Victor, Andrew, and Thomas Gallus.

The order spread by both imitation and colonisation. In England, possibly the first clerical community to adopt the observance was that of St Botolph's, Colchester. According to a later tradition, the clergy of this establishment sent two of their members to France to study the customs of St Quentin of Beauvais, an important house of canons regular which had formed its own congregation. St Botolph's had clearly turned itself into a community of canons regular by 1107, as in that year, at the request of Queen Matilda, it sent a party to colonise the priory of Holy Trinity Aldgate, on the edge of the city of London. Matilda and her husband, Henry I, were both enthusiastic patrons of the order, and during the twelfth century it spread rapidly in England. In fact, numbered by foundations, it became the largest religious institution in the country, with 274 houses, excluding alien priories, as against 219 Benedictine establishments. And it was welcomed with the same alacrity and multiplied just as fast in Germany, where it produced in Gerhoh of Reichersberg, one of the foremost Gregorian controversialists and ascetical writers of the twelfth century. Several reasons can be suggested for this rapid expansion of the canons. Many of their houses were quite small. The possibility of making a beginning with no more than half a dozen clerks and a correspondingly modest endowment attracted the lay patron with moderate means as well as parsimonious princes. In cases where a college of secular clergy formed the basis of a new establishment of canons regular, all that was initially necessary was a rearrangement of existing properties. Another factor was enthusiastic promotion by zealous bishops like Anselm of Lucca and Ivo of Chartres. A house of canons was all the more serviceable to a bishop because it was by definition subject to his jurisdiction. They formed an integral part of diocesan organisation and were subject to the bishop's supervision and visitation. This no doubt explains their popularity with episcopal patrons: there were no damaging clashes between claims to exemption and episcopal authority that so frequently crop up in the history of other monastic orders.

All the same, the label of Austin canon regular covered a wide variety of religious establishments, including chapters serving cathedral churches, the many priories situated in towns, groups of clergy running hospitals or staffing the castle chapels of princes, and, at the other extreme, enclosed communities of contemplatives living in more sequestered places, like Prémontré in the forest of Coucy or Llanthony in a remote valley of Monmouthshire. Some of the greater houses established their own congregations of daughter-houses linked by a common custumal and a loosely knit system of surveillance. The more austere congregations of Arrouaise and St Victor in France, and the less rigorous family of Saint-Ruf are conspicuous examples; and in England, both Holy Trinity Aldgate and Merton priory in Surrey had a group of colonies. But there was no systematic attempt at organisation until after the Fourth Lateran Council of 1215. This decreed that in each province or kingdom those orders which lacked a regular system of general chapters should hold a meeting of heads of houses every three years in order to regulate their affairs. Like the Benedictine abbeys, the abbots and priors of the canons regular made rather half-hearted efforts to implement this instruction in the following years. In England, the canons of the southern province appointed a committee in 1265 to draw up a common code of practice, and this body produced a collection of statutes which became known as the Statutes of the Park, after Helaugh Park, the meeting place of the chapter. But successive chapters record a general failure to implement the new legislation. In fact the attempt to enforce a uniform observance on what was a very disparate collection of establishments came to nothing.

THE PREMONSTRATENSIANS

The diverse ways in which men of the twelfth century understood the *vita apostolica* is exemplified by the Premonstratensians or Norbertines, a branch of canons regular who took their name from the mother-house of Prémontré. Their founder, St Norbert, the son of a baron in the duchy of Cleves, had been a canon of the cathedral of Xanten in Lorraine since his teens. In 1115 he resigned all his benefices and adopted the life of an eremitical preacher like Robert of Abrissel. The canons of Xanten, whom he attempted to evangelise, gave him a rough time, but he attracted the sympathy of Bishop Bartholomew of Laon, a man of the reform party, who was prepared to support his experiment and acquired for him the chapel of Prémontré in the forest of Coucy. Round this Norbert formed a group of hermits and preachers which included laity of both sexes as well as clergy. According to the narrative of the foundation, on Christmas Day 1121 the group took vows to live 'according to the Gospels and sayings of the apostles and the plan of St Augustine'.[20] In other words, they formally adopted the Rule of St Augustine; the habit they took was one of bleached wool, which later gained them the name of white canons. In 1125 Norbert, who was well known to the German court and the papal Curia, was elected to the archbishopric of Magdeburg, where he turned the chapter of secular canons into another community of canons regular. And from then until his death in 1134, he was increasingly absorbed in the creation of missionary communities in the Slav lands, where German settlement was taking place. For him, as for Robert of Abrissel, the apostolic life meant a combination of the ascetical life in community with the active role of a missionary preacher.

The community at Prémontré had already put out colonies of its own when Norbert left it, and it asked his permission to elect an abbot to succeed him. The man they chose, Hugh de Fosses, was the real architect of the order: Norbert was no legislator and as yet the community lacked any written custumal. Hugh drew up the first statutes, which he proposed to general chapters held in 1134. Because the Rule of St Augustine was a very general formula, it could be developed, as we have seen, in a variety of ways. It seems that

Norbert's conception of the *vita apostolica* based on the Augustinian Rule laid stress on preaching activity and evangelisation. But the statutes of Hugh de Fosses, which drew upon both the Cistercian Charter of Charity and the customs of Cluny, slanted the order decisively towards the more enclosed type of contemplative monasticism of the twelfth century. The observance of the white canons came to include the fuller round of monastic choral office, and the monastic regime of fasting and silence.

Norbert was a friend and admirer of St Bernard, and it was probably at his suggestion that the legislators of the order drew heavily upon Cistercian practice, so much so in fact that the white canons reproduced many of the organisational features of the Cistercians. Like them they developed the practice of summoning all abbots to an annual general chapter, held at Prémontré; they also developed the Cistercian system of filiation, by which the abbot of each monastery was responsible for visiting and supervising the affairs of its own daughter-houses. Prémontré itself was visited annually by the abbots of the three senior foundations, Laon, Floreffe, and Cuissy. Also like the Cistercians, the Premonstratensians made use of unlettered lay monks or *conversi* for agricultural work and other manual tasks. In fact, the early settlement at Prémontré had included lay converts of both sexes as well as clerks, and some of the first foundations of the order were double monasteries; but this development was stopped by an order of the general chapter of the year 1135.

Like the other Austin canons, the Premonstratensians, because of their modest requirements, attracted lay patrons and benefactors among the lesser baronage as well as among bishops, and the order rapidly put out new foundations, especially in northern France, Germany, and the Low Countries. It was imported into England about the year 1143, when Peter of Goxhill, a minor baron of Lincolnshire, endowed the abbey of Newhouse, importing a group of canons from the county of Guines to start the community. During the following century 30 abbeys of the white canons were founded in England. They resembled the Cistercians not only in their internal regime, but also in the kind of sites they chose to settle: they gravitated to waste upland areas which were suitable only for sheep farming, like the small abbey of Shap just below the Westmorland fells, or Egglestone in Yorkshire – locations well suited to the needs of an order which had made the sanctification of its own members, rather than the evangelisation of secular society, its primary objective.

The history of Prémontré presents an interesting example of the divergent interpretations that could be placed upon the *vita apostolica* lived in accordance with the Rule of St Augustine. St Norbert had apparently visualised it as an active preaching order, in which a communal life of poverty was combined with a pastoral role. And his conversion of the chapter of Magdeburg into a house of Premonstratensian canons with pastoral responsibilities inspired a similar change in the cathedral chapters of Brandenburg and Havelberg, and led to a succession of German Premonstratensian bishops. But the legislation of the general chapters of 1131–35 set the order on a different course, in which its modelled itself increasingly on Cistercian practice and withdrew from outside commitments. The change of course was viewed with misgiving by the Saxon houses, which claimed that their first allegiance was to the successors of St Norbert in the see of Magdeburg rather than to the general chapter of Prémontré. And this tension between the two parts of the order remained unresolved. The full realisation of Norbert's conception of a canonical order following a monastic regime, but committed to an active missionary understanding of the *vita apostolica*, had to await the foundation of the Dominican friars in the thirteenth century.

NOTES

1. *The Letters of Peter the Venerable*, ed. G. Constable (Cambridge, Mass. 1967), i, p. 59.
2. *De Vita Vera Apostolica*, PL 170, 644, cited by J. Leclercq in *Nature, Man and Society* (Chicago 1968), p. 206.
3. *Commentarium in Regulam S. Benedicti*, PL 102, 724.
4. 'Vita communis exemplo primitivae ecclesiae' in J. Mabillon, *Annales Ordinis Sancti Benedicti* IV (Paris 1707), 686.
5. *Pierre de Celle, L'École du cloître*, ed. G. de Martel (Paris 1977), p. 140.
6. The Apologia to William of Saint-Thierry, *S Bernardi Opera*, ed. J. Leclerq, C. H. Talbot, and H. Rochais (Rome 1959) III, pp. 63–108; and *Letters*, i, p. 56. On the chronology of this famous controversy see A. H. Bredero, 'The controversy between Peter the Venerable and St Bernard of Clairvaux' in *Petrus Venerabilis 1156–1956*, ed. G. Constable and J. Kritzeck (*Studia Anselmiana* 40, 1956), 53–71.
7. J. Leclercq and J. P. Bonnes, *Un Maître de la vie spirituelle au xie siècle, Jean de Fécamp* (Paris 1942), pp. 185–6.
8. Patricia McNulty, *St Peter Damian, Selected Writings on the Spiritual Life* (1959), p. 104. On Damian and St Romuald see, besides Miss McNulty's excellent introduction, J. Leclercq, *Saint Pierre Damian, ermite et homme de l'église* (Rome 1960).
9. *De Ordine Eremitarum*, PL 145, 333.
10. *Petri Damiani Vita Beati Romualdi*, ed. G. Tabacco (Rome 1957), pp. 55–6.
11. For Robert of Abrissel and his following see R. Niderst, *Robert d'Abrissel et les origines de l'ordre de Fontevrault* (Rodez 1952); Jacqueline Smith, 'Robert of Abrissel, Procurator Mulierum' in

Medieval Women, ed. D. Baker (Studies in Church History, Subsidia 1, 1978), pp. 175–84.

12. *Letters*, i, p. 146. Peter also expressed his enthusiasm for, and his detailed acquaintance with the observance of the Chartreuse in his *De Miraculis*: M. Marrier and A. Duchesne, *Bibliotheca Cluniacensis* (Paris 1614),pp. 1328–30.

13. *Guigonis I Consuetudines*, PL 153, 703.

14. *Ibid.* 694.

15. *Letters*, i, p. 47.

16. *PL* 152, 421.

17. *PL* 153, 752–3.

18. On the Rule of St Augustine see J. C. Dickinson, *The Origins of the Austin Canons* (1950), pp. 7–25. The most detailed study of the textual problems involved is that of L. Verheijen, *La règle de Saint Augustin* 2 vols (Paris 1967). For the early history of the canons regular see also C. Dereine, 'Chanoines, des origines au xiii*e* siècle' *Dictionnaire d'Histoire et de Géographie Ecclésiastique* xii, pp. 353–405.

19. *PL* 198, 1796; cited by J. C. Dickinson, *op. cit.* p. 179.

20. *Vita Norberti Archiepiscopi Magdeburgensis*, ed. R. Wilmans, *MGH SS* XII, 683. On the foundation of Prémontré see G. Madelaine, *Histoire de Saint Norbert* 2 vols (Tongerloo 1928). A good English account will be found in H. M. Colvin, *The White Canons in England* (1951), pp. 1–25.

Chapter 9

THE CISTERCIAN MODEL

A NEW BEGINNING

Cîteaux, and the order that sprang from it, was the outcome of the same restless search for a simpler and more secluded form of ascetical life that found expression in other new orders in the eleventh century. Like similar movements, it began as a reaction against the corporate wealth, worldly involvements, and surfeited liturgical ritualism, of the Carolingian monastic tradition. The founders of Cîteaux aimed at restoring the pristine observance of the Benedictine Rule. They drew, in fact, upon a common stock of ideas. But the order they created eclipsed all its rivals in the vigour of its growth, the number of its recruits, and the brilliance of its reputation.

Our basic source for the new foundation is a short history called the *Parvum Exordium*, which was written in 1120, probably the work of the English abbot, Stephen Harding, who was a key figure in the enterprise.[1] It all began with the secession of a group of malcontents from the abbey of Molesme in the year 1098. The leader of the group was their abbot, Robert of Molesme, who already had behind him a long and restless career as a leader of ascetics. In an earlier phase of his life, he had abandoned his post as abbot of Saint-Michel of Tonnerre to join the hermits living in the Burgundian forest of Colan. They made him their director, and after some years they settled at Molesme. It was agreed they should follow the Rule of St Benedict. But with time, the growth of endowments and the advent of new recruits brought changes. The rigorists, mainly the veterans who had come in from the forest, complained that the Rule was being diluted. In the end, a party of them about twenty strong decided to make a fresh start elsewhere; and they persuaded Robert, who first got the blessing of Archbishop Hugh of Lyons for the move, to lead them to 'the desert which was called Cîteaux', a remote site given them by the viscount of Beaune.

This then was the 'new monastery' – the early sources call it the *novum monasterium* – which was to become the archetype for a new order, dedicated to a revival of primitive Benedictine observance. But for many years the going was hard. The monks at Molesme protested to the pope about the desertion of their abbot; and Robert was forced reluctantly to return. The organisation of the new settlement was thus left to his two successors, Alberic, who was elected abbot in 1099, and Stephen Harding, who succeeded him in 1108. To begin with, the monastery at Cîteaux was housed in wooden huts built by the monks themselves. The life was austere and the site was damp and unhealthy. No new postulants came to fill the thinning ranks, and the experiment seemed doomed to extinction when, in April of the year 1112, the young Bernard of Fontaine knocked on the gate and sought admittance. The son of a landed Burgundian family, he brought with him a troop of thirty young men, including several of his brothers, whom he had persuaded to take the habit. Following this infusion of new blood there was a rapid expansion. New colonies were founded at La Ferté in 1113 and at Pontigny in 1114, and in 1115 Bernard was sent to establish a community at Clairvaux, of which he was to remain abbot until his death in 1153. Another colony was planted at Morimond in the same year as Clairvaux. As the number of abbeys multiplied, these first four foundations came to acquire a special status in the order as the four 'elder daughters' of Cîteaux, entrusted with the task of visiting and correcting the mother-house. In 1118 both La Ferté and Clairvaux founded daughter-houses of their own and the nucleus of an order began to emerge.

What was most original in the Cistercian order was its unique constitution. It was this that influenced all subsequent orders and in time coloured the thinking of the Western Church as a whole. The monastic observance of Cîteaux, on the other hand, made no claim to originality; its avowed aim was the restoration of primitive usage – a reform in the most literal sense. It was simply a question of getting back to the Rule of St Benedict, which was to be observed to the letter. The early Cistercians wanted to roll back the centuries of monastic development, to discard the elaborate rituals and circumspect compromises set out in the custumals of the eleventh century, to escape from the world of feudal obligations, and to revive what they believed to be the pure simplicity of St Benedict's plan. Of course, there is always an element of historical fiction in revivals of primitive usage. Reformers of the twelfth century knew even less than we do about the material circumstances of Italian monasteries of the sixth century. There was plenty in the Rule to justify their desire to escape from secular involvements and seek a more secluded form of religious life; there was rather less foundation in the Rule for the cult of corporate poverty and austerity and the puritanical rejection of all forms of aesthetic expression which came to prevail in the early phases of the Cistercian movement. Whether this fierce spirit of abnegation was implanted by the founding fathers or was imposed on the order by the dominating personality of St Bernard it is hardly possible to say.

It was applied to everything – to dress, food, buildings, and furniture. In contradistinction to the linen underwear and black habit of the Benedictines, the Cistercians adopted a coarse habit of undyed sheep's wool, a departure that drew a bitter aside from Peter the Venerable: 'O new race of Pharisees, who to distinguish yourselves from the other monks of almost the entire world, lay claim to a habit of unwonted colour to show that you are white while the rest are black.'[2] The same cult of simplicity decreed that the ornaments of the monastic church should be as simple as possible and made of wood or iron rather than precious metals. This puritanical attitude, which St Bernard expressed so luxuriantly in his invective against the sculptures of Cluny, was reflected in Cistercian architecture. Their early churches have a flat undecorated west façade and a simple rectangular eastern chevet and they are without towers. The circular apsidal design with radiating chapels, which the Cluniacs brought to perfection, was abandoned. The style can be seen in its purest form at Fontenay in Burgundy, a daughter foundation of Clairvaux, which was built between 1139 and 1147 under the direct influence of St Bernard, its stark arcades and bare capitals a visual reproof to the rich figure carvings of the great Cluniac churches.

A cardinal feature of the new plan was the renunciation of anything which could involve the monks in the affairs of the outside world. Cistercian foundations were located with an eye to the preservation of seclusion and strict enclosure. The sites they accepted were generally on deserted and uncultivated lands, far removed from inhabited settlements. It was a policy that had a decisive part in shaping the economy of the Cistercian abbeys. In Britain, where they settled in the sparsely populated uplands of Yorkshire and Wales, they turned to sheep farming and wool production, in which they were engaged on a large scale by the end of the twelfth century; in Germany, they played an important part, alongside the Premonstratensians, in clearing and cultivating waste lands on the eastern frontiers. They not only chose secluded areas to settle; they adopted a much more radical policy of rejecting the customary sources of monastic income. The *Exordium* says that, because such things were not mentioned in the Rule of St Benedict, the founders refused to accept the possession of churches, altar offerings or tithes, manorial rents, mills, or serfs. This total renunciation of the usual means of supporting a religious community was evidently prompted by more than a simple desire to avoid secular entanglements; it was the expression of a new zeal for the ideal of collective poverty, a new evangelism, that drew its inspiration more from the desert tradition than from a literal observance of the Rule. As the *Exordium* put it, they were the 'new soldiers of Christ, poor men with the pauper Christ'.[3]

It was the intention that the community should live by the labour of its own hands, as the Benedictine Rule had commended. The manual labour prescribed by the Rule was thus restored to its place in the monk's timetable. Cistercian writers stressed the value of physical work as an ascetical exercise as well as a means of producing food.[4] Nevertheless, they did not mean monks to be simply pious farmers. Although they dropped many of the Carolingian append-ages to the liturgy, there was still the divine office to sing and the daily masses, and time had to be made for private meditation and study. And a part-time labour force, most of which had not been inured to the physical rigours of agricultural work, was inadequate to cultivate land or tend livestock at any distance from the monastery. To meet this requirement, it was decided at an early stage that the order should both accept lay brothers or *conversi* and employ hired labour. As we have already seen, the lay brothers were to be found in other monastic institutions of the eleventh century. The *conversus* by definition was a lay convert who had come to the monastic life as an adult and who, unlike the child-oblate educated in the cloister or the clerical recruit, was usually illiterate. He was a monk in the sense that he took the monastic vows and wore the habit, though without the cowl which was the mark of the choir monk, but he did not take part in singing the choral offices; he was chiefly occupied with manual work, serving the community as ploughman, shepherd, carpenter, or mason, and he lived a separate existence from the choir monks.

The *conversi* were to be found in Cluniac establishments, and they had a special role in the arrangements of Grandmont and the Char-treuse, but it was the Cistercians who developed the use of them in a novel way and on a scale hitherto unknown. Recruited from the peasantry, they provided the permanent work-force of the monas-tery, leaving the choir monks the necessary leisure for liturgical and private prayer and reading. For the first two centuries of Cîteaux, the institution of lay brothers proved remarkably popular and recruit-ment remained buoyant; so much so that in most Cistercian abbeys the *conversi* formed the larger part of the community. At Rievaulx at the time of Abbot Ailred's death in 1167, his biographer tells us that the lay brothers numbered 500, as against 140 choir monks.[5] Cistercian building plans were specially adapted to house them. The range of buildings on the west side of the cloister was turned over to their use, providing them with a separate refectory on the ground floor and a dormitory above. At the northern end their quarters gave direct access to the nave of the monastic church, where they congre-gated for services, separated from the choir monks by a screen, for the choir was reserved to the clerical members of the community. The same segregation was observed in the cloister, where the *conversi* were confined to the walk on the west side, which was commonly separated from the rest by a wall. We can get a vivid impression of the scale and character of the lay brothers' accommodation from the surviving west range of Fountains abbey. The astonishing vista of the interior, with its petrified forest of piers and vaulting ribs, is accidental, as it was originally divided by crossing walls to provide offices for the cellarer as well as a refectory and parlour for the *conversi*; but the 300-foot-long exterior is just as impressive and bears eloquent witness to the growth of numbers: the last nine bays of the building were added towards the end of the twelfth century to lengthen the dormitory and accommodate a larger refectory, thus carrying the southern end of the range across the river and considerably beyond the line of the other monastic buildings.[6]

Not all the lay brothers were housed at any one time within the abbey. With the acquisition of scattered properties and more distant estates, it became difficult for the monk-labourers to work them while journeying to and fro every day, and so the order gradually created a system of local granges, where the brothers could reside while they were occupied on the land. The grange was a monastic farm settlement. In the twelfth century it probably comprised in most cases little more than a barn and a modest dwelling to house the relays of *conversi* who were sent from the abbey to work the estate in collaboration with a hired work-force recruited from the local peasantry. But in the thirteenth century, with the growth of wealth and the waiving of the early rules against accepting manorial revenues and serfs, many of the granges grew in size and complexity and became miniature replicas of the parent monastery, with their own dormitory, refectory, and chapel, and even a separate chamber to accommodate the abbot when he came to visit the property.[7]

The use of the *conversi* by the Cistercians looks at first sight like straightforward exploitation of the illiterate for the benefit of the more aristocratic clerical brethren. The two centuries during which the system was at its height were a period of population expansion in northern Europe, when rising land values and land hunger were making it hard for increasing numbers of peasants to scrape a subsistence living from the soil. It is probable that a proportion of those who became lay brothers were bread-converts – men who became monks to obtain food and clothing. The discomforts of the monastic regime were no worse than those a peasant had to endure in the secular world, and the living quarters were vastly superior to those of a crowded family cottage; and celibacy was not necessarily a deterrent for the younger son of a villein who had no expectation of a share in the family tenement and who for that reason was unable to marry. But to explain the buoyant recruitment of *conversi* solely in these terms would be an over-simplification. The tide of religious fervour that swept across eleventh-century Europe touched all social classes. Peasants and artisans, as well as burgesses and noblemen, pressed along the pilgrim routes to the shrines of the saints. The Cistercians provided a new channel for this enthusiasm by opening the monastic vocation to the agrarian peasantry, to whom it had been largely inaccessible. Being illiterate, the lay brother could not share in the singing of the divine office; he was expected to make a simple contribution to the spiritual life of the community by being present in the nave of the church during the offices and by regular recitation of a few simple prayers learned by heart; but his major contribution to the effort of the monastery was the labour of his hands. This did not mean, though, that his role in the monastic family was purely economic. Cistercian writers gave manual work a new spiritual significance: it was a necessary part of a life modelled on that of Jesus, and as such it was an obligation for the choir monk as it was for the lay brother. And this sanctification of labour provided the *conversus* with an ascetical ideal that was within his grasp. His work was a sacrifice accepted by God. The point was made plain in Conrad of Eberbach's tale of a lay brother who dreamed he was ploughing a field, and he saw in his dream that he was not alone: Christ walked beside him behind the plough, carrying the goad for the oxen.[8] Caesarius of Heisterbach was moved to join the order by a story of how the Blessed Virgin herself, with St Anne and St Mary Magdalen, had descended in a great flood of light to visit the monks of Clairvaux when they were toiling at the harvest in the valley, and had wiped the sweat from the brows of the monks and fanned them with their sleeves.[9]

'Brother, if you wish to find peace in the order', said Abbot Charles to Caesarius during his noviciate, 'let the simplicity of the order suffice you.'[10] It was an ideal of perfection that was common to choir monk and *conversus* alike. Many of the examples placed before the monk by Cistercian hagiography were those of simple people who had, by humility and literal devotion to the Rule, scaled the heights of contemplative prayer, such as the unlettered lay brothers of Villers, Arnulf, and Peter, or the crusader turned monk, like Gobert of Aspremont.[11] The same message was conveyed by the story Caesarius told his novices of the lay brother of Hemmenrode, the master of one of his abbey's granges, who during the office one night saw the Blessed Virgin enter the choir of the lay brothers carrying the Christ-child in her arms and proffer the babe to those of the brethren who were rapt in prayer.[12]

The use of *conversi* enabled the choir monks to devote themselves to the observance of the Rule without getting involved in the distractions and responsibilities of estate management. It was the same passion for seclusion from the secular world and the fear of incurring outside obligations that led the Cistercians to break away from the monastic tradition of the past, and paradoxically from the Benedictine Rule itself, by refusing to accept child-oblates. There were no boys in the Cistercian cloister, and there was little provision for formal schooling. A general chapter held in 1134 conceded that novices or professed monks might learn letters during the periods of the day assigned to reading; but nobody was to be admitted to the noviciate under the age of fifteen.[13] It was all part of a determination to restore primacy of place to individual prayer and spiritual reading, to renew the concept of the monastic vocation as a spiritual adventure freely chosen by the individual in response to the divine call. The one-year noviciate, prescribed by St Benedict but waived by Cluny, was revived. Caesarius of Heisterbach stiffened the resolution of his tiros with endless stories of novices who fought a heroic and victorious struggle against the efforts of the devil to make them give up the enterprise, though a few, as he admits sadly, yielded and returned to the world, like a dog to its vomit.

One of the reasons for refusing children was a conviction that teaching grammar and the liberal arts was a dangerous distraction from the proper task of the monk. St Bernard quoted with approval the maxim of Smaragdus that 'a monk's business is not to teach, but to lament'. But there was of course a 'School of Cîteaux' in a different sense. The Cistercian monastery was, in Ailred's phrase, a 'school of love'; and the knot of monks that gathered round him in the evenings at Rievaulx to hear him talk about the spiritual life had something of the quality of a seminar. The order in fact produced a school of highly articulate writers. St Bernard towers above the rest – the most influential and widely read ascetical theologian of the Middle Ages, who received the posthumous accolade of a Doctor of the Church. But in his wake there was a throng of lesser writers, men whose talent had been fertilised by his torrential literary genius, like William of St Thierry, whose treatise on *The Contemplation of God*, written while he was yet a Benedictine abbot and not yet enrolled in Bernard's army, mapped the mystical ascent of the soul to union with God in infused contemplation, or Geoffrey of Auxerre, Bernard's secretary, who became his biographer. Many of these disciples and imitators of St Bernard were men like William and Geoffrey, who had been through the schools before taking the habit; but their literary work produced in the cloister reflects the interests and the tranquillity of the monastic life rather than the disputatious speculation of the schools. Their preoccupation is with the exploration of the interior life, the states of the soul, and the relationship between human and divine love. They were not of course alone in this. The Victorines and others developed the same themes; but Cistercian writers of the twelfth century contribute a distinctive voice to ascetical literature of this sort.

GROWTH AND RECRUITMENT

What has been said about Cistercian observance only in part explains the meteoric success of the new institution. 'Like a great lake whose waters pour out through a thousand streams, gathering impetus from their rapids, the new monks went out from Cîteaux to people the West',[14] wrote Conrad of Eberbach. His excited rhetoric is excusable, for it points to a truth: the speed and extent of the expansion were in fact extraordinary. Within a generation, the obscure and struggling group of recluses at Cîteaux had grown into a mighty order. When St Bernard sought admission in 1112, it seemed doubtful whether it had a future. By the time of his death forty-one years later, it had dispatched colonies to all parts of Europe; and there existed 343 abbeys of Cistercian monks, of which 68 had been directly founded from Clairvaux. And the growth continued, though with diminishing momentum, for the following century. By 1500, the men's abbeys numbered 738 and those of the nuns some 654.[15] In a short time the new order of white monks had wrested from Cluny the moral leadership of the monastic world and had become a powerful force in both ecclesiastical and secular politics. There were Cistercian bishops and cardinals and even, in Eugenius III, a Cistercian pope. What was the explanation of this spectacular success?

One reason was the social catholicity of its appeal, a respect in which it differed from Cluny and from most of the traditional Benedictine establishments. By opening the cloister to peasants and artisans it was able to catch the tide of demographic and economic change that was transforming Western society. But it is less easy to explain the compelling attraction the Cistercian ideal had, not only for the military aristocracy, which had long been the major source of recruitment to the monasteries, but also for the intelligentsia. For the order recruited from the outset among educated clerics and Schoolmen. And it continued to do so with some success until the second decade of the thirteenth century, when it quickly lost this catchment area to the new orders of friars. Part of this attraction must be attributed to the charismatic personality of St Bernard. He was the order's foremost apologist and recruiting officer, and his image was indelibly stamped upon it. To his contemporary admirers he seemed to personify the monastic ideal. For thirty years his was the most eloquent and influential voice in the Western Church. He was the mentor of popes, the counsellor of kings and cardinals, and the maker and unmaker of bishops; his preaching roused the nobility of France and Germany to undertake the Second Crusade. Yet all this activity and his ceaseless literary output represented an extraordinary triumph of the spirit over physical weakness. His tall, slight figure was emaciated by fasting and mortification. 'In him', wrote

William of St Thierry, 'the spirit lusted against the flesh with such power that the weakly animal nature sank under the burden.'[16] He suffered from a gastric disorder, of which William spares us none of the nauseating details. He could not keep food down long after eating and he found it necessary to dig a receptacle in the ground beside his stall in choir. For a time his physical presence was so repellent to the brethren that he had to live in separate quarters.

Bernard's legendary mortifications, his reputation for sanctity, and his fame as a preacher, gave the Cistercian ideal a publicity it could never otherwise have achieved. Without him the order, had it survived, would probably not have outgrown the dimensions of a small eremitical congregation like that of Camaldoli. But the message conveyed in his sermons and letters differed only in its passionate intensity, not in kind, from the traditional summons to the monastic life. In essence, it was a call to total renunciation of the secular world, to follow Christ by embracing a life of poverty, austerity, and prayer. He was traditional too in claiming that those who observed the Rule of St Benedict were reproducing the life-style of the Apostles: 'the Apostles left all and gathered together in the school of the Saviour, in his presence . . . in hunger and thirst, in cold and nakedness, in toil and fasting. So do you', he told the brethren, 'and though you are not their equals in merit, you are to some degree made their peers by your practice.'[17] This conviction that the Rule contained a model of the apostolic life was presupposition that Bernard had in common with Peter the Venerable. The gravamen of Bernard's accusation against Cluny was simply that it had not kept the Rule.

Bernard also worked a well-worn theme in preaching that the cloister provided the only sure route to salvation. For the individual there was only one sort of conversion, and that was to the monastic life; and the call was imperative to cleric and layman alike. It was best to make haste: life was short and precarious. 'I grieve to think', he writes to Master Walter of Chaumont, a young scholar who lingers over-long in the schools,[18]

> of that subtle intelligence of yours and your erudite accomplishments being worn out in vain and futile studies, of you with your great gifts not serving Christ, their author, but things that are transitory. O what if unexpected death should strike and snatch them from you? Alas, what would you take with you from all your toil? What return will you make to the Lord for all he has bestowed on you? He will come, he will come and he will not delay, to demand what is his with interest. What will you answer at that dread tribunal for having received your soul in vain?

This appeal relied for its effect upon the common assumption, still not seriously challenged, that the Christian life could only be lived fully in the cloister and that a serious religious commitment meant becoming a monk. It was an assumption that had as yet been hardly eroded by the proliferation of the secular schools and the growing number and diversity of alternatives open to educated men. It slowly gave ground in the course of the following 100 years, but it still haunted the classrooms of the thirteenth century and lingered in the jeremiads of university preachers.

The theme is the same, but the players are different. What is interesting is that in these latter days before the coming of the friars, when men want to preach the duty of abandoning the schools for the cloister, it is the Cistercians they represent as the embodiment of the monastic vocation. Jacques de Vitry tells a Paris congregation the story of a Master of Arts who was frightened by a dream in which he was confronted by the tormented soul of one of his pupils who had recently died: the wretched youth was crushed under the weight of a cope, heavier than the tower of Saint-Germain, on which was written 'all the vain sophisms you taught me in the schools'. The master wakes in a panic, resigns his chair, and takes the Cistercian habit.[19] The tale must have gained credibility from live examples that would have been known to the congregation, including Peter the Chanter, formerly doyen of the Paris theologians, who ended his days as a monk at Longpont. Something of the revivalist note which sounds so strongly in Bernard's appeal to the young scholar can still be heard in the account of the conversion of Stephen of Lexington, who was a pupil of Edmund of Abingdon when he decided in 1221 to throw up his academic career and become a Cistercian. In the hagiographical narratives, the master has a prophetic dream; he sees his schools enveloped by a great fire from which seven flaming brands are plucked. Next morning, still troubled by his vision, he goes to the schools and begins his lecture as usual. But while he is speaking, the Cistercian abbot of Quarr enters. At the end of the lecture, seven of Edmund's pupils including Lexington, are moved by his eloquence to approach the abbot and seek admission to the order.[20]

That the vocation to the ascetical life presented itself to educated men primarily as an invitation to join the Cistercians was the result partly of the successful propaganda of St Bernard and his followers, and partly of a powerful organisation which enabled the order to promote its image at the expense of its competitors. The ideal was a potent one for an age which was in search of the lost simplicity of the apostolic life. If offered a welcome alternative to the over-elaborate and time-consuming rituals and the secular preoccupations of the older monasticism. Its advocates conveyed all the exhilarating sense of taking part in a great reform, which was also a revival, and they pushed their case with a single-mindedness which either per-suaded by the force of its conviction or repelled by its self-righteous arrogance. 'You say', writes Bernard to Peter the Venerable, with an unconvincing plea for fraternal charity between the different orders that profess the Benedictine Rule, 'you say, who can observe with equanimity the greater part of the world turning away from our old order and converting to the new enterprise of the Cistercians?' The reason for it is simple: 'we are the restorers of lost religion'.[21] But however attractive the ideal for minds of a certain type, it could not have materialised in a huge and richly endowed order unless it had been promoted and sustained by a strong organisation.

THE CONSTITUTION OF THE ORDER

The fundamental constitutional law that governed the order was contained in the Charter of Charity – the *Carta Caritatis*. An assembly of the year 1201 decreed that the Charter should be read in entirety at every meeting of the general chapter, and that every abbey of the order should possess a corrected copy of it. In its earliest form this document was the work of the English monk Stephen Harding, one of the founding fathers, who succeeded Alberic as abbot of Cîteaux in 1108. It was composed at some date before the year 1118, and in the following year it was confirmed by Pope Calixtus II. The actual form of Harding's original text has been the subject of scholarly controversy for the past thirty years.[22] It is now generally accepted that the common version of the Charter that has come down to us contains subsequent interpolations, and that the Cistercian constitution was not a master plan that sprang fully fledged from a single mind. The successive amendments and additions to the document show that the organisation of the order was shaped gradually on the wheel of experience over a period of some decades.

The remarkable thing about this process of refinement is that it seems to have taken the form of a steady movement from initial autocracy towards a system of representation. At the beginning the organisation was monarchic: the abbot of Cîteaux had absolute and undivided powers over his daughter-houses. To ensure that they were kept up to standard in their observance, the abbots of the four elder daughters were required not only to hold their own daily chapter of faults, which was a normal feature of a monastic regime, but also to visit the mother-house once a year and take part in the chapter there, where their faults of omission and commission would be disclosed. It was out of this early arrangement that the annual general chapter of the whole order developed and, in the course of time, established its position as the sovereign body. In the thirteenth century the Mendicant Orders, more especially the Dominicans, created an all-embracing and completely articulated system of representation. The Cistercians did not go so far as this, but in several ways their organisation anticipated the more sophisticated constitutional arrangements of the friars.

The Rule of St Benedict assumes that every abbey is an autonomous society governed by its own elected paterfamilias. The problem that faced Stephen Harding and his successors was how to reconcile this autonomy with the need to preserve standards and ensure uniformity of observance – to keep the original ideal of Cîteaux from dilution as new foundations proliferated. The model of the centralised Cluniac empire, in which member abbeys were reduced to dependent status, was rejected: the Charter of Charity expressly asserted that the bond which kept the Cistercian abbeys in relationship with one another and with the mother-house was not that of subordination but that of mutual love. Instead, a solution to the problem was found by creating a strong federal framework which ensured strict and uniform observance of the Rule by a system of mutual supervision. The chief agencies in this were the annual general chapter, attended by all abbots, and the system of filiation.

It was made the duty of every abbey to oversee the conduct of its own daughter foundations; and this duty was to be discharged by means of regular visitation. As new foundations multiplied, so each abbey which had put out colonies became the head of a family of daughter-houses for which it had responsibility. The abbot of the mother-house was required to visit the abbeys of his filiation at least once a year. There was a mutuality in these arrangements which is one of the most arresting features of the Cistercian constitution in its fully developed form. The business of the visiting abbot was simply to see that the Rule was being observed. He is warned by the statutes not to interfere or do anything that could undermine the authority of the head of the house he is visiting. If, in an extreme case, he has to act against an abbot, he must only do so with the advice of the fellow-abbots of the filiation. The abbots of the filiation also have a role to play when the headship of the mother-house falls vacant; they join the monks of the headless monastery to elect a new abbot. This kind of co-responsibility was in time applied to Cîteaux itself, which was at first deemed to be above correction, but was later made subject to supervisory visitation by the abbots of the four elder daughters.

Each filiation thus constituted a distinct family within the order. But these groupings were not geographical provinces like those created by the friars at a later date; they were groups determined by the historical accidents of patronage and foundation, and which therefore cut across national and political frontiers. In England, for instance, the first Cistercian foundation, which was at Waverley in

Surrey, belonged to the filiation of L'Aumône in the county of Blois, from which the colony had come; Rievaulx, harbinger of the main Cistercian immigration, was a daughter-house of Clairvaux – St Bernard sent a colony of monks in 1132, at the invitation of a Yorkshire baron, Walter Espec of Helmsley; other English abbeys belonged to the Norman filiation of Savigny. But although the order had an international structure, individual abbeys were not generally cosmopolitan in their recruitment. Clairvaux in St Bernard's time contained a number of English monks, one of whom was his amanuensis, William, who was dispatched to Yorkshire to be the first abbot of Rievaulx. The presence of English monks in French monasteries in the early twelfth century is not surprising, as the landed classes of Anglo-Norman England had territorial and cultural roots on both sides of the Channel. Some of the early Cistercian plantations in England, like Waverley, contained French monks; but once the foundations were established, they elected native abbots and recruited from the aristocracy and peasantry of their own country, and they quickly put out social roots in their own regions. Like the Benedictines before them, the Cistercians soon became an indigenous feature of the English landscape.

It is observable, though, that the system of filiation produced some mobility at the upper levels. The head of an abbey was commonly chosen from the monks of another house within the same filiation. For instance, out of six abbots who ruled Kirkstall between the years 1147 and 1231, all but one had previously been monks of Fountains, which was the mother-house, and one of them, Ralph Haget, after governing Kirkstall for some years, returned to Fountains as abbot.[23] The more energetic and successful abbots tended to be translated upwards through the filiation from one house to another and might eventually be elected to a mother-house overseas. This was what happened in the case of Stephen of Lexington. His family belonged to the new aristocracy of talent created by the Angevin kings; his father was a royal judge, one of his brothers became steward of the king's household, and another was elected bishop of Lincoln. Stephen's family connections and his own managerial capacities marked him out for rapid advancement when he left the Oxford schools to become a monk at Quarr. After only two years he was elected abbot of the daughter-house of Stanley, an abbey with which his family had a prior connection; six years later, in 1229, he was translated to the headship of Savigny, which was the mother-house of Quarr; and from there in 1243 he was elected abbot of Clairvaux.[24] But this sequence of honours was unusual. Cistercian communities rarely looked outside their own country for an abbot. What gave the order the complexion of an international organisation was the institution of the general chapter.

THE GENERAL CHAPTER

The general chapter, which evolved from the regular attendance on the abbots of the four elder daughters at Cîteaux, was the most distinctive and influential innovation made by the new order.[25] It met annually at Cîteaux on the vigil of Holy Cross Day (13 September); and all abbots were obliged to attend. Its normal president was the abbot of Cîteaux. Its primary function was to maintain observance of the Rule. In a sense, it was an enlarged chapter of faults: it received reports, imposed penalties on peccant abbots, legislated for new situations as they arose, and authorised new foundations. The duty of attendance involved much time and effort for the heads of more distant houses. The journey from the north of England to Burgundy could take four or five weeks. Obviously a system of surveillance that took an abbot away from his monastery for several months every year was self-defeating. It therefore became necessary, as the order sent colonies to ever more distant areas, to mitigate the demands on the heads of more remote abbeys. Thus Scottish abbots were allowed to attend personally once every four years and to send a representative in other years; the same privilege was extended to abbots from Ireland, Portugal, and Sicily; and those from Greece and Syria were required to come only once in five years.

As the order continued to grow, the increase in numbers attending the chapter posed problems of accommodation and procedure. Although no abbot was permitted to bring more than a single monk-secretary and a *conversus* to act as servant, the gathering must have numbered close on 1,000 men by the middle of the twelfth century, and the housing and feeding of such a huge company clearly placed a severe strain on the resources of the mother-house. In the end it became necessary to spread the burden by imposing a levy on all abbeys for the support of the chapter. The cause also attracted earmarked gifts from princes and magnates. Richard I of England donated the church of Scarborough with its endowments to meet the expenses of the chapter, and Alexander III of Scotland put up an annual subvention of £20 sterling.

Meetings of the general chapter lasted from seven to ten days. As time went on, the inflated size of the assembly made it useless for the transaction of anything but formal business, and it became necessary to set up a steering committee of abbots who were called 'diffinitors' – men appointed to hear cases and make decisions. We find traces of this procedural device already in the chapter acts of the 1140s. The composition of this committee in the thirteenth century is set out in a code called the *Institutes of the General Chapter*. It consisted of twenty-five 'diffinitors', and invariably included the abbots of Cîteaux and its four elder daughters; the other twenty were nominated by these five statutory members. It was thus an oligarchic body which gave the five senior abbots the power to control the activities of the chapter. The work of the general assembly must have been largely confined to the formal function of ratifying the acts of the 'diffinitors' and transmitting them home.

We have lingered a little over the workings of the general chapter because it represented something new, not only in the monastic tradition, but in the polity of medieval Europe. It made the Cistercians an international order with a cosmopolitan and partly representative legislature. Beside this, it played a role of some significance in Western society as a whole. Before the advent of the friars in the thirteenth century, the Cistercian general chapter was the only international assembly known to Europe, apart from general councils of the Church, which were extremely rare events. These annual meetings of abbots or their representatives from all parts of the Christian world in effect made every Cistercian abbey a post office and the chapter itself an emporium of news, a whispering gallery of Europe. Many rulers showed they were aware of its possibilities as a medium for disseminating news and propaganda. In the year 1212 Arnaud Amaury, the archbishop of Narbonne, reported to the chapter the great victory over the Spanish Muslims at Las Navas de Tolosa, in the knowledge that it would be swiftly relayed to all parts by returning abbots. In 1245 Pope Innocent IV sent the chapter a long letter explaining the grounds for his excommunication of Frederick II, sensing that in doing so he was addressing the Church at large.

In some respects the acts of the chapter reflect the widespread esteem the order enjoyed. They record a stream of petitions from outside persons, rulers, bishops, and lay lords, requesting spiritual privileges or prayers for some specified intention. The most coveted privilege, which might be granted to benefactors, was that of full commemoration at death. This meant that when the petitioner died, the chapter would notify all abbeys throughout the order, which would celebrate the Office of the Dead for the benefit of the deceased. But the clearest testimony to the impression that the organisation of the order made upon contemporaries is the fact that it was copied. It was in fact imitated, more or less, by all subsequent religious institutes. The Premonstratensians adopted it in entirety with only a few modifications; the Carthusians adopted the practice of general chapters; and the system was carried to its logical conclusion in the organisation of the friars. At the Fourth Lateran Council of 1215, the Cistercian general chapter was given the status of an approved model, when Innocent III commended it to all monasteries that lacked a similar organisation of their own, and instructed them to hold provincial assemblies every three years.

DILUTION AND CRITICISM

The simple austerity of the Cistercian observance and the fervour of its evangelists, combined with a dynamic central organisation, brought the order spectacular success. But the success was won at a cost and brought its own penalties. Its claim to be the only authentic interpreter of the Rule exposed it to the charge of arrogance and self-righteousness: 'O new race of Pharisees' – Peter the Venerable's bitter riposte was echoed by others both inside and outside monastic circles. The quest for seclusion and disengagement from the secular church took the form of an aggressive and unremitting drive for papal privileges which exempted the abbeys of the order from episcopal supervision and from other duties and responsibilities. By the end of the twelfth century it was a highly privileged order. It is observable that the manuscript archives of any Cistercian abbey, where they have survived, contain a disproportionate quantity of documents containing grants of exemption and confirmations of privileges. This privileged position, which was jealously guarded by a succession of Cistercian cardinals at the papal Curia, gained the order no love and much hostility in those sections of ecclesiastical society whose interests had been disregarded or trampled upon in the process. For instance, the exemption from the duty of attending diocesan synods, a concession made to the order in 1132 by Innocent II, came to be a source of growing friction with bishops when the Cistercians waived their original principles and started to acquire parish churches. Another privilege which was enviously regarded was that of exemption from payment of tithes on land given to the abbeys of the order. This aroused much hostility later in the twelfth century and it was in fact modified by a ruling of the Fourth Lateran Council.

We come here to one of the curious ironies of Cistercian history. An order that had originated in a protest against monastic wealth and grandeur and had placed apostolic poverty in the forefront of its programme, had by the end of the twelfth century acquired for itself an unenviable reputation for avarice and group acquisitiveness. What was the reason for this disagreeable image? One explanation can be found in the privileged status of the order. Exemption was never popular with bishops, and the numerous financial immunities enjoyed by the white monks attracted understandable animosity from those members of the clergy and laity who had to shoulder the burdens the monks had managed to avoid. A further reason for mistrust was the fact that the acquisition and successful management of great estates had made the order exceedingly wealthy. In a time of growing land-hunger and rising land values, the business acumen the Cistercians displayed in enlarging and consolidating their properties and marketing their produce earned them the envy and dislike of landed families who had been less successful. But at the kernel of the hostile criticism there lay a harsher truth than this. The rapid expansion of the order had been made possible by a flood of endowments. There was no shortage of benefactors in the early decades, and the Cistercian abbeys became large-scale landed proprietors, differing from the older monasteries only in that they exploited their estates directly by their own labour instead of leasing them. And in pursuit of their objectives they often displayed a ruthless disregard for the interests of lesser folk who stood in their way. Because they had no use for tenants, whether servile or free, they sometimes destroyed existing villages to make way for granges, and evicted the peasant occupiers, who were settled elsewhere. Investigation of the Cistercian settlement in the north of England has verified the charge of the twelfth-century satirist Walter Map: 'they raze villages and churches, and drive poor people from the land'.[26] Their preference for estates they could work themselves brought them many gifts of virgin land; but where it did not, they showed no scruple in creating the kind of estate they wanted by means of depopulation. The claims of peasants could not be allowed to obstruct the search for the desert. The seamy underside of the Cistercian ideal was the corporate arrogance and institutional egotism that often afflict religious organisations.

In the course of the thirteenth century, the ideal itself was gradually eroded as the early self-denying ordinances were one by one abandoned. As time went on, the policy of economic purity – the refusal of seignorial revenues and churches and exclusive reliance upon monastic labour – was felt to be too restrictive. Initially the pressure for change must have come from the needs of efficient estate management; piecemeal benefactions resulted in scattered properties, some of which were too remote from the monastery to be effectively exploited. At first, the solution was found by selling such properties or exchanging them for other lands nearer the home farm; from there it was an obvious step to consolidating the estate by purchasing land. The general chapter legislated against this repeatedly from 1180 onwards, but to no purpose. Abbeys with a large surplus of agricultural produce sold it and bought more land with the proceeds. At Clairvaux a spirit of aggressive enterprise took command with the advent of Abbot Guy in 1193, who vastly enlarged the property of the abbey in southern Champagne by purchasing lands, lordships, mills, and serfs.[27] The same process can be seen at work in the English abbeys. The abbots of Quarr worked steadily to round off the abbey's estates in the Isle of Wight by purchase, the exchange of more distant properties on the mainland, and the expropriation of debtors, who might be induced to surrender their heavily mortgaged land in return for a corrody or life pension.[28] After 1228 they adopted the practice of leasing properties, including a number of urban properties they had bought in Portsmouth, and rents came to have a growing place in the economy of the abbey. A similar trend has been observed in the case of Fountains Abbey.

So in the sources of their income, their economic attitudes, and their business methods, the Cistercians became indistinguishable from the older Benedictines; the only difference was that they possessed in the lay brothers a relatively tame and mobile work-force, which was an important factor in their economic success; and even this peculiarity vanished in the fourteenth century, when recruitment from the peasantry dwindled and eventually dried up altogether. Having begun as a rebellion against the established conventions of monastic life, the Cistercian movement gradually adopted the ways of the establishment it had criticised. In one respect it moved even further along the path of compromise. It had been the original vocation of Cîteaux to recall men to the primitive observance of the Rule, in which the essential tasks of the monk were a simplified round of liturgical prayer and manual labour. Between the cloister and the world a new gulf was to be fixed. It was an ideal that accepted learning in St Benedict's sense of *lectio divina* – the study of ascetical theology to provide food for meditation – but it was unsympathetic to the intellectual pursuits of the schools. The fascination the order exerted over the academic intellect was that of renunciation. But in the thirteenth century the absorption of university teachers brought a softening of this early rigorism; for men trained in the liberal and disputatious atmosphere of the schools did not shed their intellectual outlook when they took the habit. And so, by a strange paradox, the Cistercians became the first monks to set up colleges for their members in the universities.

The author of the plan seems to have been Evrard, the abbot of Clairvaux, who formulated a project of installing a small community of student monks, with a warden and two *conversi*, in a house that the abbey had acquired in Paris. But he died in 1238 before the scheme had got off the ground, and it fell to Stephen of Lexington, the Oxford graduate, to realise it on a large scale and in a permanent form. In 1245 he obtained the somewhat reserved approval of the general chapter, launched an appeal for endowments, and acquired land near the abbey of St Victor, just south of the modern Boulevard Saint-Germain, where he constructed new buildings for a monastic college.[29] The house, which was for monks attending the schools of the theology faculty, remained under the jurisdiction of the abbot of Clairvaux, who appointed the head of the establishment. By 1250 the student monks had already taken up their new quarters, and six years later the first Cistercian incepted and began teaching in the faculty. This revolution in Cistercian policy seems to have been brought about by a small pressure group of university graduates, who succeeded in pushing through their plans with the aid of powerful friends at the papal court, one of whom was the English Cistercian cardinal, John Tolet. But it provoked a backlash from more conservative abbots, who felt that the principles of the order were being betrayed: 'it has not hitherto been the custom', wrote Abbot Arnulf of Villers grimly, 'for monks to leave their claustral exercises, which most befit their profession, in order to give themselves over to the study of letters; as St Bernard says, a monk's business is not to teach, but to lament'.[30] The critics demanded a victim, and Stephen was deposed; but his fall did not bring about a reversal of his policy. His college of the Chardonnet at Paris continued to flourish; and in 1287 the general chapter decreed that every abbey having twenty monks should maintain one of them at the university. By this time the order had houses of study at the universities of Oxford, Montpellier, and Toulouse.

The entry into the new scholastic world of the universities was one of many ways in which the early principles of Cîteaux were abandoned under the pressure of a changing social environment. They did not make much impact on the academic world. After 1230, men with intellectual aspirations were much more likely to join the friars. By the end of the thirteenth century, much that was distinctive in the Cistercian vocation had been lost. In its heyday it had summoned the aristocracy and the intellectual élite of Europe to a new spiritual adventure. But the compromises that followed in the train of wealth and influence made the voice less compelling. Thanks to the strength of its organisation, the order preserved decent standards of observance in most of its houses, and it continued to constitute a formidable interest in ecclesiastical politics. But a new European intelligentsia was emerging, and it looked to other forms of religious life for the fulfilment of its ideals.

NOTES

1. P. Guignard, *Les Monuments primitifs de la règle cistercienne* (Dijon 1878), pp. 63–72; the text of the *Exordium Parvum* has been newly re-edited by J. de la Croix Bouton and J. B. Van Damme in *Les Plus anciens textes de Cîteaux: Commentarii Cistercienses, Studia et Documenta* II (Achel 1974), pp. 54–85. For a general account of the order see L. J. Lekai, *Les Moines blancs* (Paris 1957), and for an English account of its early history M. D. Knowles, *The Monastic Order in England* (1940), pp. 209–26.
2. *The Letters of Peter the Venerable*, ed. G. Constable (Cambridge, Mass 1967), i, p. 57.
3. *Exordium Parvum, op. cit.*, p. 77.
4. See the interesting discussion of this point by C. J. Holdsworth, 'The

blessings of work: The Cistercian view' in *Sanctity and Secularity*, ed. D. Bakar (Studies in Church History 10 1973), pp. 59–76.

5. *The Life of Ailred of Rievaulx by Walter Daniel*, ed. F. M. Powicke (1950), p. 38.

6. The origin and function of the *conversi* have been the subject of much discussion, see the basic investigation of K. Hallinger, 'Woher kommen die Laienbrüder' in *Analecta Sacri Ordinis Cisterciensis* XII (Rome 1956), 1–104; and J. Dubois, 'L'institution des convers au XIIᵉ siècle. Forme de vie monastique propre aux laics' in *I Laici nella Societas Christiana dei Secoli XI e XII: Miscellanea del Centro di Studi Medievali* 5 (Milan 1968), pp. 183–261. For Cistercian building plans see M. Aubert, *L'Architecture cistercienne en France*, 2 vols (Paris 1943).

7. Colin Platt, *The Monastic Grange in Medieval England* (1969).

8. This was one of many stories of the heroic age of the order collected by Conrad of Eberbach in his *Magnum Exordium*, ed. B. Griesser, *Series Scriptorum S. Ordinis Cisterciensis* II (Rome 1961), pp. 243–4.

9. *Dialogus Miraculorum*, ed. J. Strange (Cologne 1851), i, p. 24.

10. *Ibid.* i, p. 340.

11. See Simone Roisin, *L'hagiographie cistercienne dans le diocèse de Liège au XIIIᵉ siècle* (Louvain 1947), pp. 28–72.

12. *Dialogus Miraculorum* ii, p. 15.

13. *Statuta Capitulorum Generalium Ordinis Cisterciensis*, ed. J. Canivez I (Louvain 1933), p. 31.

14. *Magnum Exordium*, *op. cit.*, p. 79.

15. The expansion in terms of filiations is illustrated by the *Atlas de l'Ordre cistercien* of F. Van der Meer (1965). For the statistics, correcting previous calculations, see the article by F. Vongrey and F. Hervay, 'Notes critiques sur l'Atlas de l'Ordre cistercien' in *Analecta Sacri Ordinis Cisterciensis* XXIII (1967), 115–52. The figures for the women's houses are less sure than those for the men's because the status and observance of some nunneries are difficult to establish.

16. *Vita Prima*, *PL* 185, 250. For modern studies of St Bernard see *Mélanges Saint Bernard: xxivᵉ Congrès de l'Association bourguignonne des sociétés savants* (Dijon 1953).

17. *Sermo* XXII, *PL* 183, 595; cited by M. H. Vicaire, *L'Imitation des apôtres. Moines, chanoines et mendiants, IVᵉ-XIIIᵉ siècles* (Paris 1963), p. 30.

18. *Epistolae*, *PL* 182, 238–9.

19. T. F. Crane, *The Exempla of Jacques de Vitry* (1890), p. 12; quoted by C. H. Haskins, *Studies in Medieval Culture* (1929), p. 50. For other university sermons on the same theme see for example *Les Sermons universitaires parisiens de 1230–1231*, ed. M. M. Davy (Paris 1931), pp. 292, 295.

20. C. H. Lawrence, *St Edmund of Abingdon* (1960), p. 251.

21. *Epistolae*, *PL* 182, 414.

22. Text in *Statuta* I, pp. xxvi–xxxi; a modern translation will be found in D. Douglas and W. Greenaway, *English Historical Documents* II (1953) pp. 687–91. For discussion of the textual history see M. D. Knowles, *Great Historical Enterprises and Problems in Monastic History* (1963).

23. M. D. Knowles, C. N. L. Brooke and Vera London, *Heads of Religious Houses in England and Wales 940–1216* (1972), p. 136.
24. C. H. Lawrence, 'Stephen of Lexington and Cistercian university studies in the thirteenth century', *Journ. of Eccles. History* **11** (1960), 164–78.
25. The best account of the workings of the general chapter is to be found in J. B. Mahn, *L'Ordre cistercien et son gouvernement* (Paris 1951). The chapter acts were edited by Canivez, n. 13 above.
26. R. A. Donkin, 'Settlement and depopulation on Cistercian estates during the twelfth and thirteenth centuries'. *Bulletin of the Institute of Historical Research* **33** (1960), 141–65.
27. R. Fossier, 'La Vie économique de L'abbaye de Clairvaux 1115–1471', *École des Chartes, Positions des thèses* (1949), 57–63.
28. S. F. Hockey, *Quarr Abbey and its Lands* (1970), pp. 72–94. C. H. Holdsworth in his introduction to *Rufford Charters* I (Thoroton Soc. 1972), pp. xxxiii–lxxix, remarks on the same trend towards the leasing of lands and the acquisition of serfs after 1200, but concludes that Rufford, which was not a richly endowed abbey, did not grossly infringe the early principles.
29. Lawrence, 'Stephen of Lexington'.
30. *Ibid.* p. 176.

Chapter 10

A NEW KIND OF KNIGHTHOOD

Of all the new forms of monastic life that emerged from the religious ferment of the twelfth century none was more original or seemingly more paradoxical than that of the Military Orders. These were orders of knights, dedicated to fighting the infidel, who were also fully professed monks. They look like a contradiction in terms. Admittedly ascetical writers were much given to using military imagery, but the warfare they referred to was spiritual combat, not the warfare of this world. Monks and clergy were forbidden by the canons to have any part in the shedding of blood. How could fighting and killing with carnal weapons be reconciled with the Gospel of peace and love? Professionally the monk and the warrior stood at opposite poles. The reconciliation of these incompatible occupations in the orders of fighting monks can only be understood in the context of the crusading movement from which they sprang.

The scruples of the early Church on the subject of warfare continued to haunt the minds of medieval moralists and left their mark on the Penitentials. In a fallen world the profession of arms might be necessary, but it was dangerous to the soul. Although it was lawful in certain conditions for a Christian to engage in warfare, the individual who did so was not exonerated from the moral guilt of killing his enemies. He had still committed a sin that called for repentance and satisfaction. Burchard of Worms, the eleventh-century canonist, devotes a whole chapter of his *Decretum* to the penances appropriate to 'those who commit homicide in public war'.[1] The traditional tariff required the performance of three Lents – three periods of penance each lasting forty days – for every victim. Thus, despite the fact that William the Conqueror had obtained the prior approval of the pope for his invasion of England, the year after Hastings a papal legate arrived and imposed carefully graduated penances on all the Norman and Breton knights who had fought in the battle.

What made possible the creation of hybrid institutions like the Military Orders was the lifting of this sinful stigma from prowess in arms. Such a change in attitude was in fact brought about in the course of the eleventh century by the emergence of a new ideal of Christian knighthood. The status of the knight was gradually transmogrified: from being a professional hit-man operating on the edge of the moral law, he was slowly transformed by ecclesiastical theory into a Christian warrior fighting in the service of the Church. We can see the genesis of this change already in tenth-century liturgical formulas for the blessing of warriors and their weapons.[2] It derived impetus too from early peace movements, like the Peace of God, which were encouraged by the Cluniacs. There were attempts to limit the destructiveness of private warfare by persuading members of the knightly class to observe certain codes of conduct towards non-combatants and to defend the property of churches. But the decisive agency in bringing about the change was the First Crusade.

In a sermon preached at Clermont on the 18 November 1095, Pope Urban II summoned the chivalry of Europe to an armed pilgrimage in order to rescue Jerusalem and the other Holy Places from the hands of the infidel. And to all who participated he offered an indulgence, a remission, that is, of the canonical penance due for their sins. While the precise terms of this indulgence are uncertain, there can be no doubt about the interpretation placed upon crusading indulgences by theologians and canonists of the twelfth century: they sanctioned the principle of a holy war. In such a war, killing an enemy, provided he was an infidel, was not a materially sinful act requiring penance; it was a positively meritorious act, which remitted the temporal punishment due for sin. Death in such a war carried the rewards of martyrdom. 'The knight of Christ need fear no sin in killing the foe', wrote St Bernard, 'he is the minister of God for the punishment of the wicked. In the death of a pagan a Christian is glorified, because Christ is glorified.'[3]

The crusading indulgence represented a landmark in the medieval theory of Christian warfare. It proposed a new vocation of Christian knighthood. It diverted the aggressive and acquisitive instincts of the military aristocracy into a holy war against Islam; and in so doing it sanctified the profession of arms. The Military Orders – the societies of monk-knights – were the product of this crusading ethos. They were professionally dedicated to the holy war; and in them Christian knighthood found its apotheosis. They offered knights and sons of the baronage the fulfilment of their religious aspirations by becoming monks without having to abandon their zest for physical activity or their skills in mounted warfare. St Bernard, who presided at their inception, saw in them the ideal means of salvation for those laymen who showed no aptitude for the traditional type of monastic life.

THE TEMPLARS

Although the Order of Hospitallers had a longer pre-history, the Knights of the Temple were the first to be constituted as a military order. They were called into existence by the needs of the Latin kingdom of Jerusalem. Thanks largely to divisions among the rulers of the Muslim states in the Middle East, the First Crusade had ended in spectacular success. In 1099, after capturing Antioch, the Franks stormed Jerusalem. In the wake of the army, the leaders of the contingents created a group of Frankish principalities; and in the following twenty years these territories were extended and consolidated by further conquests. But the Latin kingdom and its satellite principalities of Antioch, Tripoli, and Edessa, maintained only a tenuous foothold on the fringe of the Muslim world. They were subjected to periodic attacks of mounting weight, and they suffered from a chronic shortage of manpower. At the end of the campaign many crusaders returned home, and later crusades did little to replenish the Frankish settler population. The majority of pilgrims were also birds of passage. It was the inability of the settler population to police the roads and protect pilgrims from brigands and Muslim raiders that persuaded a knight of Champagne, Hugh de Payns, to form a small standing militia for this purpose. Towards the end of the year 1119, he, and eight other companions of the same class who were residing at Jerusalem, formed themselves into a religious society for the purpose of defending pilgrims *en route* to the holy places. King Baldwin II of Jerusalem, evidently perceiving the potential value of this small association, took them under his wing and assigned them quarters in the royal palace, which was attached to the Temple of Solomon.

Hugh de Payns seems to have conceived from the outset that his group of knights would be soldier-monks.[4] They took vows of chastity and obedience, followed some form of community life, and assisted at the divine office sung by the canons regular who served the church of the Holy Sepulchre. The plan was an intelligible development of crusading ideology. For the crusade was a pilgrimage. In the early stages of the movement it may have offered alluring prospects of plunder and territorial gain to some of the participants; but to others, and to the churchmen who preached it, the rewards it offered were primarily spiritual ones. It was an ascetical exercise, a supreme act of self-denial, which rendered satisfaction for sins. The privations and dangers of the long journey across hostile territory were to be endured in a spirit of mortification. Battles and sieges were preceded and accompanied by prayer and fasting. It was in fact a form of penitential life, of limited duration, undertaken for the love of God.[5] Thus it realised, though in a different way, the essential principle of monasticism. To give it permanent institutional form in a special monastic order involved bridging only a small mental gap.

In the autumn of 1127, then, Hugh de Payns with some of his companions set out for Rome to seek authorisation for this novel kind of monastic institution. They were referred for a decision to a council which met at Troyes in 1128, under the presidency of the papal legate, Mathew of Albano. The council approved the plan, and the composition of an appropriate rule was entrusted to St Bernard. The Rule of the Temple clearly owes much to the Benedictine Rule, of which it contains verbal echoes, and also to the practice of the Cistercians. It bears traces, too, of the aggressive and élitist spirituality that is such a marked feature of the early Cistercian movement: 'If any knight out of the mass of human perdition wishes to renounce the world', runs the formula for the reception of novices,[6] echoing Bernard's invective against the gaudy panoply of secular knighthood.

The observance prescribed by the Rule is unremittingly monastic and coenobitical. The knights are bound by vows of personal poverty, chastity, and obedience. They are to dress soberly, to wear short hair, and to avoid all association with women – the white gown they wear is to be an outward sign of chastity. They sleep fully clothed in a common dormitory, and eat in a common refectory. They are to be present at the singing of Matins and all the canonical hours; but an exception is made for those away on active duty or tired out by their military activities; these are allowed to recite paternosters in place of the offices. It is apparent that, being laymen, they are expected only to hear the offices, not to sing them; that was to be the role of the clergy attached to the order. Similarly, the Rule makes no provision for individual reading. Instead, the brethren listen to a clerk reading to them at mealtimes and at assemblies. They are bound by the monastic regime of fasts and vigils, with relaxations made necessary by the demands of their military role: they eat twice daily, and meat is allowed three days a week. Another standard feature of the monastic timetable included with modification is the chapter of faults, which is to be held weekly on Sundays, wherever at least four of the brethren are residing together.[7]

Socially, the order reproduced the class structure of secular society. There were two classes of brethren – the knights, who were recruited from the ranks of the military aristocracy, and the sergeants, or serving men, of humbler origin. At the beginning, the brethren depended upon the canons regular or members of the secular clergy for liturgical and sacramental services. But after the order had gained official recognition, it recruited chaplains of its own, who were fully incorporated as ordained members. It also found employment in its houses for a growing work-force of cooks, servants, and artisans.

At the outset, the attraction of recruits to such a novel kind of monastic vocation and the search for endowments required a special effort of propaganda. Hugh de Payns, in a letter written for the comfort of the brethren back at Jerusalem, refers to critics of their profession who question the legitimacy of an institution of warrior-monks – subtle tempters who urge the knights of Christ to lay down their arms.[3] It was in order to confound such critics and to publicise the new order that Bernard wrote one of his most powerful and emotional propaganda tracts – *In Praise of the New Knighthood*:[9] 'there is word abroad of a new kind of knighthood, arisen lately, one that fights flesh and blood as well as the spirits of wickedness in high places'.They dwell in the Temple of Solomon; and their way of life bears all the marks of evangelical perfection. 'How blessed are the martyrs who die in battle. Rejoice, brave athlete, if you live and conquer in the Lord; but exult and glory the more if you should die and be united with the Lord.'

Bernard's appeal was to the same convictions and emotions that moved men to go on crusade; and it aroused the same kind of enthusiasm. Recruits and donations of land flowed in, and Hugh's small brotherhood grew into a large and wealthy international order. In 1139 Innocent II issued the bull *Omne datum optimum* which approved the Rule and gave the Order of the Temple a privileged status. It was allowed its own oratories and burial grounds, it was exempted from payment of tithes, and it was removed from the jurisdiction of local bishops and made directly subject to the pope. As it acquired estates, it erected houses and churches in the West. And by the middle of the twelfth century, its constitution had been articulated. The head of the order was the grand master, to whom all the brethren took an oath of absolute obedience. He was elected by a specially constituted general chapter. The lands and houses of the order were divided into provinces, each of which was directed by a master and a commander. The individual house was called a preceptory, and its head a preceptor. Probably many of these preceptories were of quite a modest size, housing only a handful of knights – not so much military establishments as depots for the management of estates and the transfer of the proceeds to the fighting brethren out East.

The idea of an order of fighting monks, once it had gained acceptance and official blessing, proved infectious. Other orders of chivalry sprang up, inspired by the example of the Templars. In Spain and Portugal, where the reconquest of the peninsula from the Moors was a major political preoccupation, the Orders of Calatrava and Alcantara were formed later in the twelfth century, and adopted many features of the Templars' observance. The Order of Santiago was another spiritual stepchild of the Templars, though it was not so much a religious order as a pious confraternity of knights, whose members continued to live as married men. The most illustrious contemporary and rival of the institute of the Temple, however, was the Order of Hospitallers, or Knights of St John of Jerusalem.

THE HOSPITALLERS

They began as a fraternity serving a hospice for poor and sick pilgrims at Jerusalem. Some twenty-five years before the launching of the First Crusade, a group of pious merchants of Amalfi had built, or perhaps simply restored, the Benedictine monastery of St Mary of the Latins on a site adjacent to the Holy Sepulchre. In order to provide for the increasing flow of pilgrims, the monks built a hospice, dedicated to St John the Baptist.[10] This hospice was staffed by a fraternity who, like the monks, were Italians, and who took monastic vows. In 1099, when the crusaders took Jerusalem, the master of this establishment was an Italian, probably an Amalfitan, named Gerard. Gerard was clearly an administrator of vision, who grasped the opportunities opened up by the Frankish conquest. He persuaded the first ruler of the Latin state, Godfrey of Lorraine, and his successor, King Baldwin I, to endow the hospital with lands and city properties in the newly conquered territories. He also extended his organisation by establishing daughter hospitals in, or close to, the ports of Italy and southern France, from which pilgrims embarked for the Holy Land. The brotherhood of the hospital began now to attract substantial donations of land in Italy, Spain, and France. The Latin patriarch of Jerusalem, himself an Italian, granted it exemption from payment of tithes on its properties. And in 1113 Gerard succeeded in obtaining from Pope Paschal II a bull which recognised the Hospitallers as a distinct order, ruled by their own master, and subject directly and solely to the jurisdiction of the pope.

The twelfth-century Rule of the Hospitallers, which cannot be dated with any certainty, drew its inspiration from the Rule of St Augustine; and the observances of the order were those of the canons regular. It was not at first a military order. It was primarily a charitable organisation devoted to the care of sick and indigent pilgrims. Its membership included both lay brethren and clerics, but not as yet professional warriors. The decision to undertake a military role was taken by Raymond du Puy, who succeeded Gerard as master on the latter's death in 1118. As a Frenchman, Raymond cannot have been impervious to the example presented by the newly fledged Order of the Temple, created by the knighthood of Champagne. But what prevailed upon him to change course was apparently the military needs of *Outremer*. The Latin principalities suffered from a chronic shortage of effective manpower. There was urgent need to reinforce its defensive capability with a standing army of professionals. This was just the service that a military order, richly endowed and constantly attracting recruits of high quality from overseas, could provide. The Hospitallers were thus drawn into an active military role by the predicament of the society they were serving. This seems to have begun in 1123, when a body of the brethren formed an emergency corps of mounted soldiers to help repel the Fatimid invasion from Egypt. After this, they were given an increasing number of military assignments alongside the Templars. They began to supply armed contingents for the king's campaigns, and they were called upon to garrison castles. In 1136 King Fulk entrusted them with the newly constructed castle of Bethgibelin, commanding the approach to the Muslim port of Ascalon; and Count Raymond of Tripoli gave them the great frontier fortress of Crak des Chevaliers to man. By 1180 the order possessed twenty-five castles in Palestine.

The reorientation of the order under Raymond du Puy meant adding to it a regular establishment of knights. It came to resemble the Templars in having a membership divided into knights, sergeants, and clerics, and a domestic labour force of hired servants. Like the Templars, too, the knights of the hospital were lay monks, bound by vows of personal poverty, chastity, and obedience; they lived a life in community, and followed the full monastic round of the choral offices, which were sung by the chaplains. Their distinctive badge was a white cross worn on the surcoat, corresponding to the red cross worn by the Templars. By the middle of the century, the order had acquired a network of establishments and vast estates in many parts of Europe. Its possessions were divided into provinces – called priories – and commanderies; and a substantial part of their yield was exported every year to support the fighting brethren in *Outremer*. The central government of the organisation, which was in the hands of the grand master, assisted by a prior and five senior officers, was located at Jersualem until 1187. Following the disastrous battle of Hattin in that year, and the collapse of the Latin kingdom, the Hospital transferred its headquarters to the castle of Margat on the frontier of Tripoli.

DECLINE AND FALL

The Military Orders were products of the crusading movement of the twelfth and thirteenth centuries. They personified the aggressive thrust and self-confident expansion of Western Christendom. The Knights of the Temple and the Knights of St John found their identity as defenders of the Latin states in the East against the counter-attack of Islam; and their fortunes inevitably waxed and waned with the rise and decline of *Outremer*. They had been born in the euphoria that accompanied and followed the First Crusade. The failure of later crusades to succour the Latin kingdom, culminating in the fall of Acre to the Muslims in 1291, and widespread disillusionment with the crusading ideal, deprived them of their chief *raison d'être*. Their predicament was symbolised by the fact that the grand masters of both orders were fatally wounded in the final assault on the city. The débâcle left them exposed to the animosity of their critics of which they had acquired many. The Hospitallers gained a new lease of life by capturing the island of Rhodes from the Greeks in 1308, and making it their new headquarters. They had in any case never abandoned their more pacific task of maintaining and staffing hospitals, and this gave them a more lasting social role. The Templars suffered a less happy fate.

Through their large international organisation, which was engaged in the regular transfer of large sums of money to the East, the Templars had acquired a subsidiary role as international bankers. They financed crusaders, made credit arrangements for travellers, and lent money to kings. They provided valuable banking facilities for the kings of both England and France. At London, the New Temple, erected by the order off the Strand, was used by the royal exchequer in the thirteenth century as a storehouse for the revenue; and the Temple at Paris discharged a similar function for the king of France. The military brethren not only offered strongholds for safe deposit; they also provided a kind of medieval Securicor service to guard monies in transit. But these services did nothing to ingratiate the order with public opinion. Its corporate arrogance was notorious. Its exemption from all jurisdiction other than that of the papacy alienated the ecclesiastical hierarchy and rendered it impervious to any form of secular control. Its vast territorial wealth made it a tempting prey to an indigent prince. When Philip IV attacked it in 1307, it found few friends to plead for it. Philip's destruction of the order was executed with an accomplished ruthlessness, cynicism, and cruelty, that evoke a comparison with the worst villainies of the modern police state: the dawn swoop, the conditioning of the prisoners by threats and torture, the preposterous confessions extorted from the grand master and others, and the burnings of those who retracted. A feeble attempt by Pope Clement V to set up an independent inquiry was brushed aside; and the approach of a royal army was sufficient to persuade the pope to issue a bull on the 22 March 1312 declaring the order dissolved. Its property was to be transferred to the Hospitallers; but the lion's share was retained by the French crown.[11]

Many factors contributed to the tragedy that overtook the Temple: the growth of royal absolutism, the weakness of the papacy, and not least, the irresponsible conduct of the Templars themselves. But in a sense they were the natural scapegoats for the failure of the crusader states, with whose destiny they had become identified. This did not mean, however, that Western society had rejected the ideal of the crusade. There was still work for a military order. The Knights of the Teutonic Order, which had been created in the Holy Land in the wake of the Third Crusade, found a new field for their activities in conquering the pagan Prussians. After the fall of Acre, they transferred their headquarters first to Venice, and then to Marienburg, close to Danzig; and they became the spearhead of German penetration of the Baltic lands, making themselves in the process a major territorial power in Eastern Europe.

NOTES

1. *PL* 140, 770.
2. C. Erdmann, *Die Entstehung des Kreuzzugsgedankens* (Stuttgart 1935), p. 73. This seminal work contains the best modern discussion of the changing ethic of warfare in the Middle Ages; see translation by M. W. Baldwin and W. Gofart, *The Origin of the Idea of Crusade* (Princeton 1977).
3. *De Laude Novae Militiae* in *S Bernardi Opera*, ed. J. Leclercq, C. H. Talbot, and H. Rochais (Rome 1959), III, p. 217.
4. G. de Valous, 'Quelques observations sur la toute primitive observance des Templiers' in *Mélanges Saint Bernard* (xxive congrès de l'association bourguignonne des sociétés savantes, Dijon 1953), pp. 32–40
5. J. Riley-Smith, 'Crusading as an act of love', *History* LXV (1980), 177–92.
6. H. de Curzon, *La Règle du Temple* (Paris 1886), c. 11, p. 23.
7. *Ibid.*, p. 215.
8. J. Leclercq, 'Un document sur les débuts des Templiers', *Revue d'histoire ecclésiastique* LII (1957), 81–90.
9. *S. Bernardi Opera*, III, pp. 213–39.
10. For the origin and constitution of the Hospitallers see J. Riley-Smith, *The Knights of St John in Jerusalem and Cyprus 1050–1310* (1967).
11. The episode is admirably reconstructed by Malcolm Barber, *The Trial of the Templars* (1978).

Chapter 11

SISTERS OR HANDMAIDS

THE PROBLEM OF THE SISTERS

'Finally', wrote the twelfth-century canon of Liège, 'we shall return to women who lead the eremitical life, rising to the holiness of nuns, and to those who sweetly take up the yoke of Christ with holy men or under their guidance.'[1] But the promised supplement to his little book on *The Orders and Callings of the Church* was either never written or it has been lost. This is a pity, because the canon's views on the place of women in the monastic movement would have been instructive, especially as he was based in Liège, where women played an unusually prominent part in the religious life of that time. Few women wrote about it themselves, and this makes the mental world of the nunneries hard to penetrate. There was the rare prophetess, like St Hildegarde, the abbess of Rupertsberg, whose mystical revelations were transmitted across Europe by means of a voluminous correspondence. But there is a dearth of the kind of narrative writing that tells us about the inner life of the men's establishments. For the most part, the experience of the women religious of the Middle Ages is communicated to us by celibate males; and they were rarely adequate spokesmen.

The nunneries of the early Middle Ages not only offered women the chance to pursue the ascetical life; they attracted endowments because they performed an important social role in providing a haven for the daughters and widows of the aristocracy for whom no suitable marriage could be found. The women who entered them expected to enjoy the society of their own kind. They were thus aristocratic and socially exclusive communities. If girls of humbler origins were admitted at all, it was only in the capacity of servants. Hildegarde defended this exclusiveness, which was still a feature of most nunneries in the twelfth century: 'what man would concentrate his whole flock in a single stable? There should be discrimination;

otherwise, if different people are congregated together, the flock may be rent asunder through the pride of the social superiors and the shame of those who are of different degree; for God differentiates between people both on earth and in heaven.'[2] This last was a rejoinder to an ingenuous observation from the abbess of Andernach that the Lord had chosen poor fishermen to found his Church, and that the Blessed Peter had confessed that God was no respecter of persons.

In the early Germanic world noblewomen enjoyed a higher political status and a greater power of disposing of themselves and their property than they came to possess at a later period. This relative independence was reflected in the masterful government of mixed monasteries by the royal abbesses of Anglo-Saxon England and Merovingian Gaul. They ruled both the men and the women of their communities with the self-assurance that was their birthright. But in the different world of the tenth and eleventh centuries the independence of women, both outside and inside the cloister, diminished. An aristocratic society, whose legal arrangements and modes of thought were conditioned by the military fief reduced women to a strictly subordinate role. And the inferiority of their status was reinforced by the male chauvinism of the Latin Church. Ecclesiastical functions were confined to men. Had not the writer of the Epistle to Timothy said 'Let a woman learn in silence with all submissiveness. I permit no woman to teach or to have authority over men?' A clergy that was required *ex professo* to be celibate stressed the moral and intellectual weakness of womankind. Ascetical literature was written largely by men, and to the male ascetic woman appeared primarily in the guise of the temptress. Paradoxically, the elaboration of the cult of the Blessed Virgin did nothing to counteract this image, for the doctrine of the Immaculate Conception, which was gaining ground at this period, exempted her from the taint and consequences of original sin and thus detached her from the normal experience of the human race.

This change in the position of women was reflected in their declining role in the monastic world. Houses of canonesses survived, and new foundations were occasionally made, because they continued to serve a social purpose for the higher aristocracy, who felt the need to provide protection and supervision for their unmarried womenfolk. Thus in tenth-century Germany the Ottonian dynasty showed an active interest in the nunneries of Herford, Gandersheim, and Quedlinburg, which housed the daughters of the Saxon aristocracy and were governed by royal princesses. Quedlinburg, the foundation of Queen Matilda, the mother of Otto I, became in fact the chosen mausoleum of the dynasty. But the double monastery of an earlier age disappeared under a cloud of ecclesiastical disapproval. When it reappeared in the eleventh century it was in a changed form: no abbess had jurisdiction over monks; the nuns were subject to the supervision of the male founders or deputies appointed by them. Women, in fact, played no active part in the initiatives that launched the major ascetical revivals of the tenth and eleventh centuries. These were movements initiated and led by men and sponsored by patrons who were interested in creating male monasteries. Those women's houses that were founded in their wake were few and undistinguished by comparison with the plethora of important foundations for monks.

It was not necessarily that fewer women were attracted to the religious life or even that their social circumstances precluded such initiatives. The problem lay partly in the mentality of the monastic reformers, who regarded contact with women as a hazard to their souls to be avoided at all costs and who were therefore reluctant to assume the responsibility of directing nuns. The other side of the problem was the attitude of the lay patrons. The lay donor who endowed a monastery hoped to reap spiritual benefits from his gift, and the most highly valued of these was one that women could not provide: women could not celebrate mass. Medieval piety increasingly emphasised the expiatory value of the mass. And as it became the normal practice to ordain professed monks to the priesthood and the institution of the private mass enabled all to offer mass daily, patrons were increasingly eager to sponsor communities of monks.

The subordinate role of women in the monastic revival is evident in the first Cluniac foundation for nuns. It came late in the day, when the Cluniac empire already numbered its colonies in hundreds. In fact, the movement was approaching its climacteric when St Hugh decided in 1056 to create a house for women at Marcigny in the region of Autun. He persuaded his brother, Count Geoffrey of Semur, to give the necessary land. Family *pietas* was a major motive: Hugh's primary purpose was to provide a religious retreat for his own mother and for the wives and female relatives of men who had been persuaded to become monks at Cluny. Marcigny was an establishment for ninety-nine nuns headed by a claustral prioress – the office of abbess was reserved for the Blessed Virgin herself, as a sign of which an empty stall was always kept for her in choir.[3] They were to follow the customs of Cluny, with the proviso that the nuns must be strictly enclosed at all times. The house had some of the features of a double monastery, for Hugh established a small community of twelve monks in the vicinity to provide the necessary sacramental services; but the spirit of the foundation was very different from that of the double monasteries of earlier times: the nuns were placed under the supervision of the prior, who was appointed by the abbot of Cluny and who was the director of both communities. Marcigny was an aristocratic nunnery, and it remained so. The Countess Adela of Blois, daughter of the Conqueror and mother of King Stephen, who had inherited her father's imperious will, was one of several members of the higher aristocracy who took the veil there. Nevertheless, Hugh clearly judged it inappropriate that the ladies should be allowed to run their own affairs and organise their own religious life without male supervision.

Marcigny, with its rigid enclosure – Peter the Venerable's jocund prison – and strict rule of life, was the prototype of a cluster of Cluniac nunneries that were founded in France, Italy, England, and Germany, in the following fifty years. Many of them were small. None of them was endowed on the lavish scale of the greater men's abbeys. Marcigny itself was in straightened circumstances when the mother of Peter the Venerable sought admission. The postulant was of course required to bring a dowry with her when she entered a convent, but the nuns could not touch the generosity of patrons as easily as the monks could. But for all their modest scale, these satellites of the Cluniac empire went some way to meeting the religious aspirations of women who wanted a more secluded and devout way of life than they could find in the older houses of canonesses like Faremoutiers or Essen.

The existence of a growing and widespread demand, especially in Northern Europe, for new forms of monastic life suited to the needs of women made itself increasingly felt and posed a special problem for the founders of the new orders of the eleventh and twelfth centuries. The presence of substantial numbers of women in his following obliged Robert of Abrissel to provide a stable residence for them at Fontevrault. The same problem faced Norbert of Xanten. Women as well as men responded eagerly to the new ideas of the *vita apostolica*, the call to voluntary poverty and the eremitical life. The preachers of the new ascetical movement who had sought solitude in the forests of Craon and Coucy found themselves the centre of colonies of enthusiastic disciples of both sexes. But it was inconceivable that women should be allowed to assume an active role in the apostolic life as it was now being interpreted. Ecclesiastical tradition disqualified them from preaching; and social convention, which accepted the mendicant holy man, would be outraged by itinerant groups of female mendicants. Their unchastity would be taken for granted. 'They say', wrote Marbod sternly to Robert of Abrissel,[4]

> that these women are disciples and followers of your peregrinations; they say you have numbers of women distributed in guest-houses and inns, whom you have deputed to serve the poor and pilgrims. Divine and human laws are both clearly against this association. Sin began with a woman and it is through her that death comes to all of us. Without doubt, you cannot long be chaste if you dwell among women.

There was a deep conviction that the only safe place for a woman who had no husband was behind the high walls of a nunnery or perpetually immured in a hermitage.

Norbert solved the problem of his female devotees by creating double monasteries. At Prémontré he established a house for women adjacent to that of the canons. But male ascendancy permitted the sisters only a subservient role. They attended the church when the canons sang the liturgical offices; otherwise they were assigned such humble tasks as serving the hospice for the poor and washing and darning the clothes of the male community. Their status was like that of the lay brothers in the Cistercian abbeys. The more aristocratic sisters, who could not be expected to do such menial work, were probably allowed to live in the house as recluses.[5] Despite these limitations, the recruitment of women remained surprisingly buoyant and for some years double monasteries proliferated, especially in the Low Countries. By the middle of the century Herman of Tournai claimed, albeit with exaggeration, that there were 1,000 sisters living at Prémontré and its immediate dependencies and that the order contained 10,000 of them. But Marbod's strictures were echoed by misogynists within the order as well as outside it. And a move began to jettison the female communities. In 1138 Pope Innocent II took the canons to task for failing to support the sisters adequately out of the common endowments, no small part of which had accrued to the order through the women recruits. The pope's remonstrance was probably connected with the fact that at about this time the general chapter, under the guidance of Norbert's successor Hugh de Fosses, took a decision to suppress double monasteries.

The abolition of the double houses did not extrude the women from the order. The chapter merely decreed that they must live in totally separate establishments well distanced from the parent abbey. The nuns were required to pack their bags and find accommodation elsewhere. Those at Prémontré had some difficulty finding a permanent home. The bishop of Laon built them a new convent at Fontenelles; but a little later they appear to have moved on to Rozières. Those of the Flemish abbey of Tongerloo were found accommodation in the distant parish of Euwen, where the abbey had some property. In some ways the upheaval may have improved the status of the nuns: they ceased to be humble handmaids servicing communities of men and became fully fledged religious communities with ends of their own; they became in fact canonesses, singing the liturgical offices and following the same monastic regime as the men's houses. But their autonomy was still limited: the parent abbeys continued to supervise their affairs by means of a *praepositus* or prior whom the abbot appointed for the purpose. And there are indications that they paid a heavy price for this semi-independence. The letters of Innocent II and his successors suggest that the parent abbeys, which retained control over the joint endowments, adopted an increasingly niggardly attitude towards supporting their female dependencies after they ceased providing the canons with material services. In the end, misogyny and a desire to be rid of the financial burden moved the leaders of the order to adopt a policy of complete disengagement. In 1197 or 1198 the general chapter took the decision to admit no more women to the order. This decision, which was ratified by a rescript of Pope Innocent III, condemned the female branch of the Premonstratensians to gradual extinction.

The Norbertines were not the only species of canons regular to offer a vocation to women in the early stages. The Flemish abbey of Arrouaise had a large community of canonesses attached to it, though here the nuns formed an independent establishment rather than comprising part of a double monastery. And this arrangement of parallel establishments was adopted by other abbeys of the Arrouaise congregation.[6] But here too the early promise of a dual order succumbed to the same forces that had disinherited the Norbertine nuns. Economic pressure, which was intensified by the growing throng of female postulants, persuaded the chapter of the order first to impose limits on the size of the women's communities and then, in the thirteenth century, to discard them altogether. Thus from 1140 onwards the new orders increasingly adopted a policy of apartheid towards their female branches. In view of this trend, it is all the more interesting that one religious organisation for women besides Fontevrault was successfully launched in the twelfth century and maintained its course in the teeth of the prevailing wind. This was the English order founded by St Gilbert of Sempringham.

ST GILBERT AND THE ORDER OF SEMPRINGHAM

Unlike most monastic innovators, Gilbert was not an ascetic in search of his own vocation. He was an educated secular clerk, the son of a Norman knight settled in Lincolnshire and an English mother. After a spell in the *familia* of the bishops of Lincoln, he was content to retire to the family patrimony and serve the two churches in his father's gift.[7] His order grew out of efforts to meet the needs and aspirations of a small group of young women in his parish who sought a refuge in the monastic life. He began by building them a house and cloister against the north wall of his church. The fact that Gilbert's provision met a widely felt social need is indicated by the interest and support he attracted from several baronial families. Grants of land tumbled in and new foundations rapidly followed. The problem of organisation then had to be faced. Gilbert does not seem to have envisaged an order of double monasteries to begin with. His first foundations coincided with the Cistercian plantations in the North, which were attracting much interest. He was in touch with Abbot William of Rievaulx and intended his nuns to follow a modified form of Cistercian observance. His own position as a secular clerk directing a monastic congregation was anomalous. The obvious solution was to disembarrass himself of his spiritual progeny by affiliating them to the Cistercian Order. With this in mind, he approached the general chapter of Cîteaux in 1147 and asked it to assume responsibility for his order. But the Cistercians had no desire to be involved with the affairs of more women's houses, and Gilbert's request was refused. This rebuff forced him to look elsewhere for a solution.

It may have been the practice of Fontevrault that suggested the plan he adopted. For, after returning empty-handed from the chapter of Cîteaux, he set about associating small communities of canons regular with each convent to serve the sacramental needs of the nuns and manage their property. The characteristic Gilbertine monastery thus contained communities of both men and women occupying separate quarters on either side of the conventual church. The canons sang the canonical hours in their own oratory and celebrated mass for the nuns in the conventual church; the nuns recited the hours in their own choir. From the first, Gilbert had recruited lay brothers among impoverished local peasants and artisans to act as bailiffs for the nuns as well as to hew and carry for them, and there were lay sisters to cook and perform other menial tasks. Gilbert's thirteenth-century biographer likens the order to the chariot of Aminadab:[8]

> it has two sides, one of men, another of women; four wheels, two of men clerk and lay, and two of women lettered and unlettered. Two oxen draw the chariot, the clerkly and monastic discipline of the blessed Augustine and the holy Benedict. Father Gilbert guides the chariot over places rough and smooth, over the heights and in the depths. The way by which they go is narrow, but the path is eternal life.

We do not in fact know much about the internal life of the Gilbertine houses in the early years. Gilbert's original constitutions have been submerged in a medley of later ordinances.[9] The developed institutes insist upon a rigid segregation of the two communities – even in the conventual church they were hidden from the sight of each other by a longitudinal screen, and at mass, communion was passed through a turn-table. But the grisly story of the nun of Watton suggests that in the earlier days contact between the sexes was less rigidly debarred than it later became. She was able to contrive lovers' meetings with a lay brother on the premises for some time before they were discovered and she was found to be pregnant. The nuns vented their rage on the body of her lover with a horrible act of revenge.[10] This incident and the troubles with the lay brothers in the

1160s may have resulted in a more inflexible regime of segregation. Before the advent of the canons it had been the practice of the lay brothers to attend the night hours in the nuns' church, but this was later stopped.

The rebellion of the lay brothers of Sempringham in 1166–67 illustrates the difficulties that beset an attempt to revive double monasteries in the twelfth century. The ringleaders were two brothers whom Gilbert had entrusted with managerial responsibilities and who probably felt they had lost status through the arrival of the canons. After being punished by him for misconduct, they daringly went to the papal Curia at Sens and laid charges against the order. The most serious accusation was that grave sexual lapses had resulted from the close proximity of nuns and canons in the Gilbertine houses. This attack came close to success: the conspirators returned from the Curia with letters from Pope Alexander commanding Gilbert to rehouse the canons and nuns in completely separate and properly distanced establishments. But Gilbert had powerful friends and admirers who rushed to the defence of his order. Five English bishops picked up their pens to rebut the charges and reassure the pope that the nuns and canons lived in strict segregation; the legate, Hugh Pierleoni, visited Sempringham and wrote a glowing testimonial;[11] and – most cogent argument of all – King Henry gave the pope to understand that he would confiscate the endowments of the order if any such radical change were made.[12] And so the double monasteries survived. The Order of Sempringham contained thirteen mixed priories, all save three of them in Gilbert's native Lincolnshire, besides sixteen houses that were for canons only. The rebels had touched a sensitive nerve. The scandal of the nun of Watton was common knowledge in the north of England, and possibly there had been other less notorious cases. But the pope's readiness to respond to charges brought by a couple of disgruntled runaways reflected the conviction of many churchmen that men and women could not be associated in the religious life without endangering chastity.

This early crisis in the order left its mark in the severity of the statutes regulating the enclosure of the nuns. The internal affairs of each house were directed by three prioresses, who ruled the community by turns. The canons were denied all access to the nuns except for the purpose of administering supreme unction to a dying sister. The ordinances contain elaborate instructions for the making and custody of the turn-table, the sole point of communication through which advice and funds could be passed. Even at mass the celebrant was hidden from the sisters by a screen. The only meeting point was the general chapter which assembled annually at Sempringham. This was attended by the prioresses as well as by the priors of the male communities, but the nuns were required to travel in a covered cart so that they could neither see about them nor be seen. This preoccupation with keeping the two sides of the order from contact had one advantage for the nuns. They were left with a rare degree of autonomy in the running of their own affairs; they had control of the moneys and the conventual seals, and the prioresses were answerable only to the master of the order, that is to Gilbert himself and his successors.

THE CISTERCIAN NUNS

In rejecting Gilbert's overture the general chapter of Cîteaux was following a policy to which it continued to cling until the beginning of the thirteenth century. The early Cistercian ethos was hostile to any arrangement involving contact with women. Abbots were forbidden to bless female novices, and the statutes fiercely debarred female visitors from the cloister. But as time went on the success of the Cistercian ideal in attracting female disciples created a problem of growing dimensions. Gilbert's nuns were not alone in their desire to be associated with the Cistercian Order; elsewhere in Europe many nunneries were modelling their observance upon the customs of Cîteaux. Yet the order steadily declined to accept any responsibility for their pastoral care. It has been observed that until 1191 the official acts of the order omitted any reference to the existence of this large company of female fellow-travellers.[13] Individual abbots gave encouragement to new foundations for women and helped with advice; but the order refused to incorporate them into its organisation. Being excluded from the official structure of the order, some groups of nunneries following Cistercian customs made a move to form a parallel organisation of their own. Before the end of the twelfth century the Cistercian abbesses of Castile were meeting in annual chapters at Las Huelgas, and the Burgundian nunnery of Tart was convening the heads of its daughter-houses to an annual chapter.

In the end, the stance of benevolent detachment became impossible to maintain. The growing demand by nuns and their aristocratic patrons for association forced the order to take cognisance of the women's houses. It may have been the pressure from Alfonso VIII of Castile on behalf of the royal nunnery of Las Huelgas that eventually overcame the reluctance of the general chapter: he was determined that his foundation should be recognised as a daughter-house of Cîteaux; and he was a valuable patron whom it was not easy to refuse.[14] In any case, after the Premonstratensians decided to admit no more nunneries to their order, more and more communities looked to Cîteaux for guidance and support. 'After this', wrote Jacques de Vitry, 'the nuns who professed the religion of the Cister-

cian Order multiplied like the stars of heaven and vastly increased
. . . convents were founded and built, virgins, widows, and married
women who had gained their husbands' consent, rushed to fill the
cloisters.'[15] Jacques himself, who was an Austin canon, had seen
seven abbeys of Cistercian nuns constructed within a short period in
his own corner of the diocese of Liège. So, early in the thirteenth
century, the general chapter yielded to the demand and began to
acknowledge that some nunneries had been incorporated into the
order. In 1213 it enacted the first of many statutes to regulate their
observance. This ordinance laid down a rule of strict enclosure and
underlined the responsibility of abbots to supervise those women's
houses which had been affiliated to their abbeys.

Only seven years after this first effort to bring some of the
nunneries under the offical control of the order, the general chapter
decreed that no more women's abbeys should be incorporated.[16] The
prohibition was reiterated in more drastic form in 1228: no more
convents were to be erected in the name of the order: 'if any convent
of nuns not yet associated with the order or not yet built wishes to
imitate our institutes, we do not forbid it; but we will not accept the
care of their souls or perform for them the office of visitation.[17] There
were probably a variety of reasons for this *volte-face*, chief among
them the sheer scale of the problem. There were many women's
houses which had been sailing under the Cistercian flag without being
subject to the disciplinary constraints of the Cistercian organisation.
During the thirteenth century, Cistercian nunneries multiplied at an
extraordinary rate, especially in Germany and the Low Countries,
where they greatly outnumbered the men's abbey.[18] It proved an
impossible task to exercise effective supervision over such a multitude of different establishments.

The chapter acts indicate that the order experienced much difficulty in trying to impose its disciplinary control upon the nunneries.
Aristocratic ladies accustomed to directing their affairs in relative
freedom did not take kindly to the constraints of a highly disciplined
organisation that was governed by men. Abbots attempting to carry
out a visitation of their affiliated nunneries sometimes found the
doors barred against them.[19] The chapter repeatedly referred to the
need for stricter enclosure of both nuns and their abbesses; in 1298
it complained that the order was being dishonoured by nuns who
went about freely outside the cloister.[20] In 1250 it received a report
on the abbey of Colonges that disclosed a situation which was far
from being unique. Colonges in Burgundy was a daughter-house of
Cîteaux. When the headship of the house fell vacant, two abbots of
the filiation went to supervise the election of a new abbess. But the
prioress refused to surrender the seals or carry out instructions. The
two abbots therefore excommunicated her and retreated. Having got
them out of the way, the convent proceeded to elect one of their own

number as abbess and installed her.[21] A year later, the general
chapter had made no headway with the problem and despairingly
reported the excommunication of the nuns to the bishop. The same
chapter that received the complaint against Colonges excommunicated another nun who was conducting herself as abbess of Bland-
ecques.[22] The problem of controlling these recalcitrant nunneries was
obviously made more difficult by the fact that they were unrepre-
sented in the sovereign body of the order. Abbesses were not allowed
to attend the general chapter. And women of high birth were disinclined to submit to dictation by a distant body of men who showed
scant understanding of their problems. When visitors informed the
abbess and nuns of Parc-aux-Dames of the chapter decrees of 1242,
the nuns signified their annoyance by clapping and stamping their
feet and walking out of the chapter-house.[23]

These difficulties, and the fear of incurring financial liability for
communities with inadequate endowments, explain the reaction of
some sections of the order against the incorporation of nunneries.
But the prohibition of 1228 evidently did not reflect a consensus, for
it failed to stick. In the Low Countries the Brabander abbey of Villers
continued to promote the foundation of Cistercian nunneries and to
provide them with spiritual direction in the 1230s.[24] And the general
chapter continued to accede to requests for affiliation of new foundations made by influential patrons. In 1248 it bowed to a request
from Queen Margaret of France for the incorporation of her three
abbeys of Le Lys, Vaux de Cernay, and Royaumont.[25] In 1250 the
dowager countess of Arundel, Isabella d'Albini, persuaded it to
accept her foundation for nuns at Marham in Norfolk.[26]

A NEW EXPERIMENT: THE BEGUINES

The official attitude of the order may have placed some brake upon
the affiliation of women's houses, but it did nothing to impede the
creation of new religious communities, which continued to multiply,
especially in Germany and the Low Countries. Some of these
modelled their observance on that of the Cistercians; others adopted
a freer, more experimental type of religious life. It was these latter
groups that contemporaries called Beguines.

The Beguines, like the Cistercian nuns, were a product of the
extraordinary spirit of religious fervour that swept through certain
sections of Western society in the twelfth and thirteenth centuries.
They were groups of laywomen living in the towns of Northern
Europe who devoted themselves to a new form of ascetical life. They
were not affiliated to any religious order, nor did they follow any

recognised monastic rule. The movement may have been prompted by the social exclusiveness of the nunneries; equally it may have represented a widespread rejection of the affluence and formalism of the established orders. But there was more to it than this. Its piety was rooted in the cult of voluntary poverty and the ideas of the apostolic life, but it flowered in a very different soil. It was an urban phenomenon. Its leaders were recruited largely among the daughters and widows of the newly affluent bourgeois of the northern cities – women like Marie d'Oignies, mystic and doyenne of the Flemish Beguines, whose patrician family of Nivelles was infuriated and frightened by her determination to renounce all her property. And whereas the traditional forms of monastic life had sought salvation in the desert, the Beguines found the milieu for their religious life in the towns. In this they resembled the friars, with whom they soon came to be linked. Like the Franciscans too, they were inspired by a new kind of vision formed in the uncomplicated minds of lay Christians – the vision of the evangelical life, or the literal imitation of the life of Christ. In his biography of Marie d'Oignies, Jacques de Vitry tells us that she was consumed with a desire to follow the Gospel and make herself a beggar, 'so as naked to follow the naked Christ'.[27]

It began with groups of devout women living in the world, in some cases remaining in their own families, who used a town church as a focus for their association. By the beginning of the thirteenth century, they had begun to form communities occupying houses in the towns of Flanders, Brabant, and the Rhineland. They took no irrevocable vows, but simply made an engagement to observe celibacy while they lived in community. They attended mass and the other offices in the parish church. A condition of membership was the renunciation of personal wealth and the cultivation of a humble and frugal life-style. They supported themselves by their own work, mainly by weaving, sewing, and embroidery; and they moved freely about the city serving the needs of the poor and the sick. Some groups resorted to more or less organised begging as a means of support.

The rapid spread of the Beguines is one of the most arresting religious phenomena of the later Middle Ages. As they gradually secured recognition from the authorities of church and state, Beguinages sprang up everywhere in the northern towns. In some cases the houses were purchased out of the funds brought to the communities by new members; in others, buildings were donated by members of the ruling nobility. By the end of the thirteenth century, Namur contained five Beguinages; and Cologne, the biggest and most populous of North German cities, had witnessed fifty-four such foundations. In Brussels, where the Beguines enjoyed the patronage of the dukes of Brabant, they were allowed to appropriate the chapel of La Vigne to their use, and they secured a right to have their own priests and their own burial ground. Here, as in other towns of the Low Countries, they came to constitute a separate enclave within the city. Some impression of the size and layout of these establishments of pious women can be gained from the Beguinages that are still to be seen at Bruges and Louvain and several other Belgian cities. Although most of its existing houses date from the seventeenth century, the Great Beguinage of Louvain presents the essential aspect of the medieval settlement – a small township within the town, containing its own streets, gardens, church, and collegiate buildings, separated from the surrounding city by a high encircling wall.

Why were so many women attracted to the movement? As a social phenomenon, the explanation for it must lie in the demography of the northern cities. The escalating demand by women both for nunneries and for alternative forms of ascetical life indicates a population imbalance. The number of marriageable women must have substantially exceeded the number of available men. Such an imbalance can be easily accounted for by normal female longevity and the inroads made upon the male population by warfare, the hazards of travel, and clerical celibacy. Just as the nuns and canonesses had provided a home for the ladies of the landed classes for whom no suitable marriage could be found, the Beguinages in turn offered a refuge to the surplus daughters and the widows of the wealthier bourgeoisie. Nor were they only a haven for the unmarriageable. The religious life offered an escape, usually the only escape, for girls who found themselves forced by their families into a marriage they did not desire. Being the children of affluent families, they were readily attracted by the ideal of ascetical poverty – voluntary poverty has no meaning except for the rich – and by the relative freedom which characterised the life in the Beguinages.

It was Jacques de Vitry who first trumpeted the virtues of the Beguines at the papal Curia. As an Augustinian canon, he had lived for a year as the neighbour, confessor, and disciple of Marie d'Oignies, and once made a bishop, he strenuously defended the new communities of women against their detractors and persuaded Pope Honorius III to authorise their way of life. And after Marie's death in 1213 he wrote her Life for the benefit of Bishop Fulk of Toulouse, so that he could show the heretical sectaries of the Languedoc what a real holy woman was like. Jacques saw the Beguines, in the way that later popes saw the friars, as a sign of fresh hope for a Church beleaguered by heresy and weakened by the ignorance and vice of the secular clergy. And there were other educated and zealous churchmen who took the same view. According to Eccleston, Grosseteste, when he was lecturing to the Franciscans at Oxford, warned them that there was an even higher form of holy poverty than mendicancy, which was to live by the labour of one's own hands, 'wherefore he said that the Beguines have attained the highest perfection of holy religion, for they live by their own labour and do not burden the world with their demands'.[28] It was a striking testimonial from one of the greatest Schoolmen of the thirteenth century. He was echoed by Master Robert of the Sorbonne, who daringly opined that the Beguines would fare better at the Last Judgement than many of the masters and theologians of Paris.[29]

Yet despite this enthusiastic promotion, the women's movement encountered much hostile criticism both from the laity and from the more conservative sections of the clergy. The spectacle of laywomen, without the sanction of any religious order, engaging in an active apostolic role was offensive to both male chauvinism and to clerical professionalism. From the first they were suspected of heresy: the name 'Beguine' itself originally denoted a heretic. And although for the most part they were neither heretical nor anti-clerical, the individualistic and intensely affective piety they cultivated aroused the misgiving of ecclesiastical authorities. The laity, observed William of Saint-Amour, hammer of the friars, belonged to that order of the Church that stood in need of perfection by the ministrations of the clergy.[30] The mystical experiences and direct illumination ascribed to laywomen like Marie d'Oignies or Hadewijch, the Beguine of Nivelles, could be seen as posing a threat to his hierarchical organisation of divine grace. It was the chronic conflict between the religion of authority and the religion of the spirit.

Before the middle of the thirteenth century the reaction had set in. Criticism focused upon the lack of inclaustration or clerical supervision and the scandalous behaviour of female mendicants. In 1233 a provincial synod of Mainz attempted to stop the practice of begging by some Beguines: they were not to run about the streets; they must remain in their houses, live by the work of their hands, and be directed by their parish clergy.[31] Another synod at Fritzlar in 1244 alleged frequent sexual lapses among younger Beguines and ordained that for the future no woman should be admitted to their community under the age of forty.[32] The attitude of many of the clergy towards them was tersely summed up by Bruno, bishop of Olmütz, thirty years later: 'I would have them either married or thrust into an approved order.'[33] In the end, the conflict was resolved by a compromise. The Council of Vienne in 1312 censured 'certain women, commonly called Beguines, who lose themselves in foolish speculations on the Trinity and the divine essence . . . these women promise obedience to nobody, and they neither renounce their property nor profess any approved Rule'. Their way of life was permanently forbidden. But this was without prejudice to those faithful women who wished to live 'as the Lord shall inspire them, following a life of penance and living chastely together in their hospices, even if they have taken no vow'.[34] In other words, the Beguines would be tolerated so long as they stayed in their convents and accepted clerical supervision. Female vagrancy and similar antics were not acceptable. Most Beguinages, in fact, attached themselves to houses of Franciscan or Dominican friars, who supplied them with spiritual directors and confessors.

In its tamed form the Beguinage survived the onslaught of its critics and persecutors. In many of the cities of Germany, northern France, and the Low Countries, it remained an established and respected institution, providing a home for the sick and destitute as well as for the sisterhood. In a genuine sense, the Beguines represented a movement of women's liberation. Even after their wilder manifestations had been suppressed, their informal associations offered unmarried women a greater degree of freedom and initiative than was allowed them either in a traditional convent or in a lay household. Their simple Scriptural piety and their cultivation of mystical experience, which was often expressed in the erotic imagery of the *Brautmystik* or 'Bridal' mysticism, placed them alongside the friars as preachers of a new kind of religious experience, which was individualistic, intuitive, and lay in its inspiration.

NOTES

1. *Libellus de Diversis Ordinibus et Professionibus qui sunt in Aecclesia*, ed. G. Constable and B. Smith (1972), p. 5.
2. *Epistolae, PL* 197, 337–8.
3. G. de Valous, *Le Monachisme clunisien* (Ligugé-Paris 1935) i, p. 383. On Marcigny see also Hunt, *Cluny under St Hugh 1049–1109* (1967), 186–94, and P. Schmitz *Histoire de l'ordre de Saint-Benoit* vii (Maredsous 1956) pp. 73–4.
4. *Marbodi Redonensis Episcopi Epistolae, PL* 171, 1481–2. On Robert's relations with women disciples see Jacqueline Smith, 'Robert of Abrissel, Procurator Mulierum' in *Medieval Women*, ed. D. Baker (Studies in Church History, Subsidia I, 1978), pp. 175–84.
5. E. Erens, 'Les soeurs dans l'ordre de Prémontré', *Analecta Praemonstratensia* 5 (1929), 6–26. The status of women in the order is examined at length by H. Lamy, *L'Abbaye de Tongerloo depuis sa foundation jusqu'en 1263* (Louvain 1914), pp. 93–101; see also the observations of R. W. Southern in *Western Society and the Church in the Middle Ages* (1970) pp. 312–14.
6. L. Milis, *L'Ordre des chanoines réguliers d'Arrouaise*, 2 vols (Bruges 1969), pp. 502–29.
7. The fullest account of Gilbert's life is that of Rose Graham, *St Gilbert of Sempringham and the Gilbertines* (1903), which has still not been superseded.
8. *Dugdale Monasticon* (1825) VI, 2, ix; cited by Graham, *op. cit.*, p. 14.
9. They are printed in *Monasticon* VI, 2, post pp. 947; see the critical

observations of Raymonde Foreville, *Le Livre de Saint Gilbert de Sempringham* (Paris 1943), pp. xi–xii.

10. See G. Constable, 'Aelred of Rievaulx and the nun of Watton' in *Medieval Women*, pp. 205–226.

11. W. Holtzmann, *Papsturkunden in England* (1952), III, no. 231.

12. See the account of the incident by M. D. Knowles, 'The Revolt of the lay brothers of Sempringham', *Eng. Hist. Review* **50** (1935), 465–87.

13. By Southern, *op. cit.*, p. 316.

14. A. Dimier, 'Chapitres généraux d'abbesses cisterciennes', *Cîteaux* **11** (1960), 272.

15. *The Historia Occidentalis of Jacques de Vitry*, ed. J. F. Hinnebusch (Fribourg, Spicilegium Friburgense 17, 1972), p. 117.

16. *Statuta Capitulorum Generalium Ordinis Cisterciencis*, ed. J. Canivez, I (Louvain 1933), p. 517. On the general bearing of this decree see Sally Thompson, 'The Problem of the Cistercian nuns in the twelfth and thirteenth centuries' in *Medieval Women*, pp. 227–52.

17. *Statuta* II, p. 68.

18. For the figures see F. Vongrey and F. Hervay, 'Kritische Bemerkungen zum Atlas de l'Ordre Cistercien von Fred. van der Meer', in *Analecta Cisterciensia* **23** (1967), 137–8; cited by Southern, *op. cit.*, p. 317 n. 19.

19. See for example the cases reported in 1243 and 1244: *Statuta* II, pp. 272–3, 281.

20. *Ibid.* III, p. 293.

21. *Ibid.* II, pp. 357–8, 375.

22. *Ibid.* II, p. 359.

23. *Ibid.* II, p. 272; cited by Southern, *op. cit.*, p. 317.

24. Simone Roisin, 'L'efflorescence cistercienne et le courant féminin de piété au XIIIᵉ siècle', *Revue d'histoire ecclésiastique* **39** (1943), 342–78.

25. *Statuta* II, p. 331.

26. *Ibid.* II, p. 364.

27. *Acta Sanctorum June* V, 557. On the rise and development of the Beguines see the classic study of H. Grundmann, *Religiöse Bewegungen im Mittelalter* (2nd edn. 1961), pp. 319–54; and E. W. McDonnell, *The Beguines and Beghards in Medieval Culture* (Rutgers, USA 1954); and Southern, *op. cit.*, pp. 318–31. On Mary d'Oignies and other leaders see Brenda Bolton, 'Vitae Matrum: a further aspect of the Frauenfrage' in *Medieval Women*, pp. 253–73.

28. *De Adventu Fratrum Minorum in Angliam*, ed. A. G. Little (1951), p. 99.

29. Grundmann, *op. cit.*, p. 305.

30. *De Periculis Novissimorum Temporum* in E. Brown, *Fasciculus Rerum Expetendarum* (1690) II, pp. 18–41. William's attack was aimed mainly at the friars, cf. chapter 12 n. 30 below, but he singled out the Beguines for particular condemnation.

31. Grundmann, *op. cit.*, p. 326.

32. *Ibid.* p. 326.

33. *Ibid.*, p. 337.

34. C. J. Hefele and H. Leclercq, *Histoire des Conciles* (Paris 1915), VI, pp. 681–2; *Clement III, xi De Religiosis domibus*, c. 1.

Chapter 12

THE FRIARS

The order of mendicant friars which appeared early in the thirteenth century represented a new departure, a radical breakaway from the monastic tradition of the past. By adopting a rule of corporate poverty and refusing to accept endowments or to own property they discarded impedimenta that had long been regarded as indispensable to any organised community of monks. But their rejection of property and reliance upon begging to support themselves were only the outward signs of a more fundamental change of spirit. The Mendicant Orders broke free from one of the most basic principles of traditional monasticism by abandoning the seclusion and enclosure of the cloister in order to engage in an active pastoral mission to the society of their time. Preaching and ministering to the people was their *raison d'être*. And the message they brought was different. Assurance of salvation need no longer be sought by flight from the human hive or by attachment to the shirt-tails of a spiritual élite; those who lived in the world, whatever their status, could fulfil the demands of the Christian life by sanctifying the humdrum duties and tasks of their estate; all that was needed was that they should receive the Gospel. It was a necessary condition of this missionary programme that the old monastic principle of stability should be dispensed with. It was one of the favourite charges brought against the friars by their more conservative opponents that they were *gyrovagi* – the wandering monks for whom the ultimate curse of St Benedict had been reserved. Unlike the monk, who was bound to the house of his profession, the friar was mobile. Supported by an organisation that was international and cosmopolitan, he moved from house to house and from province to province at the dictates of his superiors, for the purpose of study, preaching, or administration. But although the Mendicant Orders embodied a revolutionary concept of the religious life, they had antecedents. The roots of the plant that flowered so prolifically in the thirteenth century lay in the religious experience and the social changes of the previous hundred years.

As we have seen, the cult of voluntary poverty and the ideas of the apostolic life had found expression in various new forms of religious life in the course of the twelfth century. There was a growing recognition that a mode of life modelled upon that of the Apostles should involve not only the renunciation of worldly goods but also commitment to active evangelism. It was this perception that stirred individual ascetics like Norbert of Xanten and Robert of Abrissel to combine mendicancy with the role of the itinerant preacher. But their vision of the *vita apostolica* was a personal one which they did not succeed in communicating to the institutions they founded. Both the Order of Fontevrault and the Premonstratensians canons conformed in fact to the accepted norms of monastic organisation. It was later in the century that the cult of voluntary poverty combined with the idea of apostolic preaching of 'metanoia', or interior conversion, to inspire a more revolutionary form of religious life which was adopted by a number of more or less organised groups of preachers in the towns of France and northern and central Italy. The early friars were only the most conspicuous and successful of these groups of zealots. To understand the dynamics of these new religious associations we need to look at the social environment from which they sprang.

THE SOCIAL CONTEXT

In the two centuries before 1250 Western Europe had experienced a prolonged period of economic and demographic expansion which had both solvent and stimulating effects upon the religious life. As commercial wealth and industrial activity grew, urban populations increased and the physical area of many towns was enlarged. In northern Italy and Flanders, where a thriving textile industry was organised on a capitalist basis, and in the Rhineland, several cities underwent an expansion to a point where they had begun to attain the dimensions of a modern town. Rapid urban growth, the expansion of international trade, the rise of a new bourgeoisie deriving its wealth from commerce, and the creation of an international community of learning, all tended to break down the isolation of local communities and to produce a society that was more mobile, more critical, and, at the upper levels, more affluent than before. It is a truism that city populations provided the most fertile seed-bed for religious dissent and anti-clericalism. Recent studies have suggested that in the thirteenth century scepticism about some of the fundamental dogmas of faith was commoner even among the rural peasantry than was once believed. Nevertheless, the closely regulated and enclosed society of the rural manor exerted on the individual an almost irresistible pressure to conform; whereas town living, with its relative freedom from customary constraints, its political turbulence, and the constant stimulus of competition, fostered a more critical mentality and provided readier opportunities for the communication of ideas.

Another feature of economic growth was the appearance of a literate·section of the laity. Literacy was ceasing to be a clerical monopoly. Commercial activity demanded of its practitioners at least some degree of formal literacy; and in fact, by the end of the twelfth century, the ability to read and write the vernacular, and to a lesser extent Latin, was quite common in the larger Italian towns. The rise of an articulate town-dwelling laity, critical of the intellectual and moral shortcomings of the clergy, and unsympathetic to the claims and assumptions of monastic spirituality, presented the medieval Church with a pastoral challenge it was ill-equipped to meet. The diocesan and parochial structure of the Church had developed to serve the needs of a rurally based population. Its clergy, apart from an educated élite which was absorbed by the schools and the ecclesiastical bureaucracy, were largely recruited locally from the ranks of the free peasantry, and educationally most of them were only a little above the level of their rustic parishioners. The numerous churches that were to be found in many medieval towns were generally appropriated to monasteries or collegiate bodies and were too poorly endowed to attract the services of educated clerks. The predicament of the thirteenth-century Church was rather like that of the British Railways in the mid twentieth century – its layout reflected the economic and social needs of an earlier age. Of course, the analogy can be pushed too far. In the thirteenth century, the majority of the population still resided in the countryside; but the significant growth points were the towns, and thenceforward modes of Christian piety and forms of the ascetical life would be determined by the religious experience of townsmen.

It was this gap in the pastoral equipment of the Church that the friars were to fill with such brilliant success. Thomas of Celano, the biographer of St Francis, tells that Pope Innocent III had a dream the night after his first encounter with Francis. In his dream he saw the Lateran basilica (the mother-church and head of all the churches of the West) crumbling and on the point of collapse, when a little man wearing a habit of sackcloth and a cord crossed the piazza and shored up the tottering edifice with his back.[1] The dream had a symbolic reality that was vindicated by history. As Innocent perceived, in the new world that was emerging the Church was faced with a major crisis. Heresy was widespread. In the Languedoc the Catharist heresy had taken root under the patronage of the landed classes and was organised as a counter-church with its own hierarchy. The towns of northern Italy had long been nurseries of various heretical sects, against which the secular clergy could make no headway. The bourgeoisie and the swelling population of artisans offered a ready audience for free-lance itinerant preachers who moved along the trade routes in increasing numbers. New and radical forms of lay piety were appearing, which drew their inspiration from first-hand study of the New Testament, now circulating in unofficial vernacular translations, and which posed a potential threat to the hierarchical structure of the Church. The question was whether this unruly flood of enthusiasm could be canalised and made to serve the cause of orthodoxy. Innocent was playing for high stakes when he gave his qualified approval to certain groups of mendicant lay preachers, but it was a gamble that succeeded.

The friars were only one among several groups of itinerant evangelists. The common inspiration of these groups came from a fresh and more radical interpretation of the apostolic life. Poverty, voluntarily embraced, was an essential part of it, and so was the idea of a preaching mission to proselytise the unconverted. But a new dimension was perceived in the old ideal. The authentic apostolic life was now seen to be one modelled upon the earthly life of Jesus as it was revealed in the Gospels – the imitation of Christ. The mental leap was easier for the literate layman whose mind was unencumbered by the medieval traditions of Biblical exegesis. It was a rediscovery of the literal sense of the Gospel.[2] And in fact the initiative in forming groups of evangelists came in many cases from the more affluent and articulate sections of the urban laity. Peter Waldes, the founder of one such group, was a wealthy merchant of Lyons when, soon after 1170, he renounced his property and embarked upon a career of itinerant preaching. Most of his followers, the Waldenses, who subsequently drifted into an anti-sacerdotal position, were drawn from the same social milieu. It was the class that produced St Francis of Assisi, the son of a rich cloth merchant, and his first followers, and the leading spirits of the Humiliati in northern Italy.

The Humiliati were a religious fraternity, dedicated to the new style of apostolic life, which had gained a substantial following in the cities of Lombardy and the Veneto. Jacques de Vitry, ever a sharp-eyed reporter of the religious scene, noticed their success in recruiting among the urban patriciate, some of whom joined their communities, while others remained in their own homes with their families but 'living in the religious state and persevering in sobriety of life and works of mercy'. He also noticed that their lay members had been authorised to preach: 'Their brethren, both clerks and literate laymen, have authority from the supreme pontiff who has confirmed their rule, to preach, not only in their own congregation but in the city squares and secular churches.'[3] The decision to authorise lay preaching legitimated an extraordinary breach in the sacerdotal professionalism of the medieval Church. To more conservative churchmen lay preaching usurped the function of the official ministry. It was synonymous with subversion and heresy. The initial reaction of authority had been to stamp on it. And both the Humiliati and the Waldenses, along with heretical sects, had been included in a general condemnation by Pope Lucius III in 1184. It was left to the shrewd intelligence and inspired pragmatism of Innocent III to rehabilitate the Humiliati and to reconcile the orthodox section of the Waldenses led by Durandus of Huesca.

In their spirit and organisation the Humiliati bore some resemblance to the orders of friars. They associated voluntary poverty with evangelism; and their organisation, as it was approved by the pope, comprised three orders, the first consisting of tonsured clerics, the second of lay people living the coenobitical life, and the third of lay disciples pursuing a life of regular devotion in their own homes. Both the second and third orders earned their keep by working at manual crafts. Where the friars differed was in pursuing a more radical ideal of poverty. In Milan and the other cities of northern Italy the communities of Humiliati enjoyed the security of well-endowed conventual houses. St Francis would have none of this. The scheme of evangelical perfection he proposed to his followers involved organised destitution. They were to join the ranks of the holy beggars who were becoming a scourge of the ecclesiastical establishment.

The friars, then, came on an urban scene that had grown accustomed to the visitation of wandering preachers and wild prophets and to the sight of unkempt and threadbare evangelists. They were part of this scenario themselves, and they might well have proved as ephemeral as the rest. The fact that they persisted and expanded into a European-wide organisation can only be explained by the peculiar genius of their founders and by the shrewdness of the ecclesiastical authorities who perceived their possibilities and gave them support. The two first and greatest of the Mendicant Orders originated in the early years of the thirteenth century, and they grew side by side in a kind of symbiosis. But their antecedents and the circumstances of their origin were very different. The Dominicans were founded by an Augustinian canon, and from the outset they were a clerical order, which retained many of the features of the canons regular, and had discernible roots in the twelfth-century ideology of the apostolic life. The Franciscans, on the other hand, owed their origin to the literal and uncomplicated vision of a layman.

THE FRANCISCANS

On some questions the mind and intentions of St Francis are hard to penetrate. It is one of the central enigmas of his career that, unlike St Dominic, he failed to establish a stable religious institution. Several years before his death in 1226 he resigned the direction of his order, and the work of organisation fell largely to other hands. This situation was not in itself remarkable or unprecedented. What was unique about the role of St Francis was that he became a sign of contradiction to his followers. Within twenty-five years of his death the order he had inspired was rent by controversy over his teaching and the meaning of his life, his valedictory testament to the brethren was declared null by a papal bull, and provincial ministers were ordering copies of it to be burned. And time, so far from healing the fractures, only worsened them. The schism between the Spirituals – the rigorists for poverty who claimed to be the authentic custodians of the founder's message – and the Conventuals became a permanent and tragic feature of Franciscan history.

These dissensions have always posed a critical problem for the student of St Francis because at an early stage they infected the hagiographical tradition. What is probably the most widely known image of the poor man of Assisi, the Poverello, is derived from the Little Flowers – the *Fioretti*. The publication of this work in English translation enchanted the religious imagination of Victorian England; and even today it retains much of its freshness and power. Yet it is a relatively late and partisan source – a collection in fact of Umbrian legends, which achieved its existing form about the beginning of the fourteenth century. It represents the beginning of the movement, the idyllic Franciscan morning of the Umbrian countryside, as it was seen through the eyes of the Spirituals, who had been driven into schism, and it is deeply tinged with their preconceptions and disappointments. This conflict is reflected throughout the hagiographical tradition. Celano, the first biographer of St Francis, compromised his credibility by composing a second Life eighteen years later which on important issues fails to square with the first. The wonderful cycle of frescos with which Giotto, or another, embellished the walls of the upper basilica at Assisi drew their subject-matter from the Life of the saint by St Bonaventure. This was the work of a man who had never known St Francis, a Paris theologian, who was deeply involved in trying to reconcile the conflicting parties. It was commissioned by the general chapter of the order in 1260, and in its omissions and sandpaperings it bears the unmistakable marks of the official hagiographer. Following its acceptance, order was given that the two earlier Lives by Celano should be destroyed. Even the great basilica itself and the friary of Assisi, the *sacro convento* – so strangely at variance with St Francis's own admonition that the brethren should not build large churches – became a rock of offence. A later anecdote in the Spiritual tradition has a story that Brother Leo, the old disciple and friend of Francis, visited Assisi, and seeing a marble collecting vase which Elias had put out to receive contributions to the building fund, indignantly smashed it with his stick.

To some extent the chronic controversy over Franciscan poverty has infected modern historians as well as the medieval biographers. Paul Sabatier, who published the classic modern biography in 1894, saw the early history of the movement in terms of an inevitable conflict between the pure religion of the spirit, represented by St Francis, and the religion of authority, represented by Ugolino – the cardinal protector of the infant order, who later became Pope Gregory IX: the original ideal of St Francis was progressively diluted and finally smothered by the institutional Church. This viewpoint derived some support from those sources that embodied the tradition of the Spirituals. All this means that anyone who sets out to describe the personality and teaching of St Francis must recognise that the enterprise is subject to severe limitations. But the task is not impossible. We have the guidance of a handful of Francis's own writings, including the first and second Rules and the valuable testament. And next to these, we have the first Life by Celano. Although this too displays the limitations of official hagiography, it has two important merits: it was begun within two years of the death of St Francis by a friar of the first generation who had met him – it contains in fact a vivid pen-portrait; and it was written before the outbreak of troubles in the order had tainted the wells.[4]

Francis was a child of one of the turbulent urban societies of the twelfth century. His father, Pietro Bernadone, was a rich cloth merchant of Assisi. We do not know, we can only speculate, how his mind encountered and absorbed the conflicting ascetical ideals that were abroad at the end of the twelfth century. A surviving letter written in his own hand shows that he could read Latin, though he could only write it imperfectly; he also spoke French – the lingua franca of the medieval merchant class. But at any period, ideas that are widely current can be picked up without recourse to books. It is certain that Francis had travelled in connection with his father's business, and it is probable that he encountered members of the Humiliati or other exponents of the apostolic life in the course of his journeyings. His early struggles after he had renounced the family home and the life-style of his class indicate that his mind was captivated by the eremitical ideal. In the first stage of his spiritual saga he lived as a hermit in caves and ruinous churches. At some point, after he had been joined by the first disciples, Celano reports a significant discussion they had about their way of life. They were living in a desolate spot among the tombs outside the town of Orte – the *mise-en-scène* recalls the *Life of St Antony* – and they discussed 'whether they ought to live among men, or betake them to solitary places'.[5] In his later years, the compulsion of the solitary life reasserted itself upon Francis, and he increasingly withdrew to a hermitage in the fastnesses of Mount Alverna. But the imagery of the desert fused in his mind with another and more compelling idea. This was the concept of the apostolic life which, as it was now coming to be widely understood, involved an active preaching mission. Celano pinpoints for us the moment when the idea took hold of his mind with overwhelming force. It was some time after his act of renunciation, when he was attending mass at the little church of the Portiuncula outside Assisi. It was the feast of St Matthias, and the Gospel lesson of the day was from Matthew x.7,9, describing the sending out of the Apostles: 'Preach as you go, saying, "The Kingdom of heaven is at hand." . . . Take no gold, nor silver, nor copper in your belts, no bag for your journey, nor two tunics, nor sandals, nor a staff; for the labourer is worthy of his food.' Celano says that when Francis heard this he cried, 'This is what I wish; this is what I am seeking.' And he immediately removed his shoes, made a tunic of roughest material, and began to preach to all the need for repentance.[6]

This model of the apostolic life had been the inspiration of other lay pietistic movements like that of the Humiliati and the Waldenses or Poor Men of Lyons. They too had embraced a life of poverty and devoted themselves to preaching, like many other free-lance evangelists of the time. But Francis went further in his insistence upon poverty. The brethren were to reject even the common ownership of the apostolic Church; they were to wander through the world, sleeping in borrowed barns and shacks, and begging for their daily food. How Francis understood the way of life he had adopted and taught the brethren can be most directly stated in his own words; it was the literal imitation of the earthly life of Christ as depicted by the Gospels: 'This is the life of the Gospel of Jesus Christ which brother Francis asked to be permitted him by the Lord Pope Innocent' begins the second Rule. And in the Testament he explains that 'The Most High revealed to me that I ought to live according to the model of the holy Gospel.'[7] And again, in the Rule[8],

The brothers shall appropriate nothing to themselves, neither a place nor anything; but as pilgrims and strangers in this world, in poverty and humility serving God, they shall with confidence go seeking alms. Nor need they be ashamed, for the Lord made himself poor for us in this world. This is that summit of most lofty poverty which has made you, my most beloved brothers, heirs and kings of the kingdom of heaven.

For Francis this organised destitution, the refusal to own houses, or touch money or accumulate any reserves, was not just a missionary expedient or a means to an end. It was itself the *via salutis* – the literal imitation of the earthly life of Christ, who had nowhere to lay his head. The sole model for his fraternity was to be the Gospel. They said that the first draft of a rule he submitted to the pope consisted of nothing but a catena of texts from the four Gospels.

Francis's story speaks to us of the religious experience of the town-dwelling laity in search of a spiritual identity which was denied them by the traditional monastic theology. His vision was direct, literal, and concrete, uncomplicated by the conceptual analysis of the clerk who had passed through the schools. His apprehension of God always expressed itself in concrete symbols – the speaking crucifix of San Damiano which commanded him to go and repair the church, the living crib at Greccio, and the seraph which left on his body the physical stigmata of crucifixion. These things were symbols of a new orientation of Western religious sentiment, marked by personal devotion to the humanity of Jesus, a concern with the exterior circumstances of his life, and a compassionate identification with his sufferings. The visual symbols expressed a form of direct religious experience which was no longer confined to an enclosed spiritual élite, which ignored the juridical distinction between clerk and layman, and which the teaching of the friars was to make available to the ordinary Christian living in the world.

In its genesis the Franciscan movement was a lay initiative which had sprung from an urban environment. More than in the country-side, great disparities of wealth and poverty were made conspicuous by the crowded conditions of medieval town life. Meditation upon the Gospel and the spectacle of luxury in the midst of destitution had led St Francis to reject the values of the new urban aristocracy. The Franciscan ideal of absolute poverty was a rebellion of the bourgeois conscience. A sense of guilt was manifested by the fierceness with which Francis forbade the brethren to touch money. Their voluntary destitution identified them with the most deprived sections of society. But although they recruited members from all social groups, their chief attraction was understandably to the more affluent middle class and to the clerical intelligentsia. Voluntary poverty was not an ideal that easily appealed to those who were born poor. It is certainly a mistake to regard the friars as an incorporation of down-and-outs. Francis himself and the apostles of the movement were almost all children of well-to-do merchant families. Salimbene, himself a Franciscan of the second generation, observed in his invective against the secular clergy that[9]

> There are many in both orders of friars who, if they had been in the world, would have possessed the prebends they hold, and perhaps much better, for they are just as nobly born, as rich, powerful and learned as they, and would have been priests, canons, archdeacons, bishops and archbishops, perhaps even cardinals and popes, like them. They should recognise that we have given up all these things to go begging.

The Friars Minor did have some early success in recruiting among artisans, but broadly speaking, Salimbene's boast was justified. Their ideal of evangelical poverty attracted substantial numbers of followers from the aristocracy and the urban patriciate. Their most spectacular trawl was among the students and masters of the universities, which brought them an influx of clerical recruits, a triumph fraught with momentous consequences for the future development of the order.

At the beginning, Francis and his disciples were an intimate fraternity of nomadic preachers, some clerics but most of them laymen, who moved from town to town in central Italy, preaching in the market-squares, attending services in the churches, and doing manual jobs or begging for their keep. In 1210 he took his companions to Rome and persuaded Innocent III, not without misgivings, to authorise their activities. Although he does not seem to have formulated any organisational plan at this date, it was in fact the first step in the creation of a new religious order. As numbers grew, it became the practice for the brethren to assemble at intervals and camp round the tiny church of the Portiuncula – a building lent them by the Benedictines of Subasio – where they held a chapter. It was at the Whitsun chapter of 1217 that the decision was taken to launch the brethren on a universal mission. Parties were sent to various countries, provinces were defined and provincial ministers were appointed to supervise them. The composition and style of the party that later founded the English province was characteristic. On the 10 September 1224 a group of nine, consisting of four clerics and five lay brothers, all of them barefooted and penniless, landed at Dover, having been ferried across the Channel by the monks of Fécamp. Three of the party were Italians, including their leader, Brother Agnellus of Pisa. They made their first settlement at Canterbury in a house lent them by the town corporation, and from there they quickly moved on to London and Oxford.

The urban populations were the chosen mission field of the friars. And it was in the towns of Northern Europe that the apostolate of the Franciscans began to take shape. As it did so, the paradox inherent in the idea of St Francis came to the surface and disturbed the order with a prolonged crisis of identity. The attempt to reconcile absolute poverty with the practical needs of a pastoral ministry involved heroic gymnastics of conscience. How could the friars preach and administer the sacraments if they possessed no churches? How could preachers and priests be educated for their task if they had no books and no rooms in which to study? And how could any of these essentials be acquired without funds? In the official Rule – the so-called *Regula Bullata*, which was sanctioned by Pope Honorius III in 1223 and which represented Francis's third attempt to draw up a plan for the order – he had expressly forbidden the brethren to own buildings or to use money. The practical problems posed by this prohibition forced the provincial ministers in 1230 to seek a papal interpretation of the Rule which in effect mitigated its force. They were permitted to appoint a *nuntius* or 'spiritual friend' as a trustee to receive and hold money on behalf of the brethren, to whom they could apply to pay for necessities; they were thus enabled to accept gifts of money, notably the legacies that were showered upon them by their grateful penitents. The papal privilege *Quo Elongati* authorising this concession represents the beginning of the inevitable retreat from St Francis's uncompromising ideal of absolute poverty.

The observance of poverty was not the only problem. The primitive fraternity had been largely lay in its inspiration and membership. There was no distinction of status between clerical and lay members. We do not know at what stage Francis himself was ordained; possibly he was tonsured by the pope in 1210; but he never proceeded beyond the diaconate. Brother Elias, the chosen disciple to whom Francis handed over the direction of the order, remained a layman throughout his life. But the whole concept of a lay ministry conflicted with the sacerdotal professionalism of the medieval Church. As Salimbene, himself an ordained friar, remarked, the hordes of idle lay friars he met in the Italian friaries were useless for the vital pastoral tasks of hearing confessions and dispensing the sacraments. Moreover, as the Friars Minor expanded and made settlements in the towns of Northern Europe, they came under the direct influence of, and in competition with, the Order of Preachers. In Paris, Cologne, London, and Oxford, they found the Dominicans already established; they came up against an order that, like them, was dedicated to poverty and preaching, but which was entirely clerical and had a clearly defined missionary purpose and a fully articulated representative constitution of a kind that St Francis had never envisaged. The problem was accentuated by their success among the scholars of the northern universities, which brought the Franciscans an influx of highly educated clerics.

These tensions culminated in a conflict with the minister-general, Brother Elias, and led to his deposition. In the tradition of the Spirituals, Elias was cast for the role of the Judas who betrayed the ideal of St Francis.[10] Certainly his life-style during his generalate laid him open to criticism. He seems to have developed a taste for grandeur, and abandoned any personal effort to observe the spirit of Franciscan poverty. Salimbene refers indignantly to his plump palfreys, his retinue of page-boys, and the private cook who accompanied him on his travels.[11] But other and more significant charges were laid against him. The attack upon his regime came from the northern provinces, and it was mobilised by a group of friars who were clerks and university graduates, the most prominent among whom was the English scholar Haymo of Faversham. The indictment contained the charges that he had governed the order autocratically and that he had persistently appointed lay brothers to positions of authority as guardians of houses and provincial ministers. There is no doubt that in both these respects Elias was perfectly faithful to the mind of St Francis. But the disapproval of the ministers prevailed, and after presiding over a stormy meeting of the general chapter in 1239, Pope Gregory IX deposed him. His overthrow was quickly followed by a reappraisal of the constitutions and objectives of the order. Leadership passed to the graduate clerical members, and lay brothers were debarred from holding office. In fact the Friars Minor had been subjected to a clerical take-over from within. In the ensuing phase of constitution-making they came under the powerful influence of the Dominican Order, to which we must now turn.

THE ORDER OF PREACHERS

The Order of Preachers differed both in its genesis and its spirit from the early Friars Minor. From the start, it was a clerical and learned order, a stepchild of the canons regular, in which everything was subordinated to the needs of a pastoral mission. It grew out of the situation in the Languedoc, where the founder had become involved in preaching against the Catharist heresy. Dominic was a Castilian priest, probably of aristocratic birth – a late tradition connects him with the noble Spanish family of Guzman.[12] He had been educated at the schools of Palencia, and he was a canon of Osma cathedral, the chapter of which had been reconstituted as a community of canons regular living according to the Rule of St Augustine. It was in 1203, when accompanying his bishop, Diego of Osma, on a diplomatic mission, that he made his first direct acquaintance with the strength of the Catharist heresy in the society of the Languedoc.

At this time the task of combating the Albigensian heresy had been assigned by the pope to the Cistercians; but they had had little success. On their way home in 1206, Dominic and Diego encountered the Cistercian legates at Montpellier, and decided to add their efforts. And here Peter Ferrandus, Dominic's biographer, records a significant conversation between the two parties of missionaries. Diego and his canon argued that the Cistercian abbots were hampered in their mission by their prelatical style and large retinue; only practitioners of the *vita apostolica* could hope to secure a hearing as authentic preachers of the Gospel. It was a question of competing with the *perfect*, the spiritual élite, of the Catharist sect, who were famous for their austerity and self-denial.[13] The apostolic life meant the life of the itinerant preacher, without visible property and dependent upon alms for his food. The two Spaniards persuaded the Cistercian abbots to join them. The bishop set the tone by sending his servants and clerks home with the horses. The party then set out on foot on an itinerant preaching tour, holding public disputations with the Cathar leaders in the towns of the Midi.

It had often been said that the Dominicans borrowed the ideal of absolute poverty – the rejection, that is, of even corporate ownership – and the practice of mendicancy from the Franciscans; but this is an over-simplification. Francis and Dominic admired one another. Possibly they met in Rome. But the mendicant idea was adopted by Dominic and Diego independently at a time when they could scarcely have heard of Francis. To them it was simply the practical application of the twelfth-century notion of the *vita apostolica*, which meant a life dedicated to voluntary poverty and evangelism. It was a perfectly familiar concept to an Augustinian canon like Dominic. In the case of the Dominicans we can see quite plainly the link with current doctrines of the apostolic life, which we only suspect in the case of the Franciscans. Where the Franciscan example may have influenced the thinking of the Order of Preachers was over the question of corporate ownership. In the early years Dominic acquired property in Toulouse where he founded an establishment for the preachers, and Bishop Fulk of Toulouse assigned them a portion of the tithes in his diocese. But the first general chapter of the order, which was held at Bologna at Pentecost in 1220, renounced all its properties in Toulouse and decreed against the acceptance of any properties or revenues for the future. Thus a year before Dominic's death his order declared for the principle of corporate poverty. It is possible, though we cannot be sure, that the decision was prompted by the example of the Friars Minor.

Diego returned home to die; but Dominic continued his activities in the Midi throughout the grim years of the northern Crusade against the Albigenses and the social upheaval that followed it. The house he had established at Toulouse became the headquarters of his preaching mission, where he attracted and trained a community of helpers. The nucleus of a new preaching order had now come into existence, and in the autumn of 1215 he travelled to Rome to seek papal authorisation. His reception at the Curia seems, however, to have been less than enthusiastic. Perhaps out of a desire to stem what now seemed to be an uncontrollable tide of religious experiment, the fathers of the Fourth Lateran Council, which was then assembling, proceeded to decree that, owing to the multiplicity and confusion of orders, nobody was to found a new one; any one who wished to found a new community was instructed to adopt an existing rule already approved.[14] Dominic therefore returned to Toulouse to discuss the matter with the brethren and, as might be expected, chose the Rule of St Augustine, to which he was already vowed. This left him free to plan the structure of the order as he thought best. Papal confirmation, which was obtained from Honorius III in 1216, did no more than authorise the existence of the order and confirm its possessions in Toulouse. It did not ratify any specific rule comparable to that of the Franciscans. The arrangements subsequently enacted by the general chapters, which gave the order its remarkable constitution, were never confirmed by the papacy. Nor was confirmation sought. Officially, the Order of Preachers was simply a branch of the canons regular.

When Dominic approached the Curia, the order was still engaged in preaching in the Languedoc. But in 1217 in a chapter held at Toulouse he announced the decision to scatter. There was a diaspora of the Toulouse community. Some were dispatched to Paris, some to Spain, and some to Bologna. The Preachers were thus launched on a universal mission, a fact proclaimed by a bull of Honorius III issued in 1218, which commended the brethren to prelates everywhere and invoked their support for their preaching efforts. The selection of Paris and Bologna as objectives exemplified a consistent element in their strategy – to capture the leading intellectual centres of their time. The programme was demonstrated by the course of the English mission, which was dispatched by the general chapter of 1221. A party of thirteen led by Gilbert de Fresney landed at Dover and was escorted to Canterbury by the bishop of Winchester, Peter des Roches. There they were welcomed by Archbishop Langton, who then and there invited Gilbert to preach him an impromptu sermon. He offered them a residence in Canterbury, but this was declined. They pressed on to London, and from there to Oxford, which was evidently the goal of their journey. It was among the masters and students of the newly fledged European universities that the Preachers found their most outstanding recruits, and the universities of the thirteenth century were to be the scene of their greatest intellectual achievements.

One of the gifts St Dominic had – one that St Francis conspicuously lacked – was a capacity for organisation. Although the earliest comprehensive body of statutes governing the internal life of the Friars Preachers was not enacted by the general chapter until 1228,[15] the plan they embodied was largely the creation of Dominic himself. In their domestic observance the Preachers retained most of the marks of their monastic origins. As a canon regular, Dominic had followed the usages of Prémontré, and he imposed these on his new order, including choral recitation of the divine office, a daily chapter of faults, and the Premonstratensian penitential code. Some mitigations were admitted to allow for the active role of the Preachers: manual labour was discarded; the liturgy was to be sung 'briefly and succinctly'; and any prior was authorised to dispense friars from parts of the office to enable them to get on with study or preaching. Otherwise the regime was monastic. What was revolutionary was the constitution of the order, which gave effect to the principles of representation and responsibility to an extent then unknown in either the ecclesiastical or the secular world.

The Dominican constitution embodied, in fact, a completely new conception of monastic authority. At every level the superiors of the order were not only elected; they were made responsible for the conduct of their office to their constituents. The basic unit of the organisation was the individual priory or convent. Its head – the prior – was elected by his brethren in chapter. They also elected a companion, a *socius*, to accompany their prior to the annual meeting of the provincial chapter, whose role was to carry a report on their superior to the assembly. The order was divided into provinces, and the head of each province – the prior provincial – was elected by a special session of the provincial chapter, consisting of the heads of individual houses together with two representatives elected for the purpose by each priory. The provincial prior was answerable to the chapter. As the provincial chapter was usually a large body, the Preachers quite early adopted the Cistercian practice of delegating business to a steering committee, in this case of four 'diffinitors', and this committee could receive complaints against the provincial and, if necessary, suspend him from office.

The sovereign body of the order was the general chapter, which met every year at Whitsun. In the early years, it met alternately at Bologna and Paris, the two major intellectual focuses of the Preachers, but after 1243 it chose various other sites for its meetings. The general chapter had, of course, been a feature of some monastic organisations for nearly a century. Where the Dominican chapter differed was in its representative character. It consisted of the master-general, who presided, and one representative elected by the chapter of each province. Since the order established only thirteen provinces before 1300, the general chapter must have been a relatively small body. For two successive years, only the elected representatives of the provinces attended; in the third year, the provincial priors attended instead. This nice balance between the representative and official elements was reinforced by a proviso that any new statute must have secured the assent of three consecutive chapters. Thus, in effect, the official element could exercise a veto. The head of the order, the master-general, was himself elected by an enlarged session of the general chapter. And although he held office until death or resignation, the statutes made him answerable for his stewardship to the chapter, which had the power to correct or depose him.[16] Here then was a completely articulated system of representative government, which apparently sprang fully fledged from the mind of St Dominic and his successor, Jordan of Saxony, in the years 1220–28. It succeeded, in a way that no other monastic rule had done, in institutionalising the ascetical principle of obedience to a superior without recourse to paternalism or prelacy. It proved to be a model that influenced many other ecclesiastical organisations, and not least that of the Friars Minor.

The Franciscans worked out their constitutional arrangements more slowly. To his followers St Francis was a pillar of fire, but he was no legislator. The process of legislation only began in earnest after the fall of Elias in 1239, and it was completed by the code St Bonaventure compiled and presented to the general chapter at Narbonne in 1260.[17] Much of the Franciscan structure of government was borrowed from the Dominicans, including the system of provincial chapters, and election to office. But though their debt to the sister order is obvious, the arrangements of the Friars Minor fell short of the thorough-going system of representation the Dominicans had created. Their general chapter met only every third year, and their general minister was left with less fettered powers of direction; and the process of democratic election to office only operated at the higher level; at the lower level, the guardians of friaries and the heads of the regions called custodies were designated by the provincial ministers. Something of the paternalistic spirit in which the primitive order had been governed still survived in the constitution of 1260.

By adopting much of the Dominican constitution the Franciscans ensured the continuance of the movement St Francis had begun; for the charismatic has to be translated into institutions if it is to survive. And the Dominicans, on their side, by absorbing the Franciscan doctrine of evangelical poverty, acquired from the Friars Minor a characteristic that greatly enhanced their impact upon the lay society of their time. Nor did the process of mutual assimilation and rivalry end there. The Franciscans became, like the Preachers, a clerical order, and after some initial hesitation followed them into the scholastic world of the universities. To both their patrons and enemies, the two orders came to appear almost indistinguishable except by the colour of their habits – the grey or brown habit of the Franciscans derived from the tunic of sackcloth Francis had adopted, whereas the Dominicans wore a distinctive scapular of black over the white habit of the Augustinian canon. At least one bishop – Alexander Stavensby of Coventry and Lichfield – saw no point in having them both in the same town.

THE MISSION OF THE FRIARS

Both orders made the evangelisation of the urban populations the objective of their missionary effort. In France, Germany, and England, a list of the houses they established before 1300 provides a roll-call of all the significant centres of trade and industry. 'The harvest was great of those who lacked the doctrine of salvation', wrote Bonaventure, 'but suitable and faithful labourers were few.'[18] He was defending the strategy against clerical critics who suggested the friars confined their preaching to the towns because it was there they had good residences and were well provisioned. The shaft was unfair, but it was well aimed. Only the towns could support a ministry that relied upon organised begging; for, apart from the nobility, most country-dwellers of the thirteenth century lived too close to subsistence to welcome a troop of mendicants in their midst; it was only townspeople who possessed any significant surplus of disposable wealth. The early residences of the friars consisted of disused and not always salubrious dwelling-houses within the city walls, lent them by individual patrons or, in many cases, by the borough corporations, who generally welcomed them with enthusiasm.

As Bonaventure said, the friars captured a market that was relatively neglected. The success they had with their urban congregations was the result of their effectiveness as preachers and confessors. The homily had long since ceased to be part of the normal experience of the church-going laity. Few of the parish clergy, in fact, had enough education to offer their people moral or doctrinal instruction. It was the achievement of the Mendicants to lead a revival of popular preaching that was just beginning. In their hands, sermon-making became a new art, which was inculcated in their schools and through their writings. To help the preacher perform his task, they produced a large body of didactic literature. This included the theoretical treatise, like *The Instruction of Preachers* by the Dominican master-general Humbert de Romans, replete with general observations and such obvious practical advice as 'keep a middling tempo in delivery, so as not to speak too fast or too slowly; for rushing swamps the understanding of your hearers, and slowness generates boredom'[19] and more technical aids, like the *Art of Preaching* by Thomas Waleys, and collections of model sermons, which began to circulate in large numbers. The early Biblical concordances, which were compiled by Dominicans in the thirteenth century, really belong to this class of literature – their primary purpose was to provide the sermoniser with an arsenal of texts. But the most characteristic sermon-aids were the collections of *exempla* – moralising anecdotes, drawn from the Lives of the saints or from the more workaday world, that a preacher could use to touch his audience in the quick of their experience.

It was not only their methodology that enabled the friars to talk convincingly to city congregations; their message was just as important a factor in their success. There is a sense in which they pioneered the idea of the devout life for the laity; a Christian life, that is, not modelled upon that of monks or dependent upon the vicarious merits acquired by professional ascetics, but one lived fully in the world. They offered a new theology of the secular life, which had its intellectual roots in the discoveries of the Schoolmen who were reappraising the relationship between grace and nature – as Aquinas, the Dominican, was to say, 'grace does not abolish nature, but perfects it'.[20] The new orientation is exemplified by the popularity of a genre of sermon which had made its first tentative appearance in the twelfth century – sermons *ad status*, directed to the particular spiritual needs of different classes: sermons for knights, merchants (a class hitherto despaired of by ascetical writers), masters, servants, apprentices, married people, and so forth, which took full account of their state and worldly responsibilities. This was a genre in which the friars excelled. One of the most interesting features of this preaching, which still awaits full investigation, is a more optimistic and appreciative approach to the theme of married love, a subject that in the past had often evoked virulent anti-feminism from ascetical writers.[21]

The counterpart of evangelical preaching was the hearing of confessions. 'There are some preachers who totally refuse to hear confessions', wrote Humbert disapprovingly; 'these are like farmers who gladly sow, but are unwilling to reap any harvest.'[22] This was the other side of their pastoral work in which the friars achieved great success. They were much in demand by the laity as confessors and spiritual directors in royal and aristocratic courts as well as in the city market-places. This success can be partly explained by superior training: every Dominican priory contained a lector who gave the brethren regular instruction on the theology of penance. But the phenomenon was more complex than that, and here we can do no more than hint at the explanation. Chaucer's gibe at the friar

> He was an esy man to yeve penaunce
> Ther as he wiste to han a good pitaunce[23]

was a half-truth, the product of a century of bitter polemic between the Mendicants and the secular clergy. The fact is, the friars made themselves the chief exponents and practitioners of a new school of moral theology which was developed by the doctors of theology in the schools of Paris. It was a form of casuistry, in the proper sense of the word, which escaped from the strait-jacket of the old Penitentials with their graded tariff of punishments, and placed greater emphasis on the circumstances and intentions of the penitent.[24] Its application made, of course, much greater intellectual and psychological demands upon the confessor than the older system.

From what has been said it is apparent that the pastoral strategy and method of the friars was closely connected with advances in systematic theology that were being made in the schools. They were drawn into the schools by the needs of their mission. Holy simplicity was a vocation for the desert. Preaching to the relatively sophisticated and literate town populations demanded mental agility and learning. The Dominicans had accepted the logic of this from the beginning: 'Study', ran the constitutions, 'is not the end of the order, but is most necessary to secure its ends, namely preaching and the salvation of souls, for without study neither can be accomplished.'[25] The Dominican order of priorities is well illustrated by the entry into the order of John of St Giles in 1229. He was at the time a secular master lecturing in the faculty of theology at Paris. In the course of preaching a university sermon on the evangelical counsels, he referred to the Friars Preachers as the best living exponents of the Gospel. At this point, he interrupted his sermon, left the pulpit and requested the Dominican master-general, who was present, to admit him to the order. His request being granted, he returned to the pulpit wearing the habit of a friar and finished his sermon.[26] This was more than a theatrical demonstration. The order dispensed John from the period of noviciate and allowed him to take his vows immediately, so that he could continue teaching in the theology schools without a break. Clearly he was an important catch for the order. By dispensing him from the normal requirements of their rule, the Dominicans gained for themselves a second chair in the faculty of theology. The same tactic was adopted at Oxford in 1226–27, when Robert Bacon, a secular master in theology, joined them. He too was dispensed from the noviciate, so that he could continue to hold his schools without interruption.[27]

University teaching was only the pinnacle of the academic edifice the friars erected. The Dominican order was organised as a kind of disseminated university. At the base was the priory school with its own lector. The statutes forbade the foundation of a new priory without a trained theologian, whose business it was to lecture to the brethren on the Bible, the *Sentences* of Peter Lombard, and the *Summa* of confession and penance composed by Raymond of Penaforte. No friar was permitted to preach in public until he had studied under a lector for at least three years. Within each province of the order a number of larger priories were given the status of major schools – *studia solemnia* – with a larger teaching staff to teach the subjects of the Arts curriculum. A study of the Aristotelian logic which formed a large part of the Arts course – 'the books of the heathen' as the statutes referred to them distastefully – was a necessary preparation for the study of theology at the advanced level. But the friars refused to allow their men to follow the Arts course in the turbulent society of the universities; they provided the necessary philosophical grounding in their own schools. Those who were groomed for teaching were sent to one or another of the provincial priory schools to hear lectures and take part in disputations until they were ready to embark on the theology course at one of the order's 'general schools' situated in a university. In due course they would incept as masters in the university theology faculty. This co-ordinated academic system was an extraordinary construction without parallel in the Middle Ages. It was far superior to anything that existed for the secular clergy or the laity.

The Franciscans moved into higher education more slowly and at first more reluctantly. There can be little doubt that St Francis never envisaged such a move and that he would have been opposed to it. 'We were unlettered [*idiotae*] and the servants of all', he wrote wistfully in the Testament[28]; and Celano reports him as saying 'My brethren who are led by curiosity for learning shall find their hands empty on the day of retribution.'[29] But the needs of their mission, the example of the Preachers, and above all the attitudes of the masters and students they recruited in the universities, drove them along the same road. For many years after their settlement in Oxford they arranged to have the brethren taught by a succession of secular masters, the first and most distinguished of whom was Grosseteste. The decision to go into university teaching themselves seems to have been made at Paris in the 1230s, when the English theologian Alexander of Hales sought admission to the order, and he was permitted to continue lecturing in the faculty without interruption. But at Oxford, it was not until 1247 that a Franciscan incepted in the theology faculty. This was Adam Marsh, who was already a Master of Arts when he joined the order. After this, the English Franciscan province rapidly developed a scholastic structure closely resembling that of the Dominicans. Its organisation was largely the result of collaboration between Adam Marsh and the provincial minister William of Nottingham, who picked and groomed suitable men to be lectors in friaries throughout the province.

Both the Mendicant Orders thus created an articulated and international system of advanced education. And compared with the secular schools, the system had another important advantage besides that of superior organisation. In the secular schools men taught for a few years and moved on; university teaching was not regarded as a life career. The need to acquire a benefice, to repay patrons, the competition for pupils, and the hopes of a career at the higher levels of Church or state, constantly drew men away from the schools in early middle-life. But when a man became a friar, he opted out of the race for preferment. At the schools he was free to pursue scholarship with a sense of detachment and security hardly open to his secular colleagues. And if he was successful, he might be left to spend his whole life in the academic world. These were propitious conditions for original intellectual work. They go some way towards explaining the fact that in the thirteenth century, the classical age of scholastic theology, it was the friars who produced the most original and creative scholars. The Dominicans Albertus Magnus, Aquinas, and Kilwardby, and the Franciscans Alexander of Hales, Bonaventure, and Duns Scotus, were not only men of creative genius who dominated the intellectual world of their time; they left behind them a huge mass of written work – the fruit of academic leisure and security – which is of permanent and universal significance.

THE CONFLICT BETWEEN THE MENDICANTS AND THE SECULAR CLERGY

To begin with, relations between the friars and the secular clergy were relatively harmonious. The more zealous and discerning prelates welcomed their assistance. Grosseteste, after he became bishop of Lincoln, wrote to the provincials of both orders asking them to supply him with friars who could be used to preach and hear confessions during his diocesan visitations. But as the Mendicants expanded their pastoral activities, began building their own churches, and moved into the schools, they came increasingly into collision with the interests of the secular clergy. Their success as preachers and confessors siphoned congregations away from the parish churches, and of course with the congregations went the flow of offerings and pious bequests, which were diverted into the trust funds administered for the friars. Some of the great urban preaching churches of Europe, like Santa Croce in Florence, embellished with frescos and paved with the monuments of the civic aristocracy, bear eloquent witness to their success in winning the patronage of the thirteenth-century bourgeoisie. The mounting tension was brought to the boil after 1250 when the friars obtained from Innocent IV a privilege permitting anyone, who so desired, to be buried in one of their cemeteries. This breached what had hitherto been a lucrative and jealously guarded monopoly of parish churches.

Many of the secular clergy now began to regard the friars as a threat to their status and livelihood. And their cause found an articulate voice among the secular masters at the university of Paris. Here the dispute began as a straightforward conflict of interests. Papal decree had limited the number of chairs in the theology faculty to twelve at any one time, three of which were reserved to canons of the cathedral. By the process we have seen, the Mendicants had gained control of three chairs, and looked fair to gain a fourth; and their success necessarily reduced the opportunities for secular teachers. But the conflict that broke out was more than a squabble over jobs. The friars were in the university, but not of it; and they tended to sit loose to their obligations towards the academic corporation. The flash-point came in the Lent of 1253. Following a brawl in which a student had been killed by the city watch and others imprisoned, the university decreed a suspension of teaching and threatened to secede from the town unless its privileges were respected. But the friars refused to take part in the demonstration and so were excommunicated and excluded from the university by their enraged colleagues. What had begun as an 'industrial dispute' now developed into a violent controversy, which brought into focus some of the deepest tensions and most revolutionary developments in the structure of the medieval Church.[30]

The leading spokesman of the secular masters, the Burgundian William of St Amour, did not confine his attack to the academic activities of the friars; he challenged their right to exercise any pastoral ministry at all. In his tract *Concerning the Perils of the Last Days*, which he put out in 1255, he took his stand on the theory that the diocesan and parochial structure of the Church was founded upon the Apostles and was of divine ordinance. In this divine dispensation the secular clergy alone were entrusted with the cure of souls, and this was something that no one, be he pope or anyone else, had authority to change. Taking a leaf from the *Hierarchies* of the Pseudo-Denys, he argued that it was the exclusive role of the superior priestly order to perfect and instruct others; monks, including the friars, belonged like the laity to the inferior order of those who received pastoral ministrations; they could not perform the office that belonged to their superiors. Moreover mendicancy was contrary to the example of Christ and the express instructions of St Paul.[31]

In face of this attack, the friars invoked the authority of the pope, who had authorised their ministry, and took refuge behind a paralysing barrage of papal privileges – a strategy plainly contrary to the declared will of St Francis, who had specifically warned the brethren never to postulate privileges from Rome, even for their own protection. They also produced replies to William which expounded a different system of Church order. Bonaventure, at the time a Bachelor of Theology in the Franciscan house at Paris, wrote an apologia based upon an extreme papalist ecclesiology. For him, the pope was not only the universal bishop; he was every man's parish priest. As such, he could delegate his parochial responsibilities to whom he chose; and he had chosen to delegate them to the friars.[32] Thus the controversy resolved itself into two conflicting ecclesiologies: that of William of St Amour, based upon a static hierarchy and the indefeasible rights of local churches within their territorial boundaries; and that of the friars – a dynamic theory, which reflected the rising power of the centralising papacy, and regarded the Church as a single social organism emanating from the pope. It was a theory adapted not only to developments in the organisation of the Church; it also reflected the social and economic changes of the thirteenth century, when the isolation of local communities was being eroded by the growth of international trade and new forms of communication.

William's tract was condemned by Rome, and he was forced to retire from Paris. But the university had only been the cockpit for a quarrel that continued with growing intensity elsewhere. Secure under papal protection, the Mendicants went from strength to strength. In 1281 a Franciscan pope Martin IV, provided them with the privilege *Ad fructus uberes*, which commissioned them to perform all pastoral functions in any diocese or parish without seeking consent from the local authorities. This represented the high-water mark of their privileges, and it led to a prolonged and bitter struggle. It was Boniface VIII who achieved a truce with the states-manlike bull *Super Cathedram* issued in 1300. This decreed that friars might only preach in parishes with the consent of the incumbent; that provincials would present confessors to the bishop, who would license them to act in his diocese; and that the friars might accept requests for burial, but a quarter of legacies were reserved to the parish priest. It was a workable settlement. Papal support saved the mission of the friars. And they in turn made themselves the most thorough exponents of the papalist ecclesiology of the thirteenth century. As centrally directed international orders, devoted to Rome and to the preservation of orthodoxy, they corresponded exactly to the needs of a papacy that was in the process of creating a centralised system of Church government. All the same, the conflict with the secular clergy left a long residue of bitterness, and echoes of the dispute continued to reverberate in England and elsewhere down to the Reformation. In the fourteenth century, regardless of papal privi-leges, writers of manuals of instruction for the parish clergy still ques-tioned whether a penitent who confessed to a friar had fulfilled the canonical requirements for absolution: he would be safer to repeat the confession to his own parish priest. The friars emerged victorious, but not unscathed. Chaucer's friar – the confidence trickster who sold easy penances and traded on the credulity of pious women – was a stereotype lampoon derived, by a process of literary descent, from the bitter polemics of thirteenth-century Paris.

THE ROLE OF THE NUNS

Like the earlier preachers of the apostolic life, both Francis and Dominic attracted women followers as well as men. Dominic's first foundation in the Languedoc was the convent of Prouille for women converts. One of Francis's earliest and most illustrious converts was Clare of Assisi, a girl of aristocratic family who vowed to follow him in the practice of poverty and the imitation of Christ. Jacques de Vitry, who was in Italy in 1216 observed groups of sisters – Minoresses – who worked alongside the Friars Minor ministering to the sick and destitute in the towns, but who lived apart in their own residences.[33] Francis assigned to Clare and her sisterhood the restored church and house of San Damiano just below the walls of Assisi. But if he contemplated any active collaboration by his women disciples in the ministry of the friars, the pressure of social convention and ecclesiastical disapproval must have disabused him. The Rule that Cardinal Hugolino, patron and protector of the Franciscans, gave to Clare and her disciples in 1219 provided for a regime of strict enclosure based upon the Rule of St Benedict.[34] The ideal of voluntary poverty was not a male monopoly, but female mendicancy seemed unthinkable. So Hugolino's Rule reiterated the call to personal poverty, but authorised the sisters to hold common property. This was not how Clare understood her discipleship of St Francis; and she won for herself and the nuns of San Damiano an exemption that allowed them to forgo corporate ownership. But it was a personal privilege that was not applicable to the other convents of the order. The Poor Clares thus became an enclosed monastic order of the traditional type.

The Dominican sisterhood developed in the same way. St Dominic seems to have accepted the fact from the beginning that his women converts would be strictly enclosed, and he gave them a fully monastic constitution based upon the customs of Prémontré. The crucial question which would determine their ethos was that of their relationship to the friars. For a period both the Dominican and Franciscan nuns came close to being cast off by their parent orders of friars and suffering the same fate as St Norbert's sisters in the twelfth century. The Dominican general chapter of 1228 ordered the friars to discontinue their priestly ministry to the women's houses on the grounds that it diverted them from their apostolic mission. But Dominic's own foundations of Prouille and St Sixtus at Rome succeeded in winning exemption from the ruling; and after several decades of struggle, the nuns gained from Pope Clement IV a constitution that accorded them full status as an associate order of the Friars Preachers.[35] The Clares had to overcome the same reluctance of the friars to assume responsibility for their direction. The reluctance was understandable. The preoccupation of the friars was with the evangelisation of the urban laity, and the duty of counselling numerous communities of nuns was a diversion from this task. It was an inescapable paradox that the two Mendicant Orders, which had broken out of the monastic tradition of segregation and enclosure, originated two female contemplative orders which observed a regime of strict enclosure.

OTHER MENDICANT ORDERS

The new pattern of religious life created by the Preachers and the Friars Minor had a compulsive influence upon all subsequent monastic legislators. No order could entirely escape their influence. Several smaller groups of penitents adopted some features of their organisation as well as the practice of mendicancy. Among these were the Trinitarians or Mathurin friars, a group of canons dedicated to ransoming Christian captives of the Muslims, and the Friars of the Cross or Crutched Friars, who were mainly engaged in running hospitals. And alongside these there sprang up in the wake of the mendicant mission a multitude of para-orders, consisting of fraternities of lay people, who engaged in a life of piety and works of charity while continuing to live in their own homes and plying their trades. The Franciscan Tertiaries – the so-called Third Order – was a confraternity of this kind. Its members bound themselves to attend mass regularly at the churches of the Friars Minor and to recite the day hours of the Franciscan breviary. They were given official acknowledgement in 1289 by Pope Nicholas IV who provided them with a rule. But besides these satellite organisations, two other major religious bodies fell under the spell of the mendicant ideal and produced two orders of friars which rivalled the Dominicans and Franciscans in scale and esteem. These were the Carmelites and the Augustinian friars.

The Carmelites and the Austin Friars had one peculiarity in common: they both originated as groups of hermits, and subsequently adopted the ideals and organisation of the Mendicants. In doing this they more or less successfully reconciled the active apostolic vocation of the friars with the contemplative life of the desert. In both of them, however, the original eremitical ideal persisted, often as a hampering or disruptive force. Neither order could point to any clear founder or give a satisfactory historical account of its origins.

The Order of Our Lady of Mount Carmel emerges from legend into history after the middle of the twelfth century, when groups of hermits living in Palestine on the slopes of Mount Carmel began to form an organisation under a common rule. Evidently impelled by the fall of Jerusalem to Saladin and the collapse of the Latin kingdom, they migrated in several groups to the West during the early decades of the thirteenth century, and settled in Sicily, Italy, Spain, and England. According to Eccleston, the Franciscan chronicler, the first contingent to settle in England was brought over by Lord Richard de Gray of Codnor in 1241–42 on his return from crusading in Syria. The earliest settlements were group hermitages located in remote spots like Aylesford in the Kentish weald and

Hulne in Northumberland. But within ten years strains became apparent. Younger recruits pressed the order to adopt an active role of study and preaching after the mendicant pattern. The engineer of the change was the otherwise obscure Simon Stock, an English Carmelite, who was elected general in 1247. Though he had himself come from Mount Carmel, he accepted the demand for the mendicant plan and swung the order on to its new course. The constitutions of the Carmelite Friars, approved by Innocent IV in 1250, were closely modelled on those of the Dominicans. The reconstituted order formally adopted the principle of corporate poverty and mendicancy, and with it, the Dominican structure of provincial and general chapters and the scholastic organisation of the Preachers.

The origin of the Austin Friars was similar, but better documented. They grew out of a congregation of hermits spread over Tuscany, Lombardy, and the Romagna. The leading role in uniting them was taken by St John Buoni of Mantua. After Buoni's death in 1249, leadership was assumed by a party resolved to turn the congregation into an active order of mendicant friars. The process by which the eremitical groups were persuaded to accept this conversion is obscure. Probably not all did so. At any rate, the move had papal encouragement, and the change was accomplished by an ordinance of Alexander IV in 1256, formally instituting the Order of Friars Hermits of St Augustine. They took the Rule of St Augustine as their spiritual identity card, and modelled their constitution on that of the Dominicans. Thus, the Austin Friars, like the Carmelites, moved from their hermitages into the cities and followed the Franciscans and Dominicans into the scholastic world of the universities. In the last forty years of the century, they founded priories in the towns of Spain, Germany, France, and England, but their centre of gravity remained in the Italy from which they had sprung. Italy and Sicily together contained eleven out of the seventeen provinces of the order, and it has been estimated that in the fourteenth century more than half of its membership was based in Italy,

Both the Carmelites and the Augustinians, then, originated as groups of monks following an eremitical vocation. Their conversion into orders of friars attests the powerful impact of the mendicant idea upon the religious consciousness of the thirteenth century. Once the notion gained currency that the authentic imitation of Christ involved an active ministry of preaching, it proved impossible to withstand. But the change in each case meant a radical reorientation – from the secluded contemplative life to an active missionary one. In both orders the attraction of the desert continued to make itself felt. To some extent, the Austin Friars succeeded in accommodating the eremitical life within the framework of their organisation. In Italy, their spiritual homeland, they never wholly lost touch with their original hermitages, where eremitical communities continued to live.

One of the largest and most famous of these, in the forest of Lecceto, near Siena, from time to time received recruits who had retired from the active life of the order. In 1359 an English Austin friar, William Flete, who was a Bachelor of Theology at Cambridge, got permission to retire there as a recluse. Twenty-one years later he wrote to the brethren of the English province. He had been afraid to write before, for fear of reawakening old memories and affections long since put to sleep. The burden of his message was that they should stay out of the universities and not frequent the towns or the castles of the nobility: 'peace in the cell is found; outside it, all is strife'.[36] It was the perennial theme of the anchorite; and obviously, if taken literally, it was contrary to the mendicant idea. The association of the contemplative life with an active missionary order was an uneasy marriage of incompatibles.

NOTES

1. *Thomas de Celano. Vita Secunda S. Francisci* (Quarrachi 1927), p. 141.
2. On this theme see M-D. Chenu, 'Moines, clercs, laïcs au carrefour de la vie evangélique', *Revue d'histoire ecclésiastique* **49** (1954), 59–89; reprinted in translation in *Nature, Man and Society* (Chicago 1968).
3. *The Historia Occidentalis of Jacques de Vitry*, ed. J. F. Hinnebusch (Fribourg, Spicilegium Friburgense, 17, 1972), p. 145. On the social origins and development of the Humiliati see Grundmann, *Religiöse Bewegungen im Mittelalter* (2nd edn 1961), pp. 70–97; and Brenda Bolton, 'Innocent III's treatment of the Humiliati', *Studies in Church History* 8 (1972), ed. G. J. Cuming and D. Baker, pp. 73–82.
4. There is of course a huge literature on this subject. The best modern guides to the critical problems of the sources are J. R. H. Moorman, *Sources for the Life of Saint Francis* (1940); Rosalind Brooke, *Early Franciscan Government* (1959); and M. D. Lambert, *Franciscan Poverty* (1961).
5. *Thomas de Celano. Vita Prima S. Francisci* (Quarrachi 1926), p. 28.
6. *Ibid.*, p. 19.
7. *Opuscula S. Patris Francisci* (Quarrachi 1904), p. 79; translated by Rosalind Brooke, *The Coming of the Friars* (1975), pp. 117–19.
8. *Regula Secunda, Opuscula* pp. 68–9, translated by Brooke, *op. cit.*, pp. 120–5.
9. *Cronica Fratris Salimbene de Adam*, ed. O. Holder-Egger, in *MGH SS* (1913), xxxii, p. 418. On the social catchment area of the Franciscans see Grundmann, *op. cit.*, pp. 157–69.
10. The generalate of Elias has been the subject of important studies by E. Lempp, *Frère Elie di Cortone: Collections d'études et documents* (Paris 1901) iii, and by Rosalind Brooke, *Early Franciscan Government*, pp. 83–105, 137–67. My account is much indebted to these works.

11. *Cronica*, p. 157.
12. The best modern accounts of St Dominic and the origins of the order are those of M. H. Vicaire, *St Dominic and his Times*, translated by K. Pond (1964); P. Mandonnet, *Saint Dominique, l'idée, l'homme et l'oeuvre*, 2 vols (Paris 1937); and W. A. Hinnebusch, *A History of the Dominican Order, Origins and Growth to 1550* (New York 1965).
13. For the organisation of the Cathars see S. Runciman, *The Medieval Manichee* (1947); W. L. Wakefield, *Heresy, Crusade and Inquisition in Southern France 1100–1250* (1974).
14. *c. 9, X De Religiosis III, 36.*
15. Edited by H. Denifle, 'Constitutiones antique ordinis Fratrum Praedicatorum', *Archiv für Literatur-u.-Kirchengeschichte* I (1885), 165–227.
16. *Ibid.*, 214–15.
17. Edited by F. Ehrle, 'Die ältesten Redactionen der Generalconstitutionen des Franziskanerordens', *Archiv für Literatur-u.-Kirchengeschichte* VI (1892), 1–138.
18. *Questio xix: Cur Fratres frequentius praedicant in oppidis quam in abditis locis* in S. Bonaventurae, *Opera Omnia* VIII (Quarrachi 1898) p. 370.
19. *De Eruditione Praedicatorum* in *Humberti de Romanis Opera*, ed. J. J. Berthier (Marietti 1956), II p. 400.
20. S. Thomae Aquinatis, *Summa Theologica* I, Q.I, 8.
21. For mendicant preaching on marriage see D. L. d'Avray and M. Tausche, 'Marriage sermons in *ad status* collections of the central Middle Ages' *Archives d'histoire doctrinale et littéraire du moyen-âge* (1981), 71–119. The problem is also discussed by Dr d'Avray in his Oxford D.Phil. thesis on 'The transformation of the medieval sermon' (1976).
22. *Opera Omnia* II, p. 479.
23. *Prologue to the Canterbury Tales*, line 225.
24. For the whole question of the new moral theology developed by the Paris masters see O. Lottin, *Psychologie et morale aux XIIe et XIIIe siècles* III (Louvain 1949), pp. 329–535.
25. *Opera Omnia* II, p. 41.
26. M. M. Davy, *Les Sermons universitaires parisiens, 1230–31* (Paris 1931), p. 134 & n.
27. W. A. Hinnebusch, *The Early English Friars Preachers* (Rome 1951), pp. 360–9.
28. *Opuscula*, p. 79.
29. *Vita Secunda*, c. 147.
30. The fullest and most up-to-date account of this dispute is that of M.-M. Dufeil, *Guillaume de Saint-Amour et la polémique universitaire parisienne, 1250–59* (Paris 1972). On the structural implications of the controversy see Y. Congar, 'Aspects ecclésiologiques de la querelle Mendiants–Séculiers', *Archives d'hist. doctr. et litt. du m-â.* XXVIII (1961), 35–151.
31. *De Periculis Novissimorum Temporum* in Edward Brown's *Fasciculus Rerum Expetendarum* (London 1690) II, pp. 20–2.
32. *Opera Omnia* VIII, pp. 376–7.

33. *Lettres de Jacques de Vitry* ed. R. B. C. Huygens (Leiden 1960), pp. 71–8.

34. Hugolino's original Rule for the Clares is lost, but as Gregory IX he reissued it in revised form in 1239: J. R. H. Moorman, *A History of the Franciscan Order from its Origins to 1517* (1968), pp. 38–9. On the beginnings of the order see Rosalind and C. N. L. Brooke, 'St Clare' in *Medieval Women* (Studies in Church History, Subsidia I, 1978), pp. 275–87.

35. R. Creytens, 'Les Constitutions primitives des soeurs dominicaines de Montargis', *Archivum Fratrum Praedicatorum* xviii (1947), 41–84.

36. Aubrey Gwynn, *The English Austin Friars in the Time of Wyclif* (1940), pp. 195–6.

Chapter 13

EPILOGUE: THE INDIVIDUAL AND THE COMMUNITY

Most of the forms of the religious life we have described persisted in the later Middle Ages and beyond. But when we enter the fourteenth century there are signs that the traditional version of the coenobitic life, as it was represented by the Benedictine abbeys, was being eroded by a process of gradual decay. The most obvious symptom of this malaise was the decline in the number of monks. As has already been indicated, this reduction in numbers was not so much the result of dwindling applications as of a restrictive policy pursued by the monks themselves.[1] Under the pressure of economic difficulties, many abbeys of Black Monks took a decision to impose a limitation on the size of their community and to restrict the number of recruits. The abbot and monks of Fleury agreed in 1299 to fix their numbers at forty-five.[2] In 1234, the German abbey of Corbie agreed on an optimum number of forty. The monks of Monteliou, in the south of France, fixed their number at thirty-seven in 1340, and agreed on a procedure for the future selection of postulants. The abbot was to choose a postulant to fill the first place to fall vacant, the convent would choose candidates for the next two vacancies, the abbot would fill the next vacancy, and so on alternately.[3] There was a similar arrangement at the Norman abbey of Mont-Saint-Michel, where the community decided in the thirteenth century to fix numbers at forty, so as to keep within its income. There seems to have been no shortage of applicants for the limited number of places available. In the fourteenth century the lay nobility were eager to nominate relatives and protégés; and the abbot was issuing letters expectative, accepting postulants, but imposing delays of four, five, or six years, before they were admitted to the community.[4]

An anxiety to maintain institutional grandeur and domestic living standards at a time of falling real income was the major reason for holding down numbers. But it was not the only one. As has been seen, many of the German abbeys boasted of their aristocratic exclusiveness. The only postulants they would admit were the sons and

221

daughters of the free-born nobility. Reichenau was a case in point. In the past it had contained a community of upwards of ninety. In 1339 it had only eight or ten monks. Pope Benedict XII, who castigated them for their neglect of the divine office, made no doubt that their policy of social exclusiveness was the cause of their decline in numbers.[5]

Of course, the economic difficulties that beset so many of the older abbeys were themselves signs of dwindling social support for the traditional form of Benedictine monasticism. They had ceased to attract significant endowments, and like other landlords, they suffered from the effects of the agricultural recession of the fourteenth century. There were many reasons for this shrinkage of support. The phasing-out of child-oblation deprived the Benedictine houses of their usefulness as repositories for the surplus children of the landed classes. And the adult recruit, if he was highly motivated towards the ascetical life, was likely to be drawn off by the Cistercians or the friars. In general, the life-style of the Benedictine monasteries of the later Middle Ages had some attraction for the sons of the gentry or of the burgher class who were in search of security and status; but it offered no challenge to the fervent aspirant in search of spiritual perfection.

Much has been written about the relaxed discipline in the monasteries of this period.[6] There are widespread indications of a drift away from strict observance of the Rule. It was not a question of scandalous vice – though cases were not unknown – so much as a general dilution of community life in favour of the individual. The most conspicuous breaches in the coenobitic principle were over privacy and individual ownership. In many houses the common dormitory was replaced by individual chambers; monks received a cash allowance from the common fund with which they could buy clothes, books, and luxuries; and the constraints imposed by the rules of enclosure were greatly relaxed. Monastic life in these conditions resembled that of a college of secular clergy. In some abbeys the process was pushed to its logical conclusion by dividing up the properties of the house into prebends to support individual monks.

The decline in numbers and the disintegration of community life were accelerated in the second half of the fourteenth century by the catastrophes of war and plague. The bubonic plague – the Black Death – that swept through Europe in 1348–49, and recurred at intervals, left some communities unscathed, but devastated others. St Alban's lost forty-nine monks including the abbot; the ancient German abbey of Echternach had its community reduced to seven. The Benedictines were not of course the only religious communities that were severely hit by the plague. Mortality was heavy among the friars because their urban location and their ministry to the sick made them especially vulnerable. But unlike the friaries, the worst hit

Benedictine houses rarely seem to have made good their losses. War also took its toll. In the course of the Hundred Years War, many French abbeys and priories were looted and burnt, either by the combatants or by roving companies of freebooters, and communities of monks were dispersed.

One of the features of the decline in monastic observance was the growing practice of commendam. This was the conferment of the title and income of an abbot upon a beneficiary who was not a monk but a secular prelate or even a layman. Normally the commendatory abbot received the headship of an abbey for life, and he would be an absentee. The post was simply a source of income. He might or might not display any interest in the community of monks for which he was nominally responsible. It was a device much used by the Avignon popes and their successors to increase the emoluments of the cardinals. And the power of conferring abbeys in commendam was also assumed by princes, most notably by the kings of France. In the fifteenth century, the practice of appointing commendatory abbots, though unknown in England, became widespread in France, Italy, and Spain. The plight of the great Roman abbey of St Paul's-without-the-walls was typical of that of many others. In 1409 it contained only six monks, two of whom were absent. Its abbot was a cardinal, who had received it in commendam from the pope, and who enjoyed its revenues while residing in his palace in another quarter of the city. Any semblance of regular observance in the abbey had long since ceased.[7] In 1516 a concordat between King Francis I and Pope Leo X reduced commendam to a system of exploitation, by which the king would nominate to vacant French abbeys and the pope would ratify his choice.

Like most abuses, it was a symptom rather than a cause of malaise. It reflected the diminished social esteem for the Benedictine form of coenobitical life; and it was facilitated by the internal situation of the abbeys. The abbot had long since been a prelate with secular responsibilities, occupying a palatial residence apart from his monks, and living off his own portion of the monastic estates. Where, as was often the case, he was presiding over a much reduced group of monks who had adopted the easy-going life-style of a college of secular clerks, the spiritual character of his charge had become largely invisible. In these conditions an abbacy could be regarded as a sinecure, or at best an ecclesiastical benefice like any other, and it was ripe for picking by patrons who wished to use it for their own purpose.[8]

The spectacle of total decay presented by some of the ancient abbeys was not universal. In all parts of Europe Benedictine houses continued to exist where a decent standard of life was maintained. If judged by the literal standard of the Rule, they might be found wanting. Yet it is hardly meaningful to contrast their observance with that of a much earlier age, when the demands and expectations of society were very different. Some idea of the internal life and social role of these establishments can be gained from a recent study of the cathedral priory of Durham in the fifteenth century.[9] Here numbers continued to be maintained at about seventy, of whom some forty were resident at the priory, and the rest were living in the nine dependent cells of the monastery or at Oxford, where the priory had possessed a college for its own monks since the thirteenth century. Recruits, who generally entered the cloister in their late teens, were drawn mainly from the merchant and professional classes and lesser landowners of the region. They were professed after a brief noviciate, and proceeded by the canonical stages to priestly ordination. Many of them were sent to study at the Oxford college. A high proportion of them could expect to be occupied as obedientiaries in one of the priory's administrative posts during their active lifetime. The regular round of choral office was maintained, and besides this, there were the daily community masses and the numerous private masses said for benefactors at the side-altars. Otherwise, the prevailing attitude to collective obligations seems to have been fairly relaxed. Once professed, monks were not bound to eat in the refectory, though the quantity and quality of the food provided may have been an inducement to do so. For the community lived well.

The picture of fifteenth-century Durham that emerges is suggestive of one of the wealthier Oxford colleges of the nineteenth century, when the statutes still required dons to be celibate. Prior John Wessington, who presided over the establishment from 1416 until 1446, kept up a state that a Warden of All Souls might have envied. His lodgings within the priory complex comprised eight rooms, including chapel and hall, where he entertained important visitors. The state bedroom was regally decorated with plush hangings calculated to impress secular guests. His collection of silver plate, stored in the buttery, was engraved with his arms. The stables contained two palfreys for his exclusive use; and his stud of horses was good enough to attract the envious eyes of noblemen. The monks of his community were invited in rotation to dine at his table to sample such luxuries as salmon, oysters, Malmsey, and dates. It is understandable that there was no shortage of nominations for vacant places in the monastery. Membership conferred both security and status. It offered an agreeable life in palatial surroundings, combining religious observances with opportunities for study. It also provided a variety of openings for a man with organisational talents and the possible rewards of prelacy at the summit of a successful career.

Periodic attempts were made to restore a more literal observance of the Rule in the Benedictine houses. The papacy concentrated its efforts upon organisational changes that were designed to maintain standards. The example of the Cistercians suggested the standard of observance and the means to achieve it. With this in mind, the Fourth

Lateran Council of 1215 decreed that those houses of monks and canons that were not part of an organisation with a general chapter were to hold a chapter of their order in each province or kingdom every three years. The heads of all houses were to attend and were to elect one or more of their number to preside over the assembly. They were told to seek advice on procedure from Cistercian abbots. It was a hopeful plan, but it yielded meagre results. The attempt to impose regulations by means of a general assembly conflicted with the jealously guarded autonomy of the Benedictine abbeys and was defeated by their deeply rooted conservatism.

The difficulty of overcoming the forces of calculated inertia can be gathered from what happened in England. The heads of houses in the Canterbury province held their first chapter at Oxford in the winter of 1218–19.[10] The abbots of St Alban's and Bury St Edmund's were elected presidents. Various disciplinary reforms were decreed, which were to be enforced by visitors appointed by the chapter. But after this promising start, the drive for reform lost momentum. The next chapter, called in 1222, ended in fiasco as one of the abbot-presidents failed to turn up. The third meeting, held at Northampton three years later, was attended by only fifteen heads of houses. The chapters continued to meet, but attendance remained poor. During the following 100 years, the constant reiteration of injuctions about silence in the cloister, the need for abbots to mix with their monks in choir and refectory, private possessions, fasting, and abstinence from meat, indicate that the zealots were fighting a losing battle. The general chapters of Cluny held over the same period tell a similar story.[11]

Many of the changes and relaxations that had become an accepted part of the Benedictine life were formally acknowledged and regularised by a series of constitutions issued by Pope Benedict XII in 1336. Himself a Cistercian, the most austere of the Avignon popes, he recognised the need for adaptation of the traditional framework of the Benedictine observance in response to different social pressures. In many ways the role of the Benedictine monks had changed. Their intercessory function was undercut by the growth of chantries served by secular clergy. Those who felt a strong vocation to the ascetical life were looking elsewhere, either to the eremitical orders or to newer kinds of religious organisation which allowed greater scope to the individual. Men with intellectual interests were either absorbed by the schools or drawn off by the friars. What the Benedictine abbeys offered their recruits was security, social status, and a career similar to that of the secular clergy without the distraction of pastoral responsibilities. The constitutions of Benedict XII acknowledged these conditions. They mitigated some of the asperities of the Rule, authorised a reduction in the liturgical offices that had been added in the early Middle Ages, and laid down rules to ensure that the education of monks was not inferior to that of the secular clergy. Every Benedictine establishment was required to provide a qualified master to teach the brethren grammar, logic, and rhetoric – the basic subjects of the Arts curriculum of the universities; and abbots were to send at least one out of every twenty monks to university. This last requirement did no more than place the stamp of official approval upon a practice that had been gathering momentum during the previous eighty years. In the course of the thirteenth century, Cluny and Fleury had both established monastic colleges at Paris, alongside the Cistercian College of Saint-Bernard, and the chapter of the English Black Monks had provided for the foundation of Gloucester College at Oxford. The old dichotomy between the cloister and the schools, so fiercely preached by St Bernard, was forgotten. The monk-graduate was becoming a familiar feature of the scholastic landscape.

Apart from this relatively relaxed version of the Benedictine life which had now gained official approval, a number of groups endeavoured to revive a more austere and literal observance of the Rule. One of these was the Olivetan congregation of the fourteenth century. Its founder, Bernard Tolomei (d. 1348) of Siena, had retired with two friends in search of solitude on Monte Oliveto, a forested promontory twenty-two miles south of Siena, before he turned to the coenobitical life of the Benedictine Rule. In time, Tolomei's hermitage gave birth to a new congregation of abbeys, distinguished by the severity of their observance: the regime involved a sparse diet without meat, continuous silence, and regular manual work. Standards were maintained through a system of strict supervision exercised by the mother-house. In order to ward off the threat of commendatory appointments which had caused havoc elsewhere, the Olivetan customs debarred the holding of office for life and required abbots to be elected for a term not exceeding four years. The Olivetans were largely an Italian group – by 1400 the congregation had eighty-three houses in Italy – and in the fifteenth century they provided the inspiration for another observant congregation which stemmed from the reformed abbey of Santa Giustina of Padua. Here too, abbots were appointed for a fixed term, normally for three years, and the autonomy of individual houses was curtailed by a general chapter, which appointed all superiors. In 1504 the reform of Santa Giustina was adopted by the abbey of Monte Cassino, an accession that brought the congregation added prestige and a new name. North of the Alps, a movement to restore strict observance of the Rule began with the reform of the Austrian abbey of Melk, which imported monks from Subiaco in 1419.

These drives for monastic revival had their successes, but inevitably they fell far short of achieving a universal impact. For, by the fourteenth century, the number of monastic foundations in existence vastly exceeded the needs of those few men and women who were moved by a personal vocation to the ascetical life. Moreover, those who were in search of such a commitment were turning away from a version of monasticism that no longer seemed to meet their requirements. It was not simply a question of relaxed observance. The crisis of coenobitic monasticism in the later Middle Ages had deep roots in the religious psychology of the period. The rise of urban populations had created a new reservoir of recruits to the religious life. And the piety of townspeople, like their social attitudes, was more individualistic, more introverted and more critical, than that of people whose experience was dominated by the immemorial routines and collective work of the countryside. The Benedictine life of the tenth and eleventh centuries was a closely structured life dedicated to collective ritual. It imposed upon the individual a crushing load of vocal prayer and exterior observances in a community environment, which allowed no opportunity for solitude and left little time or energy for private meditation or introspection. Discontent with this form of observance had impelled numbers of people in the twelfth century to break away from existing religious institutions and search for a new kind of regime that was simpler and freer, in which the individual could develop a more inward life of his own. It was the growth of this more individualistic piety, the quest for personal religious experience, in the later Middle Ages that diverted the enthusiasm of the devout away from the structured life of exterior observances that was associated with the traditional Benedictine monasticism.

It was not only the contemplatives who experienced a desire for privacy and greater individual freedom. Many of the relaxations in the regime of the older abbeys, such as the jettisoning of additions made to the divine office in former times, private apartments, and opportunities for study, were a concession to this desire. But the clearest sign of this flight from the constraints of the older type of coenobitical life was the rise of new eremitical congregations like the Celestines. The Celestine Order took its name from Pope Celestine V who, before he became pope in 1294, had founded a group of hermitages in central Italy. He himself was so ill at ease in the world of affairs that he was easily prevailed upon to abdicate the papacy and retreat to his hermit's cell. Another indication of the same trend was the small but steady growth in the number of Carthusian foundations made in the fourteenth and fifteenth centuries. It was an outward and visible sign of the spiritual kinship between the eremitical ideal and the religious individualism of the townsman that at this period patrons of the Carthusians began to erect Charterhouses in the centre of cities like London, Paris, and Cologne.

The quest for the interior life and disillusionment with the traditional structures of the monastic orders took their most striking form in a religious movement that gained rapid ground in the towns of Holland and North Germany in the last two decades of the fourteenth century. The originator of this movement, which became known as the *devotio moderna*, was Gerard Groote, the son of an affluent cloth merchant in the Dutch town of Deventer.[12] After graduating in Arts at Paris and picking up prebends at Aachen and Utrecht, Groote was apparently launched upon a conventional clerical career when, in 1374, he threw it all up to try his vocation with the Carthusians of Munnikhuizen. But having been ordained to the diaconate, he concluded that he was not cut out for the solitude of the Charterhouse and left the monastery. The rest of his life was spent as a preacher and the spiritual director of a growing company of disciples. His fierce denunciations of clerical vice and worldliness gained him few friends in the ecclesiastical hierarchy and in the end, a year before his death, he was forbidden to preach.

The message he gave his followers can be gathered both from their reminiscences and from his own autobiographical writings, letters of direction, and sermons. Although he has been fired by contact with John Ruysbroek of Groenendael, the greatest of the Flemish mystics, and had translated some of his writings, Groote's own teaching bore no resemblance to Ruysbroek's profound analysis of the unitive experience of the contemplative. What he taught was a simple affective piety, based upon devout reading of the Scriptures and regular meditation upon the human life of Christ. It was a plain man's version of the spiritual life, not given to theological speculation and suspicious, if not contemptuous, of intellectual analysis. What mattered was interior conversion, the renunciation of personal wealth and ambition, a humble perseverance in everyday tasks. The main road to perfection lay through voluntary poverty, both material and spiritual. Some of his hottest invective was provoked by the spectacle of convents in which nuns were allowed to enjoy a personal income allotted them by relatives.[13]

The communities of men and women that stemmed from Groote's spiritual crusade embodied this ascetical programme. He had made over his parental house in Deventer to a sisterhood whose way of life was not unlike that of the Beguines. They took no vows and wore no distinctive dress; members of the community were free to leave when they wished. They elected their own superior annually. They earned their livelihood by taking in hand-work. The first of the men's communities was formed with the help of a disciple of Groote's, Florence Radewijns, who held a vicarage in the church of St Lewin, at Deventer. Radewijns's house in Enghe Street became the residence of the first community of what became known as the Brethren of the Common Life. In the following years similar groups sprang up in many of the towns of the Low Countries and North Germany.

Although the Brethren of the Common Life followed a strict

regime of prayer and work, they differed in most other respects from any of the traditional religious orders. In accordance with Groote's mistrust of binding religious vows, they maintained a free association unconfined by vows or any recognised Rule. They included both clergy and laymen on the same footing; and they adopted no distinctive religious habit. Like most ascetical teachers, Groote was convinced of the spiritual value of manual work and, in any case, work of some sort was necessary to support a community, even in the frugal style of men devoted to the ideal of poverty, for Groote abhorred the practice of begging. Possibly it was his own well-attested enthusiasm for books – it was the only form of impedimenta he refused to forgo – that suggested the most suitable kind of gainful occupation for the Brethren. At all events, book production, the copying, illumination, and binding of texts, became their favoured task. It was a trade well suited to their needs: it could be pursued apart from the world, and in silence; and in the cities of Northern Europe there was a buoyant market for the product.

The customs of the Brethren reveal a simple unceremonial regime which combined some of the outward features of the old monasticism with a greater degree of personal independence.[14] They recited (the word used is 'read') the canonical hours in common, but the emphasis was upon the interior prayer-life of the individual. Systematic meditation upon prepared themes was practised at intervals throughout the day: 'When roused from sleep, I rise at once and begin to meditate upon the theme to be prepared . . .. At 7 o'clock I go to the work allotted me, concentrating upon meditating the theme. . . .' Each works, studies, and prays in his own cell. There is no binding rule of silence, but frivolous or useless conversation is to be avoided: 'It is expedient for me to avoid distractions through the day. Therefore I do not wish to leave my cell without cause, nor to go and look for an occasion to talk with guests or strangers, except when advised.' The day closed with supper, followed by Compline. The last act before sleep was the private examination of conscience.

As had happened to the Beguines, groups of men and women living the common life without vows or affiliation to any recognised religious order aroused the suspicion and hostility of the clerical establishment. It was possibly in order to neutralise criticism from this quarter that Groote formed a plan to establish a community of canons regular. There was nothing inconsistent in this. Although he denounced the failings of monks and nuns, he was moved by zeal, not contempt for the monastic life; his letters show that he directed many devout people to the cloister. The Rule of St Augustine, with its generalised precepts about chastity, mutual charity, humility, and obedience, and its lack of specific regulations, clearly commended itself as an appropriate formula for the kind of community that had gathered round Radewijns. The project materialised in 1387, after

Groote's death, with the foundation of a house of Augustinian canons at Windesheim, near the town of Zwolle. The nucleus of the establishment was formed by a group of Brethren of the Common Life, who decided to bind themselves by formal vows.

Groote's mission thus originated two parallel and closely linked movements, one consisting of communities of devout men and women, practising the common life without obedience to any formal rule, plying a trade or teaching children, and living in the world of the small northern towns but not of it; the other a monastic congregation which, outwardly at least, conformed to the traditional norms of a religious order. In the end it was Windesheim that did more to disseminate and perpetuate the spirit of the *devotio moderna*. For it became the mother-house of a large congregation, whose daughter-houses in Germany, France, and the Low Countries far outnumbered the humble communities of the Common Life. By the year 1500, eighty-seven monasteries had been incorporated into its family, and many more had come under its influence. And the piety it practised and taught was what it had received from Groote and Radewijns – a spirituality based upon systematic meditation on the human life of Christ, preoccupied with the interior life of the individual: 'Seek a suitable time of freedom. to yourself; as someone said, whenever I have been among men, I have come back diminished as a man.'[15] 'Be watchful and diligent in the service of God, and meditate frequently on why you came hither.'[16] It was a practical, emotive piety, which inculcated the virtues of humility and hiddenness from the world and was generally impatient with learning and speculation: 'Quietly relinquish an excessive desire for knowledge, for therein is to be found great distraction and deception.'[17] 'What advantage is it to you to dispute profoundly concerning the Trinity, if you lack humility?'[18] These were the commonplaces of the school which found their most famous expression in the *Imitation of Christ* by Thomas à Kempis. Thomas (c. 1380–1471) became a canon of the Windesheim congregation at Zwolle, and his book was really designed for the instruction of novices under his care. Its theme is the interior life nurtured by devout meditation on the human life and passion of Christ. Conceptually it was not original, but it expressed the essence of the *devotio moderna*; and it outlived its immediate purpose, to become a classic of Christian literature.

'If anyone should ask you to what religious order you belong', wrote Stephen of Muret to the Brethren, 'tell him the order of the Gospel, which is the basis of all rules.'[19] To the modern observer of the medieval centuries, the most astonishing thing is the rich variety of religious institutions that sprang from meditation upon an identical premiss. These varied forms of monastic and para-monastic organisation provided an institutional framework for every type of religious experience between the two poles represented on one hand by the total isolation of the hermit, and on the other by the active pastoral mission of the friars. As we have seen, the claims of the eremitical and the coenobitical life were not mutually exclusive. The Benedictine abbeys trained and sent out anchorites; the Order of Camaldoli institutionalised the practice; and the Carthusians reconciled the vocation of the solitary with his need for the support of a community. As St Benedict had appreciated, the individual who moved out of a religious community to live in a hermitage was not necessarily demonstrating discontent with the coenobitic life. He might be moved to become a recluse by a process of personal spiritual development that could only find ultimate fulfilment in solitude, away from the closely structured regime of the community.[20]

Nevertheless, the decay of many ancient monastic establishments, accompanied by new experiments in community living, point to a prolonged crisis in the religious life of the later Middle Ages. And this crisis was only one part of a turmoil that afflicted the ecclesiastical world as a whole. For there was always a dialectic between monasticism and the world the monk had abandoned. The forms taken by religious institutions at different periods were conditioned by the demands and expectations of the society that supported them. And the great social and economic changes that overtook Western society after the middle of the thirteenth century, especially the growth of urban populations, produced a new kind of religious sentiment, which experienced the ascetical vocation as primarily a search for individual fulfilment. For many people, both among the clergy and the educated laity, the traditional forms of the coenobitic life did not seem to offer a way of satisfying this aspiration. Orthodox critics as well as heretics accused the monks of idleness and excessive wealth. And this dissatisfaction was deepened by a widespread disillusionment with the institutions of the secular Church, whose claims to spiritual authority were weakened by a manifest failure of hierarchical leadership, culminating in the disaster of the Great Schism.

A few sought refuge in the hermit's cell; some found fulfilment of their ideal in free religious associations like the Brethren of the Common Life; others, of whom St Catherine of Siena was a conspicuous example, found a way to fulfil their spiritual vocation as lay people in the secular world, pursuing the contemplative life but standing outside the organised religious institutions of their time: 'my cell', she wrote, 'will not be one of stone or wood, but that of self-knowledge'. The monastic bodies that continued to flourish were those which succeeded in accommodating this quest for personal identity.

The crisis of the fifteenth century was not a terminal disease, for both the eremitic and the coenobitic forms of monastic life survived the storms of the Reformation, and both are still with us. But

monasticism survived by undergoing an exterior and interior transformation. Because associations devoted to the performance of
liturgical ritual no longer met the religious demands of society nor
provided convenient homes for its surplus children, and because the
number of monastic establishments vastly exceeded the needs of
those few who had a personal vocation to the ascetical life, social and
economic support fell away; the number of monasteries dwindled,
and monastic property was transferred to other purposes. In England
the process was a catastrophic event, involving many personal trage-
dies. Within the cloister itself, there was a necessary adjustment
between the needs of the individual and the claims of the community.
Such adaptations were made inescapable by changes in the outside
world: a Rule designed for monks in late antiquity or in the twelfth
century could not be applicable in every detail to recruits of a later
age, whose intellectual and psychological formation was very
different. As Stephen of Muret had observed, no Rule was absolute
except that of the Gospel, which was the starting-point of the
monastic ideal.

NOTES

1. Above, Ch. 7.
2. Figures from U. Berlière, 'Le nombre des moines dans les anciens
    monasteres', *Revue bénédictine* XLI (1929), 231–61; XLII (1930), 19–
    42.
3. 'Le recrutement dans les monastères benedictins aux XIIIe et XIVe
    siecles', *Academie royale de Belgique, Classe des lettres, Mémoires*,
    XVIII (1924), fasc. 6, p. 13.
4. Nicole Simon, 'L'Abbaye au XIVe siecle' in *Millénaire monastique du
    Mont Saint-Michel*, ed. J. Laporte (Paris 1966) i, pp. 174–9.
5. Berlière in *Revue bénédictine* XLII (1930), 21. Cf. the discussion of the
    aristocratic element by F. Rapp, 'Les abbayes, hospices de la noblesse:
    l'influence de l'aristocratie sur les couvents bénédictins à la fin du
    Moyen-Age' in *La Noblesse au Moyen Age*, ed. P. Contamine (Paris
    1976), pp. 315–38.
6. For example P. Schmitz, *Histoire de l'ordre de Saint Benoit* iii (Mared-
    sous 1948), pp. 63–86; M. D. Knowles, *The Religious Orders in
    England* (1955) ii, pp. 167–74.
7. I. Schuster, *La basilica e il monasterio di S. Paolo fuori le Mura* (Turin
    1934).
8. On the history of commendam see *Dictionnaire de droit canonique* ed.
    R. Naz, III (Paris 1942), 1029–85.
9. For this and the following paragraph see R. B. Dobson, *Durham
    Priory 1400–1500* (1973).
10. See W. A. Pantin, ed. *Chapters of the English Black Monks* (Camden
    Society 3rd series, xlv, xlvii, and liv, 1931–37).

11. G. de Valous, *Le Monachisme clunisien* (Ligugé-Paris 1935) i, pp. 271–4.

12. On Groote see T. P. Van Zijl, *Gerard Groote, Ascetic and Reformer* (Catholic University of America, Studies in Mediaeval History, NS No. 18, 1963), and the authoritative study of Georgette Épinay-Burgard, *Gerard Grote, 1340–84, et les débuts de la Dévotion moderne* (Veröffentlichung des Instituts fur europäischen Geschichte, 54 Mainz 1970); his sermons are edited by J. G. J. Tiecke, *Werken van Geert Groote* (Gronigen 1941); his letters by W. J. M. Mulder, *Gerardi Magni Epistolae* (Antwerp 1933). For the Brethren of the Common Life see E. F. Jacob, *Studies in the Conciliar Epoch* (1943), pp. 121–38.

13. *Epistolae*, no. 45, p. 177.

14. *Consuetudines Fratrum Vitae Communis* ed. W. Jappe Alberts (*Fontes Minores Medii Aevi*, No. 8 Gronigen 1959).

15. Thomas à Kempis, *De Imitatione Christi* i, c. 20.

16. *Ibid.* i, c. 25.

17. *Ibid.* i, c. 2.

18. *Ibid.* i, c. 1.

19. *Sermo de unitate diversarum regularum*: E. Martene, *De Antiquis Ecclesiae Ritibus* iv (Antwerp 1728), p. 877, cited by M. D. Chenu, *Nature, Man and Society* (Chicago 1968), p. 239.

20. Cf. the observations of G. Constable, 'Eremitical forms of monastic life' in *Atti della settimana internazionale di studi medioevali Mendola, 1977* (Milan 1980), pp. 263–4.

GLOSSARY

Accidie term used in ascetical literature for spiritual sloth, boredom, and discouragement.

Advocate lay protector and legal representative of a monastery.

Almoner officer of a monastery entrusted with dispensing alms to the poor and sick.

Ambulatory aisle or passage-way encircling the choir of a church.

Anchorite a solitary or hermit.

Antiphoner a choir-book containing the liturgical chants used in singing the canonical hours.

Apostolic life the manner of life followed by the Apostles, especially as it was understood in the eleventh and twelfth centuries.

Appropriation legal act by which a parish church with its endowments were donated to a monastery, which appointed a vicar or chaplain to perform the pastoral duties.

Apse semicircular or polygonal east end of a church, terminating the chancel.

Arch-cantor early title for choirmaster in a greater church, e.g. St Peter's, Rome.

Archdeacon subordinate of a bishop with responsibility for supervising the diocesan clergy and holding ecclesiastical courts within his archdeaconry, i.e. in the territory of his jurisdication.

Ashlar large blocks of dressed stone used in building.

Austin The English form of the name 'Augustinian' as in 'Austin Friars', i.e. friars following the Rule of St Augustine.

Benedictional a liturgical book containing formulas for blessing of people and objects.

Benefice a permanent ecclesiastical living.

Brautmystik a type of mysticism that expresses itself in the imagery of human espousal.

Breviary book containing the complete order of the divine office for every day.

Calefactory warming-room in a monastery.

Canonical hours the services sung or recited at the seven fixed times of the day; cf. *Opus Dei*, office, etc.

Canonical penance periods of penitential discipline, usually expressed in days or years, imposed for various sins as set out in the ancient Penitentials, q.v.

Canons regular communities of clergy following a monastic rule, especially the Rule of St Augustine, see Ch. 8.

Cantor monk or clerk whose liturgical function is to lead the choir.

Capitulary term used for written decrees or instructions issued by the Carolingian rulers of Gaul.

Capitulum Latin term for a chapter, e.g. of the Bible or of the Rule of St Benedict, and hence for the daily assembly in a monastery at which a chapter of the Rule was read, cf. **chapter**.

Cartulary a book or register containing copies of the deeds or charters relating to the lands, churches and other properties of a monastery, or of any other establishment.

Casuistry a system of moral theology which takes full account of the circumstances and intentions of penitents and formulates rules for particular cases.

Catharist related to the dualist heresy of the Middle Ages which regarded the flesh and the world of physical phenomena as intrinsically evil.

Cellarer officer of a monastery entrusted with the general provisioning of the community.

Census a form of regular money tribute paid by some monasteries to Rome; also paid to Cluny by its dependent houses.

Chancel the eastward section of a church, containing the main altar and choir.

Chancery the secretarial office of a king or bishop.

Chapter the daily assembly of a monastic community at which a chapter of the Rule was read, faults were confessed, and business was transacted. Also the term for a body of clergy serving a cathedral.

Chapter-house the special hall in a monastery, normally situated adjacent to the church on the east side of the cloister, where the daily chapter was held.

Chevet the east end of a church, comprising chancel and apse.

Circatores name given to the roundsmen at Cluny and some other monasteries, whose function was to perambulate the premises at intervals to ensure that the Rule was being observed and that nothing irregular was taking place.

Civitas a Roman city, with its own municipal government, which in many cases became the location of a bishop's see.

Claustral prior the abbot's second-in-command, responsible for the internal life of the monastery.

Co-arb co-heir of the founder of a Celtic monastery – the usual position of the abbot of an Irish monastery.

Coenobitical the term for monastic life in community, as opposed to the life of hermits; cf. **eremitical**.

Collegiate Church a church served by a corporation or college of clergy, of which a cathedral is one type.

Commendam in the later Middle Ages, the practice of granting the headship of a monastic house as a perquisite to a secular clerk or bishop.

Compline a short service, the last of the day offices, which terminates the monastic day.

Confraternity association with a monastic community granted to the member of another monastery or to a lay person, conferring a special commemoration in the prayers of the community and a share in its spiritual privileges.

Conventuals the name given to that section of the Franciscan Order that accepted the need to modify the practice of absolute poverty enjoined by St Francis, so as to build churches and permanent friaries.

Conversus: (i) an adult convert to the monastic life, as opposed to one reared in the monastery from childhood. (ii) a lay brother, especially a Cistercian lay brother, see Ch. 9.

Corrody a pension, in the form of board and lodging or money, or both, granted to a lay person by a monastery, often at the request of the king or patron of the house, who billeted retired servants and retainers on the monastic establishment in this way. Hence 'corrodian' – the recipient of such a favour.

Crossfigill an ascetic exercise practised by Celtic monks, which involved standing in prayer for long periods with the arms outstretched in the form of a cross.

Custodian in the Franciscan Order, the head of a custody, the subdivision of a province.

Custody in the Franciscan Order, the subdivision of a province.

Custumal a book setting out in detail the practice of a particular monastery, with instructions for the celebration of the divine office and for the other activities of the monastic day, compiled to supplement the general prescription of the Rule. Also a compilation recording the manorial customs and rents due from an estate.

Dean(i) in early monastic use, a monk appointed by the abbot to supervise a group of ten brethren; (ii) at Cluny, a monk officer in charge of one of the abbey's granges; (iii) in general ecclesiastical use, the head of a cathedral chapter; also the senior priest and supervisor of a rural deanery.

Decretum a common title for a collection of canon law, arranged thematically, in use from the eleventh century onwards.

Demesne that part of an estate that a landlord retains in his own hands and exploits directly, as opposed to portions of the estate that are leased to tenants.

Devotio moderna a form of individual piety that originated in the Low Countries in the late fourteenth century and is associated with the teaching of Gerard Groote of Deventer (1340–84) and the Brethren of the Common Life. Its characteristics were an affective devotion to the person of Jesus, fostered by meditation, indifference to the institutional aspect of the Church, and mistrust of theological speculation.

Diffinitors a term used by the Cistercians and the Dominicans for those members of the general chapter who drafted legislation and steered the assembly.

Diploma technical term for an elaborate type of charter used in the early Middle Ages to confer land or privileges, characterised by a pious and often lengthy preamble and clauses anathematising those who in any way diminish the gift.

Dorter the monks' dormitory.

Dowry in monastic use, a gift of land or an entrance fee, normally exacted by a nunnery as a condition of accepting a new member. Canon law forbade the exaction of dowry, but permitted voluntary gifts. In the case of men's houses, it was normal practice for a postulant to bring an endowment with him, see Ch. 7.

Eigenkirche the German expression for a church in private ownership, or a proprietary church – the condition of most rural churches in the early Middle Ages.

Eremitical the mode of monastic life followed by hermits, either singly or in groups, from the Greek *eremos*, meaning a desert, see Ch. 1., as opposed to monastic life in community.

Eucharistic prayer the central prayer of the mass.

Evangelical counsels the recommendations found in the Gospels to embrace celibacy, poverty, and obedience, as a means to attain spiritual perfection, which formed the basis of the monastic life.

Exemption a privileged status obtained by some monasteries which freed them from the jurisdiction of their local bishop and made them directly subject to the papacy.

Familia The household establishment of a bishop or abbot, consisting of his clerks and domestic servants.

Filiation a monastic organisation that made each monastery responsible for supervising its daughter foundations; a group of abbeys linked in this way to a common mother-house – a system developed by the Cistercians, see Ch. 9.

Florilegia an anthology, especially one of patristic texts; such collections were widely used by medieval theologians.

Garth the open central space, normally a quadrilateral, enclosed by a cloister.

General chapter an assembly comprising the heads or representatives of all the houses, or of all provinces, of a religious order.

Glebe land constituting the endowment of a parish church.

Grange a monastic farm settlement at some distance from the abbey, supervised by a monk and staffed by lay brothers, created to cultivate one of the abbey's estates.

Guardian in the Franciscan Order the superior of a friary.

Gyrovagi a pejorative term for wandering monks or clergy, who lived the life of professional guests, a term used by St Benedict and subsequent medieval writers.

Hundred in England, a subdivision of the shire for administrative and judicial purposes with its own court, which originated in the Anglo-Saxon period.

Indulgence a commutation of a certain period of canonical penance, authorised by a bishop, enabling the penitent who had repented and confessed his sin to substitute for his penance some specified acts or works of charity, such as pilgrimage to a shrine or a contribution to the building of a church.

Infirmarian officer of a monastery in charge of the infirmary.

Infirmary part of a monastery, commonly situated to the east of the main complex, with its own dormitory, chapel, and refectory, which housed the monks who were sick or who were too old and infirm to take part in the normal monastic round.

Interdict a sentence laid upon a territory or an establishment, ordering the administration of the sacraments and all public liturgical rites to cease until such time as the sentence has been lifted. An exception was normally made for the baptism of infants and the absolution of the dying.

Introit verses of Scripture, often from the psalms, sung at the beginning of the mass, varying according to the day of the year.

Judge-delegate a prelate commissioned by the pope to hear and determine an ecclesiastical case locally in its country of origin.

Lauds the service of the divine office immediately following Matins. (Confusingly, it is commonly called 'Matins' in medieval texts.)

Laura the term for a type of eremitical settlement first found in Palestine and Egypt, in which the cells or caves of the ascetics are clustered round a common centre.

Laus perennis a practice, found in some Gallic monasteries of the seventh century, by which successive choirs maintained throughout the day and night a continuous and unbroken round of psalmody and liturgical song.

Lectio divina 'sacred reading', i.e. the reading of the Scriptures and the Fathers prescribed by the Rule of St Benedict as one of the most important occupations of the monastic day.

Lectionary a book containing the lessons to be read in choir during Mass and the divine office.

Lector 'reader', i.e. one who has been ordained to the minor order of lector; in a monastery, the monk entrusted with reading the lessons in church or in the refectory.

Legate an ambassador, usually a cardinal, dispatched by the pope to a territory with plenary powers (some archbishops, including the archbishops of Canterbury, claimed to be *legati nati* or standing legates in virtue of their office).

Legenda 'legends', viz. readings or lessons from the Lives of the saints, especially those used in the second Nocturn of Matins on saints' days.

Liber vitae a book kept in a monastery, often placed on the altar, in which were inscribed the names of benefactors and all those who had a particular claim upon the intercessory prayer of the community.

Martyrology a list of the martyrs, read during the office of Prime.

Master-general the head of the Order of Preachers or Dominican Friars.

Matins the first office of the day, sung during the night, commonly called Nocturns in medieval texts.

Mendicant Orders i.e. begging orders, the general term for the orders of friars, so called because they refused to own corporate property and depended upon organised begging for their support.

Mensa term used of that part of a monastic estate that was allocated to the direct support of the community and to supplying its table.

Metanoia a term used in ascetical literature for interior conversion and change of heart, involving the orientation of the personality towards God.

Minister-general the head of the Franciscans or Friars Minor.

Minor orders the four lesser orders to which a man might be ordained i.e. those of acolyte, lector, exorcist, and doorkeeper, as opposed to the three major orders of priest, deacon, and subdeacon. In medieval canon law celibacy was only required of those in major orders.

Minorite a Friar Minor or Franciscan.

Missal a book containing the complete order of mass, including both the 'ordinary' (unvarying parts) and the 'proper' (the parts that varied according to the liturgical calendar). In the early Middle Ages the proper of the mass was distributed over a number of separate books, such as the lectionary which contained the lessons, and the gradual which contained the chants.

Missi a term used in the early Middle Ages for emissaries or inspectors-general sent out by the king.

Mixed rule an expression denoting monastic practice, especially in the seventh century, by which religious communities followed observances taken from several Rules, especially from those of St Benedict and St Columbanus, rather than any single Rule.

Neophyte a novice or new recruit.

Nocturns sections of the office of Matins. In the monastic office each Nocturn consisted of three Psalms followed by four lessons; on important festivals Matins comprised three such Nocturns and thus included twelve lessons. In medieval texts Matins is commonly called Nocturns.

Nones the liturgical office sung or recited at the ninth hour of the day, i.e. at about 3 p.m.

Novice a member of a monastic community under training who has not yet taken vows.

Noviciate the period of training undergone by a recruit before taking monastic vows. The Rule of St Benedict prescribed a noviciate of one year before a recruit was permitted to make his profession.

Nuntius in Franciscan usage, an intermediary or trustee authorised to receive and hold monies donated to the friars.

Nutritus a monk reared in a monastery from childhood (see **oblate**), as opposed to a *conversus* – an adult convert to the monastic life.

Obedientiary a monk in charge of one of the administrative departments of a monastery, such as the cellarer, the sacrist, or the infirmarian.

Obit a commemoration, often in the form of mass, celebrated on the anniversary of a person's death, especially for deceased benefactors and members of a religious community.

Oblate a person given in childhood to a monastic community by his parents, to be brought up as a monk. The practice of child-oblation is already in evidence in the Rule of St Benedict.

Octave the eighth day, or the period of eight days counting inclusively, that followed a liturgical festival.

Office or 'divine office', the services sung or recited at the canonical hours of the day. The monastic office was somewhat longer than the office sung in secular churches.

Official a legal officer appointed by a bishop or an archdeacon to perform certain acts on his behalf. In the thirteenth century the bishop's Official presides over the diocesan court, and the archdeacon's Official presides over the tribunal of the archdeaconry.

Opus Dei 'the work of God' – the expression used by St Benedict to refer to the divine office (see **office** above).

Opus signinum a crude type of mosaic paving used in Roman houses in late antiquity.

Orders the various grades of the Christian ministry, viz. the four minor orders of acolyte, lector, exorcist, and doorkeeper; and the three major orders of priest, deacon, and subdeacon.

Ordinal a liturgical book containing the rites used in ordination.

Ordo (pl. *Ordines*) a book of directions, describing the ceremonies for the celebration of mass and other liturgical rites, Also a book setting out the order of the divine office for every day of the year.

Pallium a yoke-shaped band of white wool, embroidered with crosses, worn by the pope and also by some archibishops, symbolising in the latter case the delegation to them of metropolitan jurisdiction over the other bishops of their province. It was conferred by the pope and normally had to be collected from Rome in person.

Paruchia in the usage of the early Celtic Church, the area and the churches, including distant territories, over which a monastery had spiritual jurisdiction.

Peculiar term for a parish or other area not subject to the jurisdiction of the bishop within whose diocese it is situated, but subject to the jurisdiction of a bishop or some other ecclesiastical body in another diocese.

Pelagian relating to the heresy of Pelagius (*c*. 354–*c*. 419), who denied the transmission of original sin and emphasised the primacy of human endeavour in achieving salvation.

Penitential a treatise setting out the penances, or acts of satisfaction, appropriate to various sins, which a penitent was required to perform after he had repented and confessed his faults to a priest. Similarly, the section of a monastic Rule that prescribed penances for various faults or breaches of monastic discipline.

Placebo et dirige the first words of the opening antiphons of Vespers and Matins respectively in the Office of the Dead; hence, in medieval usage a term denoting the entire Office of the Dead.

Polyptique term for an early type of written survey or description of an estate.

Postulant a person seeking admission to a religious order.

Praepositus literally 'a person placed at the head of others' or provost: the term used in the Rule of St Benedict to denote the prior (see **prior** below).

Prebend a portion of the property or income of a cathedral or collegiate church allocated to a canonry in such a church.

Precentor a cathedral dignitary responsible for the choir and the liturgical functions in the cathedral church.

Preceptory a house of the Knights Templars.

Prime the liturgical office sung or recited at the first hour of the day, i.e. at sunrise.

Prior in an abbey the second-in-command or officer next in rank after the abbot; the superior of a religious house that did not have the status of an abbey.

Proctor a legal representative of any person or bodies of persons able to act for them in the ecclesiastical courts.

Proprietary church a church in private ownership, the property of a landlord or of a monastery – the condition of most rural churches in the early Middle Ages (see *eigenkirche* above).

Provincial or 'provincial minister', the superior in charge of a province of the Friars Minor; in the case of the Dominicans called a 'prior provincial'. The name and the office has been adopted by many subsequent religious orders.

Quadragesima literally 'the fortieth': the Latin term for Lent, a period of approximately forty days (in fact forty-six days) before Easter.

Quinquagesima the last Sunday before the beginning of Lent.

Rabbinics the study of Jewish law and theology.

Rector in medieval canon law the incumbent of a parish who is entitled to receive the great tithe. Where a parish church had been appropriated to a monastery (see **appropriation** above), the monastery became the corporate rector of the church.

Reeve an officer placed in charge of a borough or, on a manor, a peasant foreman appointed to superintend the peasant labour force.

Refectory the dining-hall of a monastery.

Regular clergy clergy who are monks, living under a monastic Rule (*regula*), as opposed to secular clergy who live in the world and do not belong to a religious order.

Regularis Concordia the concordance or code of monastic rules compiled for the English Benedictine houses in the year 970.

Reliquary a vessel or container, often made of precious metal and richly ornamented, used to contain the relics of a saint.

Rere-dorter the lavatory of a monastery, so called because it was usually situated at the back or far end of the dormitory.

Retro-choir part of a church at the east end of the choir, behind the high altar, commonly used as the location for the shrine of a saint.

Rood-screen screen dividing the nave from the choir of a church, so called because it was normally surmounted by a rood or crucifix.

Sacramentary a type of liturgical book used in the early Middle Ages, containing the prayers said by the celebrant of the mass and the other sacraments. The lessons and the verses sung by the choir were contained in separate books.

Sacrist the monastic officer responsible for the altars, sacred vessels, and fabric of the church.

Scapular part of a monk's dress, consisting of a broad band of cloth, open at the sides and hanging down front and back, worn over the habit.

Scholasticus the clerk in charge of a cathedral school, called in some cathedral bodies the chancellor.

Scriptorium the room or other place in a monastery where writing was done and manuscripts were copied.

Secular canons the secular clergy serving a cathedral or collegiate church, as opposed to canons regular, who were clergy living under a monastic rule.

Sext the liturgical office sung or recited at the sixth hour of the day, i.e. about midday.

Socius literally 'companion'; among the friars, a fellow-friar elected to accompany the provincial to meetings of the general chapter.

Spirituals the name given to that section of the Franciscans that refused to modify the instructions of St Francis on absolute poverty and who consequently refused to possess permanent buildings, as opposed to the 'Conventuals' who accepted the need to compromise in this respect.

Studium generale a term of art, which appeared in the thirteenth century, denoting a school of universal status, used especially of universities. In canonical theory it indicated a privileged status which could only be conferred on a school by the pope. Its special mark was the right of its graduates to teach in any other school of Christendom without further examination.

Stylite an ascetic who lived on top of a pillar.

Temporalities the landed estate and other properties belonging to a church or religious body, especially the estates of a bishopric, in respect of which the bishop owed secular duties to the king.

Terce the liturgical office sung or recited at the third hour of the day, i.e. about 9 a.m.

Tertiary a member of a Third Order, a confraternity of lay people attached to the friars, who bound themselves to follow certain religious observances of the friars, including recitation of the day hours of the divine office.

Tithe a tenth part of the produce of the land and the product of labour which had to be paid to every parish church. Monasteries generally secured exemption from payment of tithes from their land.

Tithing any group of ten persons; in early monastic usage, a group of ten monks supervised by a monastic officer called a dean. It was a means of devolving command in large religious communities.

Tonsure the ritual clipping of the hair of the head by which a young man received clerical status.

Troper a musical book containing chants used in the liturgy other than those contained in the antiphoner.

Translation in the case of a bishop, his transfer from one see to another, a change which in classical canon law could only be authorised by the pope. The term was also used to describe the process by which the bodily remains of a saint were removed from their tomb to a place of honour above or behind the altar of a church. Originally it was an act that signified canonisation; from the thirteenth century, it was a solemn act carried out following canonisation by the pope.

Vespers the liturgical office of the evening, otherwise called Evensong.

Vicar the incumbent of a parish church which has been appropriated to a monastery or some other ecclesiastical body which receives the great tithe. The vicar receives a fixed portion of the endowments of the parish and offerings, and once instituted by the bishop, he enjoys security of tenure; hence a 'perpetual vicarage', meaning a benefice of this kind.

Vigils in early monastic literature the term for Matins, i.e. the office sung during the watches of the night.

Vita apostolica see **apostolic life** above.

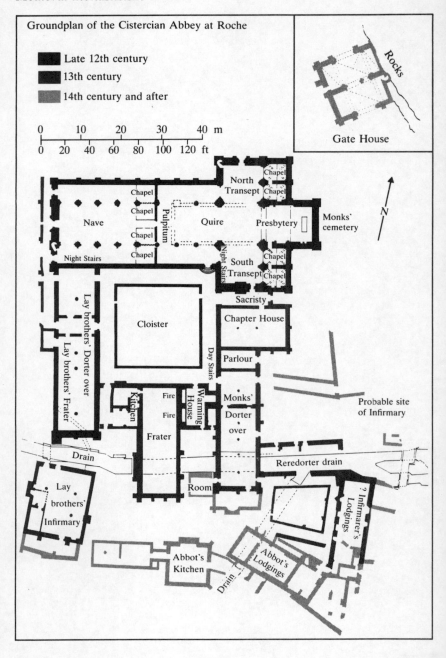

Groundplan of the Cistercian Abbey at Roche

■ Late 12th century
■ 13th century
■ 14th century and after

0   10   20   30   40 m
0 20 40 60 80 100 120 ft

Rocks

Gate House

North Transept

Chapel
Chapel

Chapel
Chapel

Nave

Pulpitum

Quire

Presbytery

Monks' cemetery

N

Night Stairs

Chapel
Chapel

Chapel
Chapel

Night Stairs

South Transept

Chapel

Sacristy

Lay brothers' Dorter over

Lay brothers' Frater

Cloister

Chapter House

Day Stairs

Parlour

Kitchen

Fire

Fire

Warming House

Monks' Dorter over

Probable site of Infirmary

Frater

Drain

Reredorter drain

Lay brothers' Infirmary

Room

? Infirmarer's Lodgings

Abbot's Kitchen

Abbot's Lodgings

Drain

The plan of Roche Abbey, near Sheffield in Yorkshire, illustrates the standard lay-out of a Cistercian monastery. The abbey was founded in 1147 by two members of the lesser baronage, Richard de Bully of Tickhill and Richard FitzTurgis. It was colonised by monks of the Cistercian Order from Newminster in Northumberland, which itself had been colonised from Fountains Abbey as recently as 1138. Roche was thus part of the first wave of Cistercian settlement in the north of England. It was one of the more modestly endowed Cistercian houses of Yorkshire, containing towards the end of the twelfth century some 20 choir-monks and about 60 lay brothers.

The lay-out of the monastic buildings of Roche presents a standard plan which can be seen at Fontenay, Fountains, and many other Cistercian sites. In its essentials it derived from the classical plan of the Benedictine monasteries. This uniformity of design reflects the fact that the general chapter of the Order supervised the foundation of new abbeys, and would only authorise occupation after the buildings had been inspected and approved. The buildings are grouped on the south side of the abbey church round a quadrilateral, of which the open space in the centre – the cloister garth – is surrounded by a covered cloister-walk. The range of buildings along the west side of the quadrilateral, which like the church was constructed in the twelfth century, housed the lay brothers. Their dining hall and living room was on the ground floor, and their dormitory ran the whole length of the range above. In the east range the most conspicuous building on the ground-floor was the chapter house, where the monks met daily for monastic business. The monks' dorter (or dormitory) on the floor above extended the full length of the range and adjoined the church at its north end. Access from the dorter was by the night stairs, which led down into the south transept of the church. The reredorter (the latrine) juts out from the end of the dormitory over the running stream which provided drainage for the whole monastery. The monks' frater (dining hall) was on the south side and, in accordance with the standard Cistercian pattern, was set at right-angles to the cloister-walk. The kitchen and warming house on either side of it were originally the only parts of the building provided with a fireplace.

The clutter of buildings on the other side of the stream include the infirmary and the separate establishment of the abbot, which was added in the fourteenth century.

INDEX

Medieval monasticism

Gregory of Tours, 17, 36
Groote, Gerard, of Deventer, 228–9
Grosseteste, Robert, bishop of Lincoln, 188, 211, 212
Grottaferrata, Basilian monastery, 128
Gualberto, St John, founder of Vallambrosa, 129
guests, reception of, 24, 107–8
Guigo (Guiges) du Pin, author of Carthusian customs, 134, 136
Guines, Premonstratensian abbey, 143
Gundrada, Countesss, 86
Guy, abbot of Clairvaux, 162
gyrovagi, 24–5

Hackington, collegiate church, 121
Hadewijch of Nivelles, 189
Hadrian, abbot, 25
Haito, abbot of Reichenau, 70
Hamo, Reeve of Canterbury, 111
Hartlepool, Celtic monastery, 51, 52
Hattin, 173
Havelberg, chapter of, 144
Haymo of Faversham, OFM, 202
Helaugh Park, 142
Hemmenrode, Cistercian abbey, 151
Henry I, king of England, 141
Henry I, king of France,
Henry II, king of England, 133, 137, 183
Henry II, Emperor, 92
Henry III, Emperor, 83
Henry IV, king of Germany, 83
Henry of Blois, bishop of Winchester, 108
heresy, in Languedoc, 194; in north Italian towns, 194–5
Herford, Benedictine nunnery, 177
Herman of Tournai, 180
hermits: early groups in Egypt and Palestine, 1, 4, 5–7; St Basil on the eremitical life, 9; Cassian's teaching on, 13; in the Rule of St Benedict, 23–4; in the Celtic Church, 39–40; supported by parish churches, 128; the eremitical movement in Italy in the 11th and 12th centuries, 128–31; in France, 132–3, 134; of Mount Carmel, 216; at the origin of the Austin Friars, 216–17
Hersfeld, Benedictine abbey, 65
Hexham, Wilfrid's foundation, later Augustinian abbey, 53
Hilarion, St, 5
Hilary, St, of Arles, 14, 15
Hilary, St, of Poitiers, 12
Hilda, St, abbess of Whitby, 50, 52–3

Hildebrand, 126, 130, *see also* Gregory VI
Hildegarde, St, abbess of Bingen, 176
Hildemar, commentator on the Rule of St Benedict, 72
Hilduin, abbot of Saint-Denis, 66, 103
Hillin, canon of Cologne, 103
Hinton, Carthusian priory, 137
Hirsau, Benedictine abbey, 84–5, 98
Honoratus, St, founder of Lérins, 14, 15
Honorius III, Pope, 188, 201, 204
Hospitallers, Knights, *see* Military Orders
Hubert Walter, archbishop of Canterbury, 121–2
Hugh of Avallon, St, bishop of Lincoln, 137
Hugh, St, abbot of Cluny, 80, 81–4, 87, 110, 178
Hugh, archbishop of Lyons, 146
Hugh de Fosses, abbot of Prémontré, 142–3, 180
Hugh, bishop of Grenoble, 134
Hugh de Nonant, bishop of Lichfield, 122
Hugh de Payns, founder of the Order of the Temple, 169
Hugh Pierleoni, papal legate, 183
Hugh du Puiset, bishop of Durham, 121
Hugolino, cardinal, protector of the Franciscans, later Gregory IX, 198, 215
Hulne, Carmelite settlement at, 217
Humbert, cardinal, 130
Humbert de Romans, Master-general of the Dominicans, 208
Humiliati, of Milan, 195–6, 199
Hundred Years War, 223
Hungary, evangelisation of, 91

imitation of Christ, 187, 195, 199; *The Imitation of Christ* by Thomas à Kempis, 230
Immaculate Conception, doctrine of, 177
Inden, Benedictine abbey, 69
indulgences, 62, 168
Ine, king of Wessex, 52
infirmary, its place in the monastery, 107–8
Innocent II, Pope, 89, 161, 180
Innocent III, Pope, 119, 122, 160, 181, 194, 196, 201
Innocent IV, Pope, 160, 212, 217
Investiture Contest, 82–4
Iona, Celtic abbey, 39, 50, 51, 57; its paruchia, 42–3